GW00644911

THE
INUIT
WAY

THE
INUIT
WAY

A JOURNEY ACROSS
GREENLAND AND
THE CANADIAN
ARCTIC ARCHIPELAGO

E. A. S. COOPER

JB

First published in the UK in November 2022 by
Journey Books, an imprint of Bradt Guides Ltd
31a High Street, Chesham, Buckinghamshire, HP5 1BW, England
www.bradtguides.com

Text copyright © 2022 E. A. S. Cooper
Edited by Ross Dickinson
Cover illustration/cover design by Neil Gower
Photographs copyright (see below)
Layout and typesetting by Ian Spick
Map by David McCutcheon FBCart.S
Production managed by Sue Cooper, Bradt & Jellyfish Print Solutions

ISBN: 9781784779641
British Library Cataloguing in Publication Data
A catalogue record for this book is available from the British Library
Digital conversion by www.dataworks.co.in
Printed in the UK by Jellyfish Print Solutions

Photographers All photographs by Edward Cooper unless otherwise stated.
Alec Greenwell (AG); pictures provided from the RGS archives (RGS).

To find out more about our Journey Books imprint, visit www.bradtguides.com/
journeybooks

AUTHOR

Edward Cooper is a trained close protection officer, a remote medic and an award-winning explorer. In 2010 he worked as a volunteer paramedic, providing life-saving treatment in some of the most dangerous townships of Cape Town, South Africa. In 2011 he was a member of the Engelandvaarders, a team of adventurers that kayaked 185 kilometres across the North Sea. In 2012 he was asked by Sir Ranulph Fiennes to support his team on the Coldest Journey expedition to Antarctica. In 2015 Ed led an expedition to Greenland to investigate the impact of climate change on Inuit hunting methods in Qaanaaq before sledging 450 kilometres across the Canadian Arctic Archipelago to Haig-Thomas Island. He has written articles on his adventures for some of the UK's leading newspapers and magazines.

Ed holds a master's in International Relations from the University of Cambridge. He works extensively across the public and private sector where he specialises in supporting the development of organisational capacity and resilience across the globe. This has involved working with some of the most conflict-torn countries on the planet including Syria, Somalia, Ukraine and Bosnia.

ACKNOWLEDGEMENTS

To the people of Qaanaaq who taught us so much. To all the expedition's supporters and to everyone else that helped me along the way – above all to my parents, my wife and our daughter.

CONTENTS

INTRODUCTION

The bear, or 'nanok' as the Inuit had spoken of it, stood there, undeterred. Its head was bowed, and its large white body set in a hunter's crouch. The small black orbs of its eyes stared straight at me. Clouds of mist hung about its frame where the watery heat of its breath met with the freezing polar air. Red smoke from the pen flare I had fired earlier drifted at its feet, almost static in the windless environment. The bear had held the flare in contempt in much the same way as it had with the other deterrents that my co-sledger Alec and I had already deployed. Shouting, clapping, banging pans were met with a mixture of curiosity and disdain. My attempts to scare it off were based on my earlier studies of a situation I never thought I would experience. I vividly remembered the story of the British Schools Exploring Society 2011 expedition to Norway where one of the younger members of the group, Horatio Chapple, a seventeen-year-old boy, had been ripped from his tent and killed. The bear had walked through the camp's tripwire: a mechanical perimeter of metal poles each set with a charge designed to go off with a bang when activated. The tripwire was incomplete and the leaders had replaced missing parts with paper clips. One of the party had tripped the wire a few days before and it had not activated. Although the team leaders were aware of a bear in the area and that the tripwire was not working properly, they set no polar bear watch and so, when the tripwire failed to activate, there was no warning to the eighty-strong team of schoolchildren before it attacked. Despite the shouting and screaming of the awakened group, it continued to maul and injure members of the young party. The group's single rifle was a relic from World War II and the team leaders had only limited training in its use. They tried to fire at the bear and in the pressure of the situation didn't to fire at the bear and in the pressure of the situation didn't notice that the rifle's safety mechanism was still in place. Finally, one of the team leaders who had already received horrendous injuries during the attack managed to discharge a single round and killed the animal. The attack left Horatio dead and four other members of the team with serious injuries. Members of the party were still having fragments of teeth removed from their skulls on their return to Britain.

The events were recent and wedged deep within my subconscious. I had studied the reasons why it had gone wrong and done everything I could to make sure I would be ready if a bear attacked. The temperature was in the minus forties and I was standing south of Axel Heiberg Island in the Arctic Archipelago, in a place aptly named on the map as 'Bear Strait'. We were hundreds of kilometres from the nearest settlement. There would be no rescue when the bear attacked. The sound of the approaching bear's paws crunching against icy snow had caused us to leap from our tent in just our base layers. Adrenaline coursed through my body, driven by a primal level of fear, and the cold seeped through the thin wool of my clothing. I was quickly becoming hypothermic. I pulled the shotgun to my shoulder and aimed at a lump of sea ice next to the polar bear. Despite the danger, I didn't want to kill the bear, just make it clear that we weren't a good target. I had been warned by Mikael, an Inuit hunter, that to scare the bear I needed to shoot next to it so it could see the bullet hit the ice. Otherwise, it might mistake it for an iceberg breaking up. 'The crack of a gunshot and the cracking sound of an iceberg are all the same to a bear,' he had said. I checked my aim and pulled the icy trigger with my numb, frost-bitten finger. There was no bang. No ignition of the cold powder. Just an empty click of the misfire as the hollow sound ricocheted off into the emptiness. My heart stopped. The bear moved forward.

Four years earlier, I had been working in London as an underling in a large, global accounting firm. It wasn't where my heart lay but it was the next step in the conformist route that had taken me through school and university and then into work. Paths that I didn't want to take but that I felt aligned to what society expected of me. Even though every bone in my body wanted to walk its own path through life. Like many, I was persistent in forcing myself into situations that never appealed to me and that left me feeling trapped, just because they felt safe.

I had very nearly had the courage to take a more fulfilling path. I graduated in 2009 in the midst of the financial crisis where jobs were scarce. I spent the summer after leaving university recovering from a dislocated shoulder and filling out dozens of online applications for graduate jobs that I wasn't interested in. All of which ended in apologetic emails telling me that I hadn't got the job. Even the navy wouldn't have me. I watched the doctor examine my still ineffective shoulder and quietly write down a negative result in her notes. I moved to France in frustration, looking to add a language to my woefully inadequate CV in the hope that this might set me apart from the hundreds of thousands of other recent graduates who had also applied in vain. Organisations were cutting costs and pushing people out the door, not letting them in.

I joined a French school in Antibes in the south of France. During the day I cleaned up after the children of wealthy Europeans. At night I took the train to Nice, a few kilometres east of where I was staying. There I worked side by side with my Senegalese friend Abdullah on the door of an infamous Irish bar just off the Promenade des Anglais. My shift went on into the early morning and I would steal sleep at the bus stop near the station while I waited for the first train to depart for

Antibes and I could start my day all over again a few hours later. It was a spartan life with barely a penny to my name, but they were happy times. I met a man who had come to the school to study. His name was Pierre, and he was the head of security at a large gold mine in Mali. He had been a major in the South African Parachute Regiment and I was left in awe at his daring exploits working in tunnels beneath African sands, spending Christmas listening for the hushed scratchings of would-be robbers as they tunnelled in from outside the wired perimeter in search of the rich veins of gold that flowed underneath. I was too fresh to really consider the deeper story. That these impoverished locals were simply trying to access resources that a large, foreign corporate was extracting for its already wealthy and faceless shareholders. The proceeds that should have trickled down likely lost through a mire of corrupt government officials. Pierre sensed my interest and asked me to come and join him. My qualities were limited to youthful enthusiasm and before he could employ me, he suggested a training school in Cape Town. It was a place that helped ex-service personnel retrain as close protection officers for deployment to the multitude of war zones that were raging across the Middle East. There they would operate as private security for diplomats and private organisations turning a profit by rebuilding the buildings and towns that their own governments had recently destroyed. In the pre-9/11 world they might have been called mercenaries, but the professionalisation of the industry had replaced this term and all the connotations of bloodshed that went with it with the more palatable 'close protection officer'.

With Pierre's backing my application was accepted by the training provider, a rarity for someone who lacked any previous military experience. I saved my money, packed my bags and moved to Cape Town where I joined teams of recently serving soldiers from all over the world who had been lured by the prospect of significant financial rewards. Marines and paras from the UK, Frenchmen from the infamous Foreign Legion and American naval intelligence officers. As a non-soldier my first course was to train as a medic. Pierre had told me that without previous combat experience this would be the only way that I would be hired by any of the many private security organisations working in Iraq or Afghanistan.

The course was a mixture of classroom-based learning and on-the-ground training. The school operated its own ambulance that deployed its students – who were protected with heavy body armour and pepper spray – to some of the most violent townships in the city. The instructors all carried guns. For the first time in a long time, I felt fulfilled. I had found a purpose in life, and I was surrounded by people for whom I had a profound respect. We scuttled through the narrow corridors and corrugated iron frames of poorly built houses laden with our heavy equipment. I responded to car accidents, coaxed diabetics out of comas with shots of glucose and carried end-stage HIV patients to hospitals around the city. Our job was not to cure but to package up and deliver. We adhered to the 'The Golden Ten Minutes' rule, the time we had to arrive on scene and stabilise a patient to give them the greatest chance of survival. It opened my eyes to the inequality that existed in South Africa: privileges as simple as receiving life-saving hospital treatment didn't exist there.

We were called to the scene of a homeless man who had become unconscious, his airways clogged by the tuberculosis that raged inside him. I gave him oxygen and in the back of the ambulance he finally came round. He grabbed my hand. 'Don't let me die,' he rasped, his eyes looking with desperation into mine. 'You won't die,' I said. I knew that I couldn't save him, but I wanted to reassure him and ease the rising panic. We raced through the streets, blue lights flashing, and arrived at the gates of a large white and newly built hospital. I hadn't been to this one before; normally we delivered to the sparsely funded buildings that operated close to the townships. We were deeper in the city today. The studious-looking doctor at the gate regarded the patient. 'You can't leave him here,' he said in a thick South African accent. I looked at the patient who still grasped my hand, his knuckles white in a combination of effort and fear. I turned to my instructor. 'What's he talking about?' I asked, but the doctor heard me and replied instead. It was the football World Cup and the hospital had been built to service the thousands of foreign visitors that would flow to the country in a few weeks' time. It wasn't meant for people like this man.

The hospital beds lay empty, and we pleaded to the doctor to let him in. Finally, the man gave in with a sigh. 'OK,' he said, 'you can put him over there.' He gestured to a corner of the newly furnished room that would be out of the way. It was close to midnight and the roads of Cape Town were clear as we headed back from the hospital in the ambulance. As we sat, now patient-free, in the back of the vehicle, my instructor explained that tuberculosis amongst the homeless was hard to treat. Many would only take the antibiotics for a short while before stopping, which meant the disease could re-emerge in them and spread to others, stronger than before. It was a concept based on the idea that antibiotics start by killing the weaker elements of the bacteria, the bugs that are most easily wiped out by the antibiotic. A half-finished treatment left the tougher bacteria which, if the treatment was stopped early, would then multiply and create a more drug-resistant strain of tuberculosis. The next time round, the infection would be even harder to treat. Whether it was right or not, the doctor thought he was only protecting the other patients and I wasn't qualified to challenge that.

However, I still struggled to reconcile to the idea that they could turn away anyone in need of life-saving treatment.

I completed my training after a few months. I had done well as a medic and was received on the close protection course based on this performance. We had all been novices on the previous course, but the protection course was different. I was the youngest person and the only civilian, surrounded by a group of hardened war veterans. My inexperience was never held against me. I worked hard and was slowly accepted by the group. I learnt a lot on the course, but I was just as interested in the people that I trained with. Especially what they thought of the choices in life that had brought them here. I became close friends with one of the older members of the course, a quick-to-anger ex-para covered in winged tattoos and a large totem pole bearing blackened skulls at its base that ran the full length of his back.

He became a mentor, a man I looked to for all the answers to the big life questions that haunted me. His name was Jim and I found myself asking questions that still echoed around in my ruminating mind. The big one being what I was going to do with my life. He told me that security paid better than the army, but he had purchased a bigger house and spent more on luxuries for his family which had meant greater expenses. He had become caught in a cycle of having to take on security jobs, sometimes with organisations that he didn't trust or had poor reputations. It had sometimes meant getting on planes that he knew he might never come back on. 'What would you have rather chosen,' I asked one day. 'This life or an easier one like becoming an accountant?'

'I would be an accountant,' he responded without hesitation. The conversation moved on and I carried on drinking beer with him at the local bar, but I continued to mull his answer over in my mind. It wasn't the one that I had been looking for.

I continued to progress through the course, long days spent on the range learning to fire pistols and assault rifles, administer advanced trauma responses and everything else I had to know to become a close protection officer. The training ended with a final operation. A three-day protection detail for a wealthy businessman in Cape Town. I was asked to lead the team. It was a surprise to me and everyone in the group. It was an operation littered with errors that were mostly down to my own lack of experience. Three long days ensued before I was able to collapse on a well-worn couch in the accommodation that the school provided. I sat there talking through the cacophony of errors that had taken place during the operation. Jim sat on an equally worn armchair opposite me, silent and listening intently. Then, unprompted, he said: 'You know, you're a man now.' The words hit me hard. It wasn't something that I had ever doubted. I had been more worried about what I was going to do after the course ended. The sentence tumbled into me and stayed deep within my core. It was another waypoint to adopt in my search for a life that meant something to me. What did it mean to become a man? In Africa, I had heard of an old tradition amongst the Masai that when a boy was old enough, he was sent out into the wilderness carrying only a spear. His sole purpose was to kill a lion. It was a rite of passage known in Maa as *olamayio*. A path to manhood. If he succeeded, he earned that right. In the Mandan tribe of North Dakota, boys would be carried aloft on ropes held by splintered wood pierced through their flesh. Bloodied and unconscious, each boy would eventually be brought down, offering the smallest finger on one hand for amputation as a sacrifice to the gods. If he had endured the terrible pain with courage, the splinters would be torn from his body and, from then on, he would be known by all to have become a man.

In the UK I felt that the rite of passage to manhood was more transient. Our ancient traditions had been forgotten long ago. Unlike the Masai or Mandan tribes, the line to manhood felt blurred. Was it the first time you were allowed to drink a beer in the pub? Maybe the time when you lost your virginity or perhaps when you got your first job? Each of those transient moments paled in comparison to a single tribal event. A challenge that had been created to push a person to their limits. If you passed you could be confident that you had what it took to make your own way in the world. It was a test that no-one was telling me to take but it was something that I wanted for myself. It felt tied to everything else I was searching for. Fulfilment, meaning and, most of all, a purpose.

CHAPTER 1

LOST

I returned to England, the same but different. Lack of funds drove me to London and without a clear path forward I remembered Jim's advice and joined a large, global accounting firm. It was a safe, sensible choice that provided a long career and importantly meant I would avoid the dangerous cycle of the security world that Jim had warned me of. I hadn't abandoned my ambitions to join the military. South Africa had left me with a deep respect for those that served, and I wanted to make sure that I stayed close to people with those same values. I joined a local army unit in North London as a reservist. I was a trooper, the very bottom rung on a tall ladder. I got some fulfilment in continuing my medical training with them and spending days walking long distances across the undulating, boggy terrain around the Brecon Beacons. Part of my training took me to Kiruna in the north of Sweden along with a small team of highly experienced patrol soldiers. We were accompanied by two army instructors who took our little pack along the Kungsleden or 'King's Trail': a 400-kilometre route through some of the most beautiful landscapes in the world.

We skied from hut to hut, meeting the local Sámi people that played host. Each day we would travel through the valleys, surrounded on each side by steep mountains covered in ice and snow. In the evenings we would arrive at small outcrops of wooden huts that were dotted at intervals along the route. We scooped out water through scraped-out holes in the ice that covered the lakes nearby. We collected large bundles of wood and used it to heat the saunas that were present at every stop-off point. It was a chance to ease our aching muscles before crawling into our wood-fired huts, the bunk beds stacked five high in places so that we could rest before starting the same thing again the next day. It was good to experience some of the lower temperatures of Sweden, which at times reached -25°C on the coldest days. Clear blue-sky days were punctuated with rougher weather, where the wind picked up, visibility dropped, and the tracks turned to ice where the snow had been blown off it. At one point a huge storm hit us with winds of up to 120 kilometres per hour. When this happened, we hunkered down in the huts, waiting for the storm to blow through. It was during the rougher days when we couldn't travel that we would carefully venture out to learn winter survival techniques from the two instructors. I learnt how to build snow walls, we practised setting up emergency shelters with a plastic bivvy and we crawled into caves that we had carved into the side of snowdrifts to keep warm. I was by no means an expert by the time we finished but it would stand me in good stead for what was to come later.

Despite the gradual progression at work and the new phases of training with the reserves there was still something niggling at me. I was living a privileged life in the city. I had a nice girlfriend and lived in a small but cosy apartment on the edges of Battersea Park, but there was still a void in life which left me unfulfilled. As if I was standing on a precipice, knowing that the way forward was to move across it but not understanding how. It was in the midst of this dilemma that I was invited to plan an expedition by a close friend of mine, Alec Greenwell. What started out as a new Guinness World Record attempt to be the fastest to kayak across the North Sea – some 180 kilometres – turned into the bigger story of retracing the journey taken by a group of people called the Engelandvaarders.

The Engelandvaarders were refugees who fled Holland during the German occupation in World War II using any means available to them. They travelled in small wooden dinghies, sneaked on board coal ships and paddled rowing boats and kayaks across a treacherous sea under the constant vigil of enemy planes and warships to escape to the shores of England. Of the thirty-two that attempted it by kayak, only eight made it across to England's shores. Some drowned, some were killed by strafing enemy aircraft and the rest were picked up by patrolling German boats that took them back to Holland where they were interned for the rest of the war. Of the eight that made the crossing, only three survived the war. I had never set foot in a kayak nor paddled so far. It would be an arduous journey and possibly the challenge that I was looking for. A way across the void. My rite of passage to manhood.

But it wasn't. I paddled one hundred arduous kilometres, just over halfway, before falling foul of the support boat – a towering old forty-two-tonne fishing trawler which caught me in its stern and bowled me over. I only just missed the whirl of its large propeller and the rigid inflatable that it towed behind it as it passed over me. I hung there in a state of numb consciousness, upside down in the middle of the North Sea, before hauling myself out and calling it a day.

The expedition had been a success as far as the story was concerned: some of the team had made it and some hadn't, just as it was back in 1940. It was telling that only three of the six made the crossing. My own personal disappointment at having to pull out ignited a desire within me to find a new challenge. The kayak hadn't given me that single defining moment. That pathway to manhood. I felt that I still had something to prove to myself, and I wasn't the only one.

One year later, on a weekend back at home in Orford, a small fishing village where I was visiting my parents on the Suffolk coast, it was Alec once again who planted the seed for an adventure. This time in the Arctic. It was Friday and we were in the depths of a winter characterised by warm coal fires, comfortable armchairs and early bedtimes. The crowds of tourists that normally flocked to witness the quaint charms of Orford in the summer were notably absent from its narrow country lanes that night. My phone rang. It was Alec.

'What are you up to?' he asked.

'Nothing,' I said as I finished cleaning the shotgun which I had been using to hunt wildfowl along the Alde-Ore Estuary that snaked its way past Orford and out into the North Sea.

'You keen for a beer?' Alec asked.

'Yes,' I replied, pleased to have some company that night. 'See you at the Jolly in ten.'

'See you there,' he said and put down the phone.

The Jolly Sailor was our local pub. Built in the 16th century, it rested a stone's throw from the river's quay. Its dark red weathered bricks had provided a home from home for the fishing folk that had made a living from North Sea fishing for centuries. I walked down the unlit street and felt the fresh evening breeze on my cheeks. I arrived at the pub just as Alec was pulling up in his car. He jumped out and with a beaming, mischievous smile said, 'I've got something to show you that I think you'll like.'

Despite being in his mid-twenties, Alec had maintained an infectious schoolboy zeal for life which often manifested itself in some sort of adventure. 'Come on then,' I said, my interest piqued, and we ducked our heads under the low door frame and stepped down into the dimly lit pub. It was empty other than a few old souls playing checkers at the long wooden table by the window. That had always been the locals' table. As if to re-enforce the point, there was a painting of the pub hanging above the broad open fireplace with the very same locals playing the same game from many years before.

'What are you having?' I asked Alec as I approached the bar.

'The usual,' he replied. I ordered two pints of Adnams Broadside: a traditional brown ale that always made me feel like I had gone back in time to some carefree era.

The barmaid placed two fresh pints on the bar. 'Do you want to pay now or put it on the tab?' she asked.

'I think we'll start a tab,' I said. Having a drink with Alec was rarely a single-pint occasion. We walked past the old men playing chequers and into a separate, smaller room that barely had space for the long table that lay across the middle. It was cosy, to say the least. The walls were adorned with black-and-white photos that harked back to Orford's days as an east coast fishing power. In one photograph, a large basking shark was hanging from its tail. It was at least twice the length of the man stood next to it. I had grown up swimming in the murky depths of the Ore and the photograph always gave me second thoughts about the idea of swimming in the same water as that giant beast.

We sat down and I took a sip of my beer before putting it down.

'So,' Alec said, barely able to contain his excitement.

'Go on then, what did you want to show me?' I replied with some trepidation. The last time we had discussed one of Alec's ideas I had ended up underwater, trapped in my kayak in the middle of the North Sea.

Alec pulled out an old hardback book with a worn blue cover and passed it to me across the table. I took the book and began carefully thumbing through the pages that had yellowed with age. Alec proceeded to explain that the book was written by his great-uncle, a man named David Haig-Thomas who had lived with the Inuit over several years. He had made the epic 2,400-kilometre journey by sledge from Greenland through what is now the Canadian Arctic Archipelago (also known as Nunavut). The journey had taken Haig-Thomas from London to the Inuit town of Thule. After wintering with the Inuit, he travelled by dog sledge across the fractious open waters of Smith Sound, through a narrow, snow-covered valley that traversed the southern end of Ellesmere Island, then along the sea ice south of Axel Heiberg Island where multiple dangerous encounters with polar bears nearly lost him his life. Accompanied by his Inuit companion, Nookapinguaq, Haig-Thomas discovered a new island nestled between Cornwall and Amund Ringnes islands to the west of Axel Heiberg.

'Now this is the best bit,' Alec said once he had finished laying out the story. 'My great-uncle left a note which is buried under a cairn on this island,' he said. 'He didn't tell us what he wrote, and no-one has found the note since.' He let a pause hang in the air for dramatic effect.

'So, you want to go to this island and dig up this note?' I asked.

'Yes, he marked it with a broken ski pole. I think we should go there and find out what it says. What do you think?'

So that was the plan. We would go to the Arctic, travelling across the sea ice to a place that had recorded some of the harshest winter temperatures and strongest winds of anywhere in the world, to find a note that someone had marked with a broken ski pole over seventy years ago. It was a completely unachievable and utterly mad idea, but I was naïve and the adventure had the ring of escapism that I craved. 'Alright,' I said hesitantly, with a continued feeling of trepidation. I knew very little about the Arctic other than what I had read in adventure stories. Experience had taught me that it was unlikely that Alec had considered the effort or risks involved in carrying out a polar expedition of this scale, but I was happy to play a support role at first. I don't enjoy the limelight, and it was Alec's idea after all.

We cemented our pact with a whisky nightcap in the dimly lit side room of the Jolly Sailor in Orford. We would go to Greenland, find a sledge with dogs to pull it and an Inuit guide. We would retrace the 2,400-kilometre route that Haig-Thomas had completed in 1938. With no experience of the area, of travelling by dog sledge or of living in some of the most debilitating conditions that could be imagined, and with the alcohol firmly combating my sense of reason, it seemed like a completely achievable thing to do at the time.

I had found with the Engelandvaarder expedition that to get support it was critical to be able to give companies strong media coverage in return. The formula was simple: more media equalled more sponsorship. You needed someone that was willing to stand in front of the cameras and present in front of large audiences. Just the idea of doing any of that filled me with nervous chills. It might sound odd that someone would be willing to travel to a hostile place with such limited experience but not be OK with standing up and saying a few words in front of an audience. I didn't know it then, but it soon became clear that if we had any intentions of going to the Arctic, I would be the one who would need to make it happen. That meant facing up to my fear and becoming comfortable with playing a more visible role.

The moment came in 2013. To garner funds for the expedition I applied to an organisation called the Scientific Exploration Society (SES). A mentor of mine, Barry Moss, had worked with the organisation for many years and had told me of a new flagship award sponsored by the Swiss watch manufacturer, Zenith. Barry helped me to navigate the process and, when the results were announced, our expedition had won. He called me into the office to let me know. 'Congratulations Ed,' he said, 'we're really proud of you.' The award came with a £7,500 grant and a watch from Zenith.

'Thanks, Barry – that's great news,' I replied.

'There is one thing,' he went on. 'Can you prepare a short piece for the awards night as you'll have to give a small presentation of around a minute.'

My heart sank; I didn't think I could stand up in front of all those people. The awards fell on a date when I had also been asked to accompany a British Army 'adventurous training' expedition to America. 'I'm actually away that date, Barry, is that going to be OK?' I said, hoping that I could still receive the award and not have to go through the agony of the presentation.

'I'm afraid not,' he responded. 'Part of the award is that you have to attend the ceremony in person.'

I know it sounds mad but the idea of giving up that amount of cash and a fancy Swiss watch was preferable to the idea of standing up for one minute and talking about the expedition. 'Uh, I'm not sure,' I stammered before Barry cut me off.

'You're really going to be letting us down if you pull out now,' he said.

The money was one thing but letting Barry down was another. 'OK,' I said, 'I'll do it.' There was no turning back now and I made the decision there and then to fully commit to my role as leader. I spent the next four months attending sessions at something called Toastmasters in the evenings after work. The sessions were designed for people that had a similar phobia about public speaking and, as each session went by, I became more and more confident. Having the courage to overcome that phobia was the first step in many.

The idea of embarking on a new adventure reinvigorated me. Following in the footsteps of the heroic stories of the past and engaging with a completely new environment in the Arctic just might provide that single challenge, a tangible progression to manhood. A way to mark the transition and prove to myself that I had crossed the threshold.

CHAPTER 2

HAIG-THOMAS AND THE CANADIAN ARCTIC ARCHIPELAGO

In an old grainy newsreel from 1938, narrated by a gentlemanly English voice, we see images of Haig-Thomas and his Inuit[1] guide, Nookapinguaq, travelling by dog sledge across the ice foot along north-west Greenland. Everyone is cheery and smiling at the camera. The atmosphere belies the extraordinary achievements of Haig-Thomas and his Inuit guide. They faced extreme temperatures and attacks by polar bears, and almost starved. The final shot is of the island itself which the commentator proudly announces has been claimed in the name of Great Britain.

The more I researched Haig-Thomas the more I understood what an incredible character he was. He seemed a man destined for greatness but as with many of his contemporaries his potential was cut too short, too soon. By the time he was thirty-five he had rowed in the Olympics, travelled with the explorer Wilfred Thesiger in Abyssinia (now Ethiopia), and journeyed to the Arctic with Edward Shackleton,

---

1 Haig-Thomas referred to the Polar Inuit or Inughuit as 'Eskimos'. In this context, the term refers to the indigenous people of north-west Greenland. It is one of the smallest indigenous groups in the world and numbers less than one thousand people. Nowadays the term 'Eskimo' has fallen out of use and in modern times it is perceived by many as offensive. In his book *The Last Kings of Thule*, Jean Malaurie spelt the name phonetically as 'Inouit' which he translated as 'the man par excellence' or 'men without peers'. For the sake of the reader I have abbreviated the full name 'Polar Inuit' to simply 'Inuit'. This term can also be used to refer more broadly to the Arctic indigenous populations of Canada, Alaska and Greenland.

the son of the Antarctic hero Ernest Shackleton. He died serving his country as a commando during the D-Day landings in World War II. In his book on the expedition, *Tracks in the Snow*, he wrote:

> *As far as I could hear from the news, which we could never get very clearly, war would break out in a few days. It seemed a pity that perhaps the results of our expedition would never be worked out — but whatever happened I had had those wonderful fifteen months in the Arctic, even if, in a few weeks' time, I was riddled with machine-gun bullets.*

It was a premonition that was played out far too accurately on D-Day. Haig-Thomas was reassigned to the 6th Airborne Division from his own unit, No. 14 Commando, shortly before the bombardments commenced. He was parachuted behind enemy lines on 6th June 1944 and was walking along a track when he was ambushed by German soldiers and killed in a hail of bullets. He was found with an *oosik*, a walrus penis bone, strapped to his waist – a bullet had passed right through it. It's something that his family still have. An odd choice perhaps but the fact that he had taken this into battle represented the deep connection he retained with the Arctic. To me it signified the respect that he continued to hold for the Inuit who had taught him so much.

It was Haig-Thomas's experience with Thesiger in the dry and brutal heat of Abyssinia that drove him to the Arctic.

> *It was to get a contrast to the stifling heat of Abyssinia that I first decided to go to the Arctic. We had been riding all day, our ponies were too exhausted and parched with thirst to carry us farther. We stumbled along over the rough, boulder-strewn ground, down the side of a valley where the Abyssinians had promised there would be water. Our eyes were full of dust, and our heads throbbed from the glare and torturing heat. But, alas! The pools had long since dried up, and there was no water to relieve our raging thirst. For six dreary hours we trudged along, leading our ponies, till we came to a so-called lake. Here, though no water was visible, by pressing a tin into the mud we collected some black liquid. Of course we couldn't drink it until it had been boiled, and it was while I was waiting that I made up my mind to go to the Arctic, where the rushing streams and icy snowdrifts would ensure that I should never again suffer from thirst.*

In search of adventure in colder climates, Haig-Thomas joined up with Edward Shackleton's Oxford University Ellesmere Land Expedition as their chief ornithologist. It was on this first expedition that his respect for the people of Greenland was seeded. Shackleton's team had ignored the advice of the locals, travelling with overloaded sledges and large dog teams, much to the disappointment of the Inuit that accompanied them. They succeeded in wearing out the dogs but not much else.

Haig-Thomas, seemingly frustrated with the inability of the team to learn from the locals, left them and travelled south, spending the summer with an Inuit family and looking for the elusive nest of the snow goose (a lifelong fascination). During this time, he learnt all he could of Inuktitut, the language of the Polar Inuit, and the techniques of living and not just surviving in the Arctic. As the summer came to an end and the ice crept in, he left Greenland and caught a boat back to England. On his way out, Haig-Thomas visited Ahpellah, an elderly and well-known hunter in the area. When he arrived at the man's tent, Haig-Thomas was moved to see that he was dying. They sat talking and the man began to tell him the story of the hunting trips that he had been on in his younger days. The old hunter recounted the story of the giant skeleton of a prehistoric animal that he had found in the 'lands beyond'. Haig-Thomas's interest was instantly sparked.

On the long journey back to England I thought of what the old man had told me. I looked at the map and saw that the 'lands beyond' must be the Ringnes Islands, where he had probably seen the fossil bones of some prehistoric monster. It would mean a sledge journey of some 1500 miles from Thule and back.

The expedition to return to Greenland and search for these bones was launched in 1937. But it was not the only focus. Haig-Thomas would also take two scientists with him. First, John Wright, a surveyor and meteorologist by trade. Haig-Thomas had been impressed by the story of John standing between his dog team and a polar bear with only a pickaxe to defend himself. Next was a friend of John's named Richard Hamilton. John and Richard had recently returned from a scientific expedition to Svalbard in Arctic Norway. Richard, who had already started his investigations of the ozone layer and the ionosphere on his previous expedition, was keen to continue these in Greenland. Wright's focus was to conduct survey mapping of the area around Thule and the east coast of Ellesmere Island. So, while Haig-Thomas's main focus was the skeleton, his team of scientists had a thoroughly modern mission. They would carry out research into the ozone layer and map changes in the glaciers around Thule. It was in Thule, which lies in the north-west of Greenland, that they made their base for the rest of the summer. Haig-Thomas and his team made observations of the Moltke Glacier in Thule and of the glaciers they came across on Ellesmere Island. They determined that the glaciers were indeed retreating. They were also told by many of the hunters that the sea ice cover had also reduced. It was something that scientists were able to prove decades later[2]. Thule itself no

2 John Wright returned to Thule in 1993 and resurveyed the Moltke Glacier determining that it had retreated by more than six kilometres from its 1937 position. The UN Environment Programme published findings in 1994 that supported the suggestions of Haig-Thomas and his team that the glaciers were melting. The evidence was based on data that only covered the period from 1965 to 1989. Data such as that provided by John Wright, which was produced decades before this, could still be very useful to researchers looking at climate change today.

longer exists as a town but is now the home of the US 21st Space Wing. In the 1950s the whole town's population was relocated by the Danish government one hundred kilometres north to a small settlement called Qaanaaq to make room for the US military[3]. It was therefore to Qaanaaq that I would venture when I formed my own expedition in 2015.

Haig-Thomas's journey was littered with extraordinary accounts of his surroundings. He recounted some of the most beautiful nights of his life spent waiting out the low winter temperatures and preparing for the sledge journey in the spring. He narrated in stunning detail his time sledging under the stars, his way illuminated by the Northern Lights, the tracks of his sledge leaving two golden lines in its wake as it stirred up the phosphorescence that sat just below the newly formed sea ice. His tale is a positive one. He had fallen in love with the country and the people that lived in it.

His reservations were focused on the Danes' continued influence in the country. Greenland was a protectorate of Denmark which gave them responsibilities for governing the country and its people. In the southern settlements, Haig-Thomas described the Inuit, living in Danish-style wooden houses, too close together, trodden mud and sewage surrounding them. He met a priest who talked of a young couple newly married and who wanted a divorce. The priest explained that no-one had ever got divorced in Greenland and that doing so may set a dangerous precedent – soon everyone might want to get married, he exclaimed.

3 In 2003, a Danish court ruled that the move was a serious and unlawful act against the local population. I was told by one lady that in order to be moved they were asked to provide their last names. Apparently, no-one had a last name up to that point so the local priest handed them out randomly instead. It was why many of the Inuit in Qaanaaq had Danish last names.

The authorities stepped in and told a made-up story that they used to play on the goodwill of the Inuit couple in question. The king of Denmark had fallen sick, caused by the news that his subjects in Greenland were getting a divorce. Hearing this, the newly-wed couple were distraught to have caused such pain and agreed to be sent by the authorities to another village. On their own and away from the problems that had triggered this state of affairs, the newly-weds decided to make a go of it and forget the idea of divorce. The village they were sent to was chosen for the high population of elderly inhabitants and so apparently no further distractions meant that whatever had caused the upset in the first place was possibly forgivable. 'Now they are one of the happiest married couples, with a large family, and divorce still has not come to Greenland,' the priest said proudly.

For Haig-Thomas the priest's story was evidence of the paternal way in which Denmark sometimes viewed its relationship with the Greenlanders. A relationship which he viewed with some scepticism. His own approach valued local methods and knowledge and his tales were written in a way that made it clear that he didn't believe the Danish authorities had learnt this lesson. He saw their interference as a continuation of colonialism and an attempt by Denmark to develop Greenland in their own image[4].

The team left Thule in February as the darkness of winter began to clear. Nookap had a considerable reputation in the area and was

4 In 1951, the Danish went a step further when they undertook a social experiment to see whether they could 'civilise' a group of children from Greenland. The twenty-two children aged between five and eight were taken from their families to Denmark. The idea was that these 'Little Danes' would return as the future leaders of Greenland. The experiment was not successful. Many never saw their families again. It was later determined that more than half suffered negatively from the experience. Out of the twenty-two, only six are still alive. They received an apology from the Danish prime minister in 2022.

known to have sledged 2,900 kilometres in just eighty days on a previous journey. From Thule they first headed north to Etah along the ice foot that ran beside the Greenland coast where they met an American expedition, the MacGregor Expedition, and their three-masted ship, the *General A. W. Greely*. It had been named after another infamous American explorer, Adolphus Greely. Greely was appointed the commander of the Lady Franklin Bay Expedition which set out to establish a meteorological observation station at Lady Franklin Bay on the north-east side of Ellesmere Island. He was perhaps an odd choice to lead the expedition having served in the land forces during the American Civil War and without prior experience of the Arctic. The expedition landed in 1881 without issue and established a base that they named Fort Conger[5], which would become their home for the next two years, after which they planned to be picked up by a relief ship.

In the summer of 1882, two of Greely's group along with their Inuit guide Thorlip Christiansen claimed the record for the 'Farthest North': a record previously established by Sir George Nares's British Arctic Expedition five years earlier, which also wintered at Lady Franklin Bay. However, things went downhill from there when the planned relief expeditions were unable to reach the team. By 1883 their stores were running low, so Greely abandoned camp and travelled south to a place called Cape Sabine on Smith Sound, eighty kilometres

---

5 Fort Conger was also where the American explorer Robert Peary made camp in 1899, along with a substantial accompaniment of Inuit guides, for one of his many attempts on the geographic North Pole. It was arguably one of Peary's least successful expeditions. When his colleague, Matthew Henson, took his boots and socks off, seven of Peary's toes snapped away. Peary's response to Henson's concern was to say: 'There's no time to pamper sick men on the trail... a few toes aren't much to give to achieve the pole.'

of which they travelled on a floating iceberg using the currents of the sound. It wasn't until 1884 that Greely and his party were rescued. Of the twenty-five that had started only seven were saved. Many died from starvation, stores becoming so low that they supplemented their rations with candle wax, the soles of their boots and bird droppings. A line in Greely's journal gives some insight into the ordeal: 'To die is easy; very easy; it is only hard to strive, to endure, to live.' One man, Private Henry, was shot on Greely's orders for stealing food. Another, Corporal Ellison, died on the ship home after both of his legs had to be amputated due to frostbite. Stories of cannibalism dogged the expedition after their return and indeed some of the recovered bodies were found to have knife marks where the flesh had been cut from their bodies.

During Haig-Thomas's time with the American party in Etah he heard news that Hitler had invaded Austria. Haig-Thomas noted that it felt like the whole expedition party was under a dark cloud with the looming prospect of a European war on the horizon. The team were powerless, however, and there was no prospect of returning home as the sea ice had already firmly set in.

From the hut at Etah they headed across Smith Sound for Bache Peninsula on the east coast of Ellesmere Island. A journey that should have taken six to seven hours would take them almost a week of hard sledging. The new ice that usually spanned the whole way across Smith Sound had formed much further north than in normal years and the route would be much more treacherous. It was on the coast of Ellesmere Island that Haig-Thomas left John and Richard and continued with Nookap to the 'lands beyond': an area to the west of the island where Haig-Thomas believed that he might find the skeleton that Ahpellah had told him of.

The small team met with an abundance of wildlife. The sea ice was littered with the tracks of snow hares, wolves and bears. He described it as 'an Arctic zoo'. They set up their tent when they stopped and laid new food depots with meat from the animals they hunted. These should have come in handy on the return journey but, by the time they came back, many of these caches would have been broken into by wolves and polar bears. Haig-Thomas and Nookap would be pushed close to starvation as a result.

The next few weeks of the journey were dotted with hardships that Haig-Thomas breezed over. It's an approach very much at odds with most accounts of polar travel. Temperatures remained between -35°C and -40°C and they felt the cold bitterly. He described the cold nights causing his back to shake in such great jerks that he thought his spine would break. It was a cold that I would get to know very well when I made my own journey. But amidst the pain he continued to focus on the incredible wildlife, flora and landscapes around him.

Wildlife and landscapes that on more than one occasion almost killed him. At one point they narrowly avoided being eaten by a mother polar bear. At another, Haig-Thomas almost fell to his death while being lowered over the edge of a cliff by Nookap. Throughout their adventures, the bond between the two explorers remained unbroken, the level of trust throughout palpable.

The old book that Alec had lent me became a close companion through the expedition planning stage. I began to feel an affinity to Haig-Thomas. He was modest in his exploits which, unlike some more modern accounts of adventure, made the Arctic feel accessible. His vivid descriptions of life in the polar north and his deep respect for its people were an enticement to experience it for myself. Haig-Thomas had become a mentor; his approach to travelling in the Arctic and his heavy reliance on local knowledge a framework for the way I wanted to travel. His book was my guide to the Arctic and the Inuit who lived in north-west Greenland.

The more I understood of Haig-Thomas, the more I realised that if the expedition was to be successful I had to ensure that we did it in the same spirit as he did. I wanted to use the time I spent up there to learn as much as I could from the people that lived in the Arctic. It was an unusual approach to take when most expeditions tend to do their training beforehand, prior to a short, sharp drop into an alien and frozen land and an equally rapid extraction once they have finished. We would need real time living out there, understanding the environment and learning from the Inuit how to operate in their land before we set off for Ellesmere Island.

Haig-Thomas never found his skeleton, but he did discover an island. His island, now named Haig-Thomas Island, lies in the south-central part of the Sverdrup Basin, a large pericratonic depression in the Canadian Arctic Archipelago that covers 310,000 square kilometres, more than half of which is water. It is a low, banana-shaped piece of land made up mostly of shale, siltstone and sandstone. The island is uninhabited and there is little in the way of flora and fauna. Even today there has been little reason to venture to the area. Extraction industries such as oil, gas and mining have tried and failed there. Exploration for hydrocarbons commenced in 1969. While major deposits of gas were discovered close by to the west on Ellef Ringnes Island, a report written in 1983 by Canadian geologists found no evidence of coal, uranium, gas or oil in their exploration of Haig-Thomas Island.

Had we been travelling in 1832 or 1994, we would have perhaps been able to claim that we were within throwing distance of the Magnetic North Pole. Discovered in 1831 by James Clark Ross, a

British explorer, the Magnetic North Pole is one of many 'North Poles'[6] and is the point at which magnetic field lines point vertically down. Like a sink without a plug, it sucks them down into the liquid core of the earth. The pull is so strong that it will drag a compass needle far off true north with deviations so massive that it becomes almost impossible to navigate. Unlike its more famous cousin – the Geographic North Pole – the Magnetic North Pole is a fidget. In the mid-1900s, scientists believed it moved only thirty metres each year. By the early 2000s its movements measured fifty-five kilometres a year. Its trajectory had taken it north, along the west side of Haig-Thomas Island. By 2015 it had gyrated hundreds of kilometres further on towards Siberia. In the last decade its movements have become so erratic that it has started to break the model on which global magnetic-based navigation relies. This is a problem for nearly all devices with a magnetic compass, including modern phones and airplanes. Recently, some scientists have speculated that there have been points in the past 20 million years where it has even switched places with the Magnetic South Pole.

Haig-Thomas wasn't the first person to journey to the area. One of the most famous names to travel there was Sir John Franklin, a naval officer and Arctic explorer, perhaps less known for his successes and more for his tragic failure. Franklin had made his name in the Arctic

---

6 There seems to be a lot of North Poles depending on what you read. The Geomagnetic North Pole, the Geographic North Pole, the Magnetic North Pole, the Northern Pole of Inaccessibility, the Pole of Cold and the Instantaneous North Pole to name a few. Then there is the charming town of North Pole, Alaska. It's a Christmas-themed town with road names that include Snowman Lane and Kris Kringle Drive. They list St Nicholas as their patron and even have a gift shop there called Santa Claus House. Every year the local post office receives thousands of letters addressed to Santa Claus. They have raised a volunteer army of elves to help write responses each year (on behalf of Santa, of course).

in three previous expeditions before a tenure as governor of the penal colony in Tasmania. Franklin's leadership capabilities – his devotion to his people and his ability to build a cohesive crew – did not transfer so well to the Australian colony with its political back-stabbing, and his career ended there. Despite a number of positive achievements that included laying the foundations for an education system in the area, his tenure ultimately ended in disappointment. It would have been an ignoble end for a man that had given so much to his country. At the age of sixty he was asked by the British government to lead an expedition to find a route through the Northwest Passage. The opportunity to lead a new expedition to the Arctic provided a chance to regain some honour. Franklin departed England in 1845 with his two ships, HMS *Erebus* and HMS *Terror*, and vanished two years later along with his entire crew. The last sighting was by a whaler in 1847 at Lancaster Sound. It spurred the start of one of the largest rescue operations in maritime history.

The search was led by his wife Lady Franklin. Tenacious and dedicated, Lady Franklin funded her own expeditions and even went to the length of contacting clairvoyants to locate her missing husband. The search uncovered the tragic outcome of the expedition: fragments of the ship's contents and the 129 souls on board were found dotted around the islands. Evidence from uncovered artefacts, diaries and accounts from Inuit in the area suggested the men of Franklin's party met a long-drawn-out death after abandoning their boats to the ice. Hypothermia, lead poisoning, scurvy and exposure to the harsh environment of the Arctic are broadly agreed to be the causes of death for the crew. There were even rumours of madness and cannibalism, with knife cuts found in some of the recovered bones of the lost sailors. Stories of the Inuit that had witnessed their demise told of men falling down dead from exhaustion on their attempted march to safety.

One of the contributions to the disaster was the British focus on using modern means rather than adopt what they perceived as inferior Inuit methods. This meant the clothing and equipment that they took was completely unsuitable for the environment. One hundred and fifty years later the world was still looking for Franklin's ships. *Erebus* was finally found to the east of Queen Maud Gulf by Parks Canada in 2014 and the *Terror* in 2016 by the Arctic Research Foundation where it lay to the south of King William Island. The images from underwater drones showed that neither of the ships had broken up in the sea ice as many had believed, but had been abandoned intact. It was a warning that if I ventured to the Arctic without listening closely to the Inuit methods of travel, I might face a similar fate.

Franklin is one of many that made their mark on the area. Haig-Thomas Island is surrounded by large swathes of water and land named after Western explorers. Amund Ringnes to the west took its name from an Oslo brewer and co-patron of the Fram expedition led by the Norwegian explorer, Otto Sverdrup, in 1900. Sir Edward Belcher was responsible for naming Cornwall Island to the south in 1852 after the Duke of Cornwall while searching for Sir John Franklin's lost ship and crew. Belcher's own search for Franklin led to his court martial when four out of the five ships he commanded had to be abandoned in the pack ice around. One of them, HMS *Resolute*, was later recovered by whalers. Wood from the ship was used in the creation of three desks, one of which, the *Resolute* desk, was presented by Queen Victoria to US President Rutherford B. Hayes. It is still used by US presidents in the Oval Office today.

The Sverdrup Islands, of which Haig-Thomas is one, were named after the Norwegian explorer Otto Sverdrup. Sverdrup's contributions to polar exploration are often overlooked but they are viewed by many as equal to Fridtjof Nansen and Roald Amundsen, his contemporaries. Unlike Franklin and many of the British expeditions of the time, Sverdrup had learnt from the Inuit. In 1892, he and Nansen were the first to cross the Greenland ice sheet by ski, a feat that many viewed as impossible at the time. At the end of the journey, Nansen and Sverdrup wintered with the Inuit and learnt many of the methods that they would use in later expeditions. In 1893, Sverdrup skippered the *Fram*, possibly the most famous ship in Arctic history. The brainchild of Nansen, their aim was to set sail in a ship purposefully designed to get stuck in the polar pack ice and let the currents take them to the North Pole. The expedition proved a huge success and the *Fram* achieved a world record of reaching the furthest north. Between 1899 and 1902, on the 'Second *Fram* Expedition', Sverdrup sailed to the west of Ellesmere Island. His three-year expedition included meeting the world-famous American explorer Robert Peary, who was in the area and attempting his own North Pole first.

Of the well-known explorers that ventured to the area, Sverdrup stood out as one of the few who managed to carry out his expedition with the rare feat of suffering few casualties while achieving great success. The only fatality was the ship's doctor who committed suicide, shooting himself as an act of freeing himself from the pressures of living in the wilderness for so long. It was during this longer expedition that Sverdrup spent seventy-two days travelling across the sea ice and mapping the area around Ellef Ringnes, Amund Ringnes and Axel Heiberg Island. Despite charting around 260,000 square kilometres in the area, Sverdrup somehow missed Haig-Thomas Island.

On his return Sverdrup claimed the almost 260,000 square kilometres of land that he and his crew had mapped in the name of Norway. In doing so he set off a dispute with Canada which had already asserted sovereignty over all known and unknown lands in the Canadian Arctic. The dispute was only settled in 1930 when Norway ceded the islands to Canada and Sverdrup took a payment of 67,000 Canadian dollars (something like 1.2 million dollars today) in recognition of his scientific work and in exchange for the records of his expeditions.

Another group of explorers arrived in the area before Haig-Thomas, Sverdrup and their European contemporaries had ever heard of the Arctic. They were a group of people called the Thule: proto-Inuit who lived in the region half a millennium earlier, between 1000 and 1300AD, and inhabited much of Arctic Canada and Greenland. They were proficient hunters who excelled in the same polar environment that claimed the lives of hundreds of European explorers several centuries later. Anthropologists believe that they developed in Alaska and migrated east across Ellesmere Island in the Arctic Archipelago to northern Greenland where they soon replaced the existing Dorset culture. The rationale for the move is not widely agreed upon. Earlier theories suggested it was due to climatic reasons affecting their food supplies during a brief stage of global warming during the medieval period. More recently, some have suggested that the Thule moved west in search of iron having learnt from Dorset wanderers of an abundance of iron that could be found in the meteorites that lay in the north-west of Greenland. With limited evidence left from this time, attempts to fill the gaps in history can seem touched with a pinch of speculation. What is more certain is that the Thule are the ancestors of the Inuit of north-west Greenland.

Thule, previously a small village and now an American airbase in north-west Greenland, was one area that they settled. In 1818, Sir John Ross made the first known contact with the Inuit that lived there. Robert Peary built a support station for his own expeditions in a protected harbour at the bottom of Mount Dundas, a flat-topped mountain that serves as a landmark for the area.

In 1910, the famous Danish explorer Knud Rasmussen, who travelled 30,000 kilometres across the Arctic by dog sledge, decided that Thule would be a good place to create a trading station. Previously an Inuit settlement known as Umanak, it was named Thule by Rasmussen, after the Greek term *ultima Thule*, or the most northerly place in the world: a name that was previously shared by Ireland when the Greek geographer Strabo, writing in the 5th century, provided an unflattering account of savage and uncivilised people living a miserable existence that he believed was 'on account of the cold'. It was also where Haig-Thomas lived and launched his expedition from. Like Sverdup, the time spent living with the Inuit reinforced Haig-Thomas's huge respect for their culture and their methods of survival in what can be a harsh environment.

Despite the rich history of Thule, I decided early on that, owing to the military presence, we would have to base our expedition in Qaanaaq, a town where many of the Inuit had been exiled to.

CHAPTER 3

THE PLACE OF A THOUSAND ICEBERGS – ILULISSAT

By 2014 I had pulled together a plan that to an outsider might look like we had a credible chance of accomplishing what we were setting out to do. Sir Ranulph Fiennes had agreed to be the expedition's patron and I had even managed to obtain the support of the SES, a smaller and, at that time, less prestigious version of the famed Royal Geographical Society. I managed to overcome my earlier nerves, deciding that courage and six months of rehearsing for a two-minute speech was a more sensible approach then hiding from it and foregoing the financial support that the SES was offering. Barry was there along with Alec, Haig-Thomas's son and two grandsons and another friend from Suffolk called Richard. With their support and a brief pep talk from Alec, I was able to deliver my speech to a crowded room and received what felt like a heady rush of applause (in fact it was more of a light trickle). What I hadn't managed to address yet was my Wikipedia-level understanding of Greenland and a complete lack of experience of polar travel. Drinking beer in the back rooms of warmly lit pubs and laying out ambitious plans while pointing heroically at different points on a map would only get Alec and me so far.

The next step was to bolster this with some practical experience. I left England for Qaanaaq later that summer to do just that. I wanted to get a feel for the place and to speak with the locals to see if what we had planned was even possible. The recce took me from London through Denmark and over to Greenland where I flew up the coast to Qaanaaq. Even now it's a journey that takes several days to complete.

My knowledge prior to arriving in Greenland had been garnered from what I had read online, in books and through brief conversations with academics and adventurers. I had preconceptions developed from an early age of a desolate world of ice, sub-zero temperatures and a culture that had been frozen in time. Greenland is one of the few places in the world still wrapped in a cloak of mystery. A glance at some world maps and you could presume it is the same size as the United States and Australia combined. This is a cartographic distortion. The earth is round, and most maps are flat. During the process of transcribing one to the other, geographies can become distorted in different ways. One of the most common of these applies to countries closest to the poles. Greenland, Canada, Russia and, on the other side of the world, the Antarctic, become giant versions of themselves. Greenland, while still vast, is a third of the size of America and one quarter that of Australia. Unlike those two continents, inhabited by a combined figure of over 350 million souls, Greenland's population is but a trifle at just 57,000 people, about the same size as Chelsea, one of the smallest districts in London. Its vast ice sheets that to date have been uninhabited cover ninety-five per cent of the country's landmass. A quarter of the population live in Greenland's capital city, Nuuk, which lies in the south-west of the island. Its second-largest city, Sisimiut, has a population of just 5,200 people. The rest are scattered along the coast where they have access to the sea and, importantly in winter, the sea ice. The small population is one of the reasons why many Greenlanders I spoke to view the island as one big family.

A legacy of its colonial heritage, fifteen per cent of the island is inhabited by Danes; the remaining eighty-five per cent are Inuit. There are three main groups of Inuit. The West Greenlanders (Kalaallit), the East Greenlanders (Iit) and the Polar Inuit (Inughuit). My objective was to spend time with the Polar Inuit in Qaanaaq, a town inhabited by those descended from the Thule Inuit that Haig-Thomas had lived and travelled with during the British Arctic Expedition. Despite a growing movement for full independence, Greenland is still part of the Kingdom of Denmark. In 1979 it achieved home rule status and in 2009 a self-government arrangement replaced this. The law of self-government gave Greenlanders the right to take over thirty-two sovereign responsibilities. In the last ten years, the only one that has been taken on is oversight across their own resources. Despite its apparent potential for untapped mineral wealth, Denmark continues to provide a standing annual payment of roughly 600 million dollars to Greenland which makes up fifty-six per cent of its total revenue. The rest comes from a combination of fishing, tourism and some mining income. To gain independence, negotiations between Denmark and Greenland will need to reach an agreement. Part of which will be deciding on what is owed for the last few hundred years of financial support.

The combination of ice, mountains and glaciers has meant that Greenland is one of the worst places in the world for a road trip. In 2014 the road system extended to a total of 150 kilometres. Compare that to the United Kingdom, an island one eighth the size, where there are over 422,100 kilometres of asphalt. Greenland has no railways, no inland waterways and almost no roads between towns. Traditionally, most travel was by sea. In the summer by boat and in the winter by sledge, when the water turns to ice and becomes a highway, linking families and friends. Perhaps most importantly, the ice connected the Inuit to their hunting grounds where the seals, narwhals, polar bears and walruses lived. Nowadays, air travel has enabled towns to connect. There are thirty-three airports in Greenland but only one international airport, Kangerlussuaq.

'Kanger' was the first place I would reach when I left London and travelled to Greenland that July. Originally built by the US after World War II, it now serves as the main transport hub for the island. The airport covers a large flat basin next to the coast and is overlooked by the golden glow that emanates from behind the steep-sided cliffs to its south. I walked down the steps and across the runway to a low, modern grey building that operated as the terminal for both international and domestic flights. I marvelled at the absence of a strict security regime that sat in distinct contrast to the European airports that I had flown through. London Heathrow then Copenhagen in Denmark. It felt like a mental weight was lifted. There were no lines of tired and frustrated passengers awaiting their passports to be checked or removing belts and phones to place in grey plastic trays. I simply walked through passport control with the briefest of glances from the uniformed official who stamped my passport before I proceeded into the main area of the building. I could not see one security camera. The UK has the largest percentage of CCTV cameras per capita in the world. London alone has almost one million of these. You are likely to be captured as many as seventy times a day just walking its streets. China's 'Skynet' and less well-known 'Sharp Eyes' systems dwarf this. The Skynet system is made up of an estimated 200 million cameras which China uses to support its social credit system among other things[7]. The subconscious and at times conspiratorial understanding between states, large businesses and us as individuals that we can be watched has slowly become a norm. In Greenland I felt an odd sense of freedom in the absence of continual digital surveillance.

The terminal was a simple affair. There were a few small shops carrying traditional merchandise such as Inuit soapstone carvings, books and photographs of glaciers and icebergs; and a single food hall, more like a school canteen than something you might expect from an international airport. There were no mass-market coffee shops or fast-food restaurants. The menu provided the basics of burgers and chips. My next flight on the journey to Qaanaaq wouldn't leave for two hours so I ordered the most Greenlandic thing I could find on the menu, which happened to be a caribou burger, and sat down on the wooden balcony overlooking the runway. It was summer, the skies were clear and blue and there was no snow on the ground and no icebergs in sight. The weather was crisp but warm enough that I took my down jacket off and sat there relaxing in the bright sunshine. The strong but not unpleasant odour of kerosene drifted across the runway from the refuelling planes and filled my nostrils. Already, my idea of a perennially frozen island was proving baseless.

A large wooden signpost stood erect in front of me on the other side of the mesh-wire fence that separated people from planes. It was painted in red and white, the colours of the Greenlandic flag. Markers

---

7 The cameras use facial recognition and big data analytics to monitor citizens and assign them with a social credit score. Credit scores are developed at an individual level. Those with higher scores benefit by being able to check in to hotels without deposits or obtain visas more easily. On the other hand, someone with a lower score may not be able to travel freely or eat at certain restaurants. The current strategy is to achieve one hundred per cent coverage across the whole of China.

hung off it like the branches of a tree. Each point marked in hours the exact time by plane from Kangerlussuaq to major cities around the world. New York lay four hours to the west, Moscow five hours and twenty minutes to the east. Tokyo was the furthest at ten hours and five minutes. It gave me a small glimmer of excitement to know that according to the sign I was now closer to the North Pole than any of those other places. Just three hours and fifteen minutes. Almost equidistant from a place that had defeated so many of those who had tried to reach it and London, where I had come from. According to the sign, London was only three hours and thirty-five minutes away. This might have been the case if direct flights existed, but they didn't and my journey had already taken two days for me to reach Greenland. That was nothing compared to Haig-Thomas and many of the early explorers who had sailed for several months to cover the same distance.

The balcony was empty, despite the sunshine, except for two lone figures sat huddled together, smoking and talking quietly. They looked European. One man wore a thin leather jacket and the other a thick flannel shirt. They seemed at ease compared to my own wide-eyed excitement at visiting Greenland for the first time. It made them stand out amongst the spattering of tourists at the airport. I was interested to see where they were going and so I plucked up the courage to ask them. 'Hello,' I said in English, giving an awkward half wave.

One of the men turned and took the half-smoked cigarette from his mouth. There was a short pause as he looked at me and I wondered whether he had understood what I had said. Then a more welcoming smile pulled across his face. 'Hallo,' he said with a Danish accent. I reached out a hand, which he took, and introduced myself. I told him about the expedition I was planning and where I was going. 'Qaanaaq, eh?' he said with surprise. 'You've got a long way to go.'

'I know – I'm not a huge fan of flying either,' I replied. 'What about you – what brings you to Greenland?'

'Me and my friend' – he looked at his friend who continued to puff quietly at his cigarette on the bench beside us, the silver smoke hanging motionless in the air – 'we work for a mining company here, we are heading to Narsaq.'

The man explained that he led a team on the Kvanefjeld Project in Narsaq and he would be taking the flight north through Ilulissat that day. The Kvanefjeld Project is one of the largest rare earth mines in the world. The three deposits together contain around a billion tonnes of mineralised ore – thought to be the second-largest deposits in the world. Rare earths are used in everything from rechargeable batteries for electric cars to computers and wind turbines. The demand for this rare material has grown exponentially as the global intention to slow the rate of climate change and find alternatives to hydrocarbons increases. The project is run by Greenland Minerals whose largest shareholder is Shenghe Minerals, a Chinese company. China is not alone in its investments in the Greenland mining boon. The UK, Australia and Canada are amongst the most prolific in terms of mining exploration in the country.

Many believe that Greenland holds some of the largest untapped reserves of resources in the world. A 2008 US Geological Survey estimated that there could be 52 billion barrels of oil off the coast of Greenland. The country is known to hold significant deposits of copper, zinc, lead, iron, cobalt and gold amongst other things like diamonds and rubies. To date, the large swathes of ice and Greenland's harsh temperatures have made it a difficult and costly place to operate in. Other parts of the world have been easier to access and therefore cheaper to work in. Increasing demand, reducing resources and the effect of climate change on ice coverage that is revealing these resources has made Greenland an increasingly attractive place for global powers and their mining companies. It has created growing friction in Greenland where many are worried about the effect these mining projects would have on the almost pristine environment that the Greenlanders have become used to. A few years after my journey I advised Renowned Films, a small British television company that was looking to get a series commissioned to send a team of Americans to Greenland to prospect for gold with pickaxes and panning gear like the early pioneers of the Klondike Gold Rush. Greenland's documented potential for mining has yet to be realised but the ambition remains for those adventurous and pioneering enough to do so.

I watched with my new friends as the twin-propped Dash 8 plane landed on the single runway and taxied up to the terminal to refuel. 'I think that's us,' said the Dane, who picked up his bag and started walking back through the terminal with his friend in tow. I picked up my own bag and followed. The Dash 8 was flying under the red and white of the carrier Air Greenland, which manages a monopoly of flights across Greenland. With the lack of roads, the smaller planes run like a bus service up the west coast of the country.

My first stop was Ilulissat. Ilulissat was the birthplace of the Danish explorer and anthropologist, Knud Rasmussen. Rasmussen led multiple expeditions to Greenland. The largest was known as the Fifth Thule Expedition. Between 1921 and 1924, Rasmussen and his team – which included two Inuit companions from Thule, Qaavigarsuaq and Arnarulunnguaq – sledged across 30,000 kilometres of the Arctic from Greenland through the Northwest Passage to Siberia. It was Rasmussen who promoted the idea that the people of the Arctic shared the same ancestral heritage. On his route he noticed that many were able to understand the same Inuktitut language that he and his Inuit companions spoke in. Like many of the successful explorers of the time, Rasmussen relied on Inuit methods of travel. It came easier to Rasmussen whose mother was Inuit. He had been driving sledge teams since the age of ten and it bode well for a career crossing the polar landscape.

The plane begun to waver in the strong crosswind as we dropped down into the picturesque airport. I held my breath. It was a rough landing and the middle-aged woman next to me was clearly shaken beneath her thick coat. I bid farewell to the two miners who remained seated, and stepped off the aircraft. The plane was only on the ground for another ten minutes or so before ambling back into the sky towards Narsaq. At the terminal I was met by Arne, the plump and jolly owner of the Hotel Avannaa: Ilulissat's most modestly priced and basic hotel. On the drive into town Arne explained that he had moved to Ilulissat twenty years ago when there had been a buzz of construction work in the town. He had stayed because he loved the climate. The idea of someone liking the climate in Greenland surprised me. Arne insisted that in the summer the temperature frequently rose to 25°C. Hot enough to relax in a T-shirt and cook outside on a BBQ while taking in the unparalleled views across Disko Bay. Ilulissat's pine-clad, slope-roofed houses gave me the impression of an alpine ski resort. The clitter-clatter of plastic-boot-fitted holidaymakers and roars of debauchery from the packed-out tables of street-side bars you might find in the Alps were replaced with the clanging of cranes and shouts from dock workers. Instead of skiing, Ilulissat's main business was its sizeable fishing industry.

There was a hum of activity rising from the large fish-processing factory around the harbour. The smell of the day's catch hung in the air. A mixture of large, bulbous trawlers and smaller fibreglass speedboats meandered in and out of the port as they made their individual contributions to Greenland's main export, fish. Once processed in Ilulissat, flat Greenland halibut and cold-water shrimp would be shipped as far afield as Japan. Not even this great island could avoid the tentacles of globalisation. It was the latest episode in a gradual move away from subsistence hunting towards a more modern-style economy. Commercial fishing has been present for hundreds of years, starting with the heavy whaling of the 17th, 18th and 19th centuries when commercial fishing from Europe killed tens of thousands of Greenland right whales. Louwrens Hacquebord, an academic from the Arctic Centre of the University of Groningen in the Netherlands, estimated that between 1669 and 1800 122,000 right whales were killed through commercial whaling activities. These activities contributed to the extermination of the right whale from the modern Arctic ecosystem. Hunted for their oil, adult whales could grow to between twelve and eighteen metres and weigh seventy-five to a hundred tonnes. They wintered in the more ice-free waters of east and south-east Greenland and migrated north in springtime to follow the receding ice which laid bare a key food source, plankton. Whalers would sight them off the south-west of Greenland in May and follow these groups as they moved up the west coast all the way to Smith Sound between Ellesmere Island and Qaanaaq. On sighting the whale, smaller boats would be launched bearing a harpoon and long line. The harpoon would be fired, and the whale tied to the boats and towed back to the ship where it would be cut up. The whale's blubber could be boiled down and used for oil to light houses and the expanding cities and towns across the world. When whales were scarce the ships might focus on seals instead. In 1766 a ship returned to the port of Hull in England carrying 400 sealskins and two years later another returned with 700 in its hold. While commercially attractive, these northern waters were also perilous. In 1830, twenty-one ships were lost. The typical crew of a whaling ship numbered from thirty to forty-five crewmen and meant that this was no small tragedy. Now commercial fishing had reached Greenland's shores. I wondered whether it was having the same impact as those earlier ventures that had done so much damage to the whale and seal populations across the Arctic.

Amongst the convoy of fishing boats going about their daily business floated an armada on a different mission. Ilulissat attracts thousands of tourists each year, lured by the prospect of witnessing climate change in action. And tourism is on the rise. Between 2015 and 2019, foreign travel to Greenland increased from 76,852 incomers to 104,782, with many travelling to places like Ilulissat in the south of Greenland. The Ilulissat Icefjord (known locally as Kangia) is one of the most productive, actively calving ice sheets in the world. Collapsing glaciers calve off hundreds of pieces of ice, the oldest around 250,000 years old, and in some cases as high as a hundred metres above sea level, that flow through the Icefjord and out into Disko Bay. Around thirty-five cubic kilometres of ice calve off here annually, representing ten per cent of all the calved ice in Greenland. It's the multitude of these smaller icebergs that gives Ilulissat its name (in Kalallisut, the main language of Greenland, Ilulissat translates as 'Iceberg'). John Wright and Richard Hamilton conducted experiments on the glaciers around Thule in 1937 to test whether, like the ones in Switzerland, they too were retreating. Haig-Thomas wrote, 'We would have to come back in the spring and record the movements of our marks, but from what we could see of the glacier we thought it was retreating.'

The sheets of ice that cover Greenland contain enough fresh water to raise global sea levels by over seven metres. As the glaciers warm, the ice melts and forms rivers of fresh water that run beneath the surface of the glacier and out into the sea. This glacial water is denser than sea water and pulls the warmer ocean water into contact with the glacier. The deeper the fjord, the more of the warmer ocean water it contains. This warmer water then undercuts the glacier which leads the glacier to calve, forming the icebergs which line Greenland's coast. The warmer the temperature, the more fresh water is produced at the surface of the glacier, increasing the flow of these subterranean rivers to the sea, which acts as a catalyst to the melting of these glaciers. In 2021, an iceberg covering 2,500 kilometres, an area seventy times the size of Manhattan, broke off Antarctica's largest ice shelf, named the Filchner-Ronne Ice Shelf, and into the Weddell Sea. That was only a third of the size of another piece of ice that broke off the same ice shelf twenty-one years earlier. Together, cumulative ice loss of over 6.5 billion tonnes in Greenland and Antarctica between 1992 and 2017 contributed to a twenty-centimetre rise in world sea levels. Five small islands in the Pacific have already been lost to sea level rises and it is predicted that another six will be lost in the future. One island – Nuatambu, home to twenty-five families – has lost half of its inhabitable area with eleven houses claimed by the sea since 2011. In England it is estimated that sea level rises will put 200,000 coastal properties in England at risk within the next thirty years.

I sat with my host that evening in the small bar at the bottom of the hotel and listened to his thoughts on the changing climate and the impact of fishing in the area. The icebergs for which the town was famous had become more numerous over the last few years. The receding ice had created a longer fishing season and small boats making two to three trips a day could bring in 600,000 DKK a year across a six-month season (roughly £50,000). This lucrative financial draw had led to overfishing and in Arne's eyes had damaged halibut stocks. 'The fish are much smaller now than they used to be,' he said mournfully. 'With less and less ice, there are now more storms than ever.' He lifted the faux-crystal glass to his lips and finished the last drops of his whisky.

The next day, I left Hotel Avannaa, driving along the road to the airport as the golden morning light glanced off the bay. The plane stood on the runway of the airport, and I boarded a couple of minutes before it had to take off. There were no lines this far up north, which was a world away from the queues and security checks of European airports. Even as we prepared to take off there were still teams of people making a last-minute dash for the flight. I was surprised that the plane was still full, and I wondered how many people could be going up to Qaanaaq at this time of year. It turned out that around half were on their way to the US airbase in Thule where they worked to support the US military presence there.

The idea to search for the note left by Haig-Thomas had drawn me to the Arctic. At first it was the challenge that appealed but more and more I wanted to understand what felt to me to be an overlooked part of the world. For me it seemed that Greenland was a litmus test for the conflicts and happenings of the wider world. Places like Ilulissat, Qaanaaq and Thule, that few have heard of, had borne the brunt of global external forces during the Cold War, the world's quest for resources, the rising great power struggles over the Arctic region and, more recently, climate change.

CHAPTER 4

THE NEW THULE – QAANAAQ

By the time we began our descent into Qaanaaq the plane had emptied. Only myself and a small group of Greenlanders remained. I sat there staring across the open water, the scattering of white dots that I had seen thousands of feet up grew into castle-sized icebergs as we descended.

In 1937, when Haig-Thomas arrived in Thule, where many of the current inhabitants of Qaanaaq had come from, he described a small settlement with a mixture of stone houses and wooden huts. Rasmussen described these huts in his own accounts of living with the Polar Inuit in 1902:

> *The first time one sees a house of this description one is struck by the little with which human beings can be content... A cave like this, skilfully built in an arch of gigantic blocks of stone, one involuntarily peoples mentally with half supernatural beings... you are seized yourself with a strange excitement at the thought of the extraordinary life that waits you in their company.*

The Inuit subsisted by hunting the local wildlife. Caribou, narwhals, hares, guillemots and Arctic char during the spring and summer months. Polar bears, walruses and seals during the winter. Every part of the animals was used. They clothed themselves in fur, used the meat for themselves and their dog teams. They used blubber for their lamps and bones to carve hunting tools and intricate pieces of art. A delicacy that still exists today is *kiviak*, a dish made from the body of a small bird called an auk which is fermented underground in the stomach of a seal.[8] Luckily, it was something I never experienced. This subsistence way of life, while attractive, could also mean that people living in the Arctic had to make difficult choices when times were bad. Rasmussen captured anecdotal evidence of infanticide and senicide in his travels. Even Haig-Thomas noted that he had spoken to a grandmother, one of the oldest women in Greenland, who was left on an island to die by her grandson only to be rescued by a Danish doctor.

During World War II, Greenland became strategically important for America. It was so important that the US took de facto control of the island from the Danish after Denmark was occupied by the Germans in 1940. Its position was important both for the natural resources it contained but also due to developments in air capabilities. An American airbase was first established in Thule in 1943. At first the Americans lived side by side with the Inuit, but the base's importance accelerated in the 1950s owing to the war in Korea. This drove growing friction between the USSR and America during the Cold War. The US reacted and undertook a global programme of base building. In 1951, an armada of twelve ships sailed from the naval station in Norfolk, Virginia to Thule in Greenland. On board were 12,000 men and 300,000 tonnes of cargo. Building the base was a colossal operation that some say was equal to the building of the Panama Canal. As a nuclear airbase its development was done in secret under Operation Blue Jay. It didn't stay secret for long, however. Jean Malaurie, a French anthropologist and explorer, discovered it

8 It is widely believed that Knud Rasmussen died in 1933 at the age of fifty-four after eating *kiviak* and coming down with acute food poisoning.

accidentally in June 1951 on his return from Ellesmere Island. In his book, *The Last Kings of Thule*, he described the arrival of the nuclear age to Greenland:

> *I advanced in the dust to the heavy rhythm of tools and machines. The most formidable air base in the world had risen in the waste in less than ten weeks... They say that the 'Blue Jay Operation', which has created this base, is the greatest military enterprise since the Normandy landings.*

In 1957 the base went from providing an early warning system for the Russian nuclear threat to a nuclear weapons site. Four nuclear missile silos were constructed on the base. In 1968, a B-52 Stratofortress carrying four nuclear weapons crashed into a frozen fjord eleven kilometres west of Thule Airbase, killing one of its crew. The nuclear weapons on board were in fact hydrogen bombs containing 1,400 kilotons of energy. The nuclear bomb dropped on Hiroshima only contained fifteen kilotons of energy. That's nearly a hundred times more powerful. It is difficult to imagine the devastation that would have occurred had the weapons detonated on impact. Luckily, none did. It was the Inuit that were called out to mount the rescue operation of the downed pilots and their hazardous cargo. During the ensuing clean-up, code-named Operation Crested Ice, all but one of the nuclear weapons were recovered. It caused outrage at the time from the Danish people towards the Americans. Denmark had voted against nuclear weapons being held on Danish territory. In 1995, feelings of anger were reignited when reviews of old government documents revealed that the Danish prime minister, H.C. Hansen, had given tacit approval for the Americans to operate nuclear weapons in Thule. In 2017, Thule Airbase received a further 40 million dollars in funding to support its role both for its protection capabilities as an early warning system for Intercontinental Ballistic Missiles from Russia and for its role in housing the US Space Command. Thule had moved from the nuclear age and into the space age.

The Inuit lived in Thule for more than 500 years when in 1953 they were forcibly removed by the Danish authorities to make space for the US military base that was to be established there. One hundred and thirty or so individuals made the journey one hundred kilometres north to a new place called Qaanaaq where they were moved into rows of drab prefabricated huts. It was because of this connection to Thule that when I travelled to Greenland I made my base in Qaanaaq, a town of almost 600 inhabitants, many of whom had descended from the Thule Polar Inuit that Haig-Thomas would have spent time with.

Qaanaaq, I soon realised, had been left far behind the modern Thule that many of its inhabitants had come from. The airport lay a few kilometres outside of town and was served by a rudimentary runway built along a shingle beach. There was no tarmac and only a simple, tin-built shed which acted as the terminal. I walked across the gravel runway, coarse grains of sand crunching under my boots. A stout Inuit gentleman with thick tinted glasses stood alone from the others. He nonchalantly puffed at his cigarette, his eyes drifting across the arrivals until he focused on me. 'You must be Edward,' he said in broken English as I got closer. The man was named Hans and he was the owner of the one and only hotel in Qaanaaq.

'How did you know?' I said, aware that I was both the only white person on the plane and also quite a few centimetres taller than the average Inuit.

Hans chuckled. 'My car is over there, you can put your bag in the back,' he said, pointing his smouldering cigarette in the direction of an old but well-maintained Land Cruiser.

Hans drove us along slowly, pulling over occasionally to allow the two or three other cars to pass us on the single-track road, each one throwing up a cloud of sand as it passed. The track ran along an exposed plain of grit and rocks that followed the side of a large bay. There were no turnings off it, just a straight line into Qaanaaq. Behind it, up in the hills, rose the Qaanaaq Glacier. Even in the summer its icy white tongue was still visible between the contours of the hills. The meltwater from the glacier ran down through the town in the form of a small, shale-lined stream.

Qaanaaq was not large: only 600 people lived there. It was a town built on a slant and organised along three main roads that lay from east to west. In the far east of the town there was a large supermarket, a sports centre, an old people's home and a small hospital. A giant satellite dish towered over the place. This was Qaanaaq's connection to the outside world, and it provided intermittent internet and phone signal for the population. It was also where the oldest houses of the town were situated: wooden prefabricated houses that were outclassed by the more recent houses that now surrounded them. Their white paint had begun to fade and flake, victims of extreme weather. Some were still inhabited by the families that had been exiled by the expansion of Thule Airbase. Malaurie had been living amongst the Polar Inuit when he came across the airbase at Thule. The noise of construction, the blasting of the land to make way for a runway, the vast armada of ships and the smell of machinery must have been overwhelming. Malaurie wrote:

The Eskimos were very upset... Measures must be taken. What? The Eskimos discussed it endlessly. 'Leave for the north? No, it's impossible (our parents, our grandparents, our great-grandparents, etc.) are buried here.' Stay? 'But in this noise we can't sleep or hunt...' And the lamentations began again.

I imagined the long trek that those first settlers made from Thule to Qaanaaq almost seventy years earlier. They had been given little warning by the authorities and were told if they didn't choose to go then they wouldn't be compensated with a house when they got to Qaanaaq. The land that they had known for thousands of years had become forbidden to them. Hunters had returned from the sea ice to find their families, many tearful and most confused, as they collected up their belongings and packed them ready for the long sledge journey north across the still-frozen water. It was May, a time when the light still shone, and the ice provided a slowly melting road of exile.

Many lived in tents at first; the houses they had been promised were still under construction. They were not completed until September when the temperatures began to plummet below zero. Some of the elderly developed coughs in their damp tents and without medical help passed on from the living world. In Qaanaaq the winds can rage. Katabatic winds that descend from the perennial ice caps and out over the fjord. Cooled into areas of high volume they tear down the slopes, driven in part by the force of gravity pouring down from the ice cap above and roaring through the town. The windiest times of the year are from July to November in the north. The fastest surface wind speed was recorded in nearby Thule in 1972 where the wind raced to a colossal 333 kilometres per hour. In Qaanaaq, the hastily built houses rocked and waved under the onslaught of one storm in 1953, the nails that held them together screeching and moaning under the strain. Some fled as their new houses were lifted up and went cartwheeling down the slopes towards the ice. It was at this modern settlement, decades later, that I arrived. A mix-match of old and new. A place where traditions were clung to while the pervasive winds of modernism strove to blow them away.

Speedboats sat motionless behind a thin rock wall that provided a makeshift harbour. Pale skin-clad kayaks and thin brown strips of drying meat were propped up on wooden towers along the water's edge, keeping them in the wind and away from the hundreds of dogs that were tethered around each house. Beyond the ageing white houses of the older part of the town sat more prefabricated housing, each adorned in a variety of bright and gaudy colours. Dark reds, bright yellows and blues. It was the only thing that set them apart from each other.

English and Spanish football flags adorned many of the houses and peeked garishly from their windows. Blue Chelsea flags seemed to dominate while the reds of Manchester and Inter Milan also had their place. Qaanaaq even had its own football pitch which was placed at the very top of the town in between the graveyard and the cliff's edge. It must have been one of the most northerly football pitches in the world.

Most of the houses had groups of dogs chained outside in packs. These were Greenland Dogs, chosen for their strength and endurance and closely protected by law. There was a ban on exporting these animals or mating with any other breed for fear of tainting what was seen as a superior animal. They were large and covered in thick, long coats of hair. I learnt that they would remain tied up like this for the whole summer until the sea ice came, when they would be taken back down to the shore. It felt cruel to someone that was used to dogs being pets, but these were working dogs. I was intimidated at first when I had to walk by these packs of tethered dogs as they lay close to the main streets that criss-crossed the town. To my untrained eyes they all looked wild and hungry. Puppies played amongst the larger dogs and were free to wander as they pleased but from the age of four months onwards it was a town rule that they would be tied up. While I never saw these dogs being aggressive, the rationale for this year-round tethering was supported by some gut-churning stories of packs of dogs getting loose and hunting down children like prey. There was even a dogcatcher that would walk through the town. Sometimes I would hear the occasional crack of a gun being fired as he carried out the unsavoury job of shooting any stray dogs that went unclaimed.

The hotel that Hans ran was at the top of the town. It was a simple place – the food was basic and the rooms felt like a boarding house – but it had a homely smell to it that made me feel at ease. Its saving grace was its unparalleled views across the bay. In the centre of the bay lay a vertiginous iceberg, so large that while most of the others had floated or melted away, its monstrous weight and size had anchored it to the bottom. It towered over the town, dwarfing the modest settlement. Its proximity made it seem even greater than the mountains around it. It was oblivious to the warm sun that beat down upon it. Its lesser-sized companions were not. I soon got used to the great thundering these towering pieces of ice made as they cracked apart, the noise ricocheting off the steep red rocky slopes that surrounded the town.

The rhythms of the days were hard to get used to. My whole life I had been accustomed to day being followed by night. In Qaanaaq during the summer the sun never went down. It just bobbed a little lower towards the horizon on a disorientating 360-degree pivot around the town. The days had no beginning and no end. I experienced the uniquely Greenlandic phenomenon of being woken up by the sound of children playing outside the hotel on the swings at two in the morning. A completely normal occurrence.

I had brought with me the copy of *Tracks in the Snow*, the book that Haig-Thomas had written in the 1930s. Qaanaaq was very different to the Thule he had stayed in. No trees grew this far north and so the Inuit had made use of local rock, grass and bones to build stone houses for the summer months. In the winter they used the snow and ice to create igloos, often with tunnels dug between them so that families could visit one another or access stores while protected from the harsh winds and cold. The igloos and stone houses of Haig-Thomas's time had been replaced with prefabricated huts nestled on concrete plinths that anchored them against the winds and movement of the permafrost ground below. They were built from imported wooden planks and filled with imported furniture and appliances: a form of housing that Haig-Thomas had mocked on his travels through the more developed southern parts of Greenland on his way up to the Polar Inuit. It was at the same time of year in 1937 that he had been convinced by the Greenlanders to take his small-engined boat to McCormick Bay, where there was a large river that the Inuit used to fish for salmon. From what he had written, fishing for salmon was a huge occasion. I had spoken to Hans about this before I arrived. Hans had promised to put me in touch with the local Hunters' Union, who I was keen to talk to and get their views on the route I was planning to take. When I arrived, Hans explained that he could arrange the meeting but that it wouldn't take place until a few days' time. I was either lucky or else deemed a useful pair of hands – my arrival coincided with a fishing trip his wife Bietcha had planned for the following day. It would be a perfect way to spend an otherwise idle few days just on my own at the hotel.

A knock on my door woke me after only a brief sleep in my new surroundings. It was Hans, who plied me with coffee and ushered me down to the shore where Bietcha and her grandson Mishookchak were already on board. My initial instincts as a traveller told me to be wary. In many other countries that I had travelled to, being ushered into a boat with a group of people you've never met and with no idea of where or for how long you are going is not normally a good idea. Anywhere else it would have felt like an odd thing to do. Arrive one day and jump on a boat with granny and grandchild the next. But I was in a different world to the one I had left. One where family seemed like everything and by staying with Hans I felt temporarily part of it. It was a privilege to be invited to second myself to this one for their annual fishing trip. Hans would not be accompanying us and perhaps he liked the idea of someone else going with his wife to help out. There seemed little to amuse me back at the hotel anyway and so I jumped on board. The boat we travelled in was owned and skippered by a friend of Hans's and, much like the other boats in the bay, it was of fibreglass construction with a large, imported engine on the back. I tried and failed to get the name of the captain as we headed out into Murchison Sound; our voices were blotted out by the high whine of the engine. The boat made good progress through the icebergs, passing Herbert Island (also known locally as Qeqertarsuaq) to our left, and I stared in awe at the multitude of auks skimming across the sea just above the waves and darting amongst the smaller pieces of ice that covered the water.

Then, out of nowhere, a thick fog enveloped us. A silver smokescreen that blinded us to the danger of the sharp, rock-like edges of the solid pieces of ice around us. I recognised a glimpse of nervousness across the face of the boat's captain. He began to steer us back towards the coast where he was able to use the land as a guide rail. The boat glided slowly over crystal-clear water. I followed the lead of the others now that we were closer to shore and leaned out over the side of the boat looking for errant rocks that threatened to smash the propeller. At one point the engine cut out and we were left stranded, but the skipper took this in his stride and within a short space of time had it working again.

The area was vast and remote, and the reality was that even though we were not the only boat on this stretch of coast, if the engine couldn't be fixed we would have been stranded for a very long time. Finally, the fog cleared, and we rounded the corner to make the final approach to a small, rock-lined beach under the red cliffs on the south side of McCormick Bay where we would set our camp. I was just short of the location where Haig-Thomas had stood shoeless in the icy water of a glacial river with the Inuit as they speared dozens of the hundreds of fish that swam past them. This was also where the explorer Robert Peary and his seven-person team, including his wife Josephine, found a home in 1891, and where they built a hut under the red cliffs to prepare for the following year's ambition to explore Greenland's ice cap. In 1892 he travelled over 800 kilometres to the north of Greenland and discovered a place he named Independence Fjord; he had arrived on 4th July and was keen to honour his American homeland. The trip gave him the right to say that he had travelled further across Greenland's inner ice than any other American or European before him. Even Nansen, later to become a competitor for the first to reach the North Pole, congratulated him. It was the first of many trips to the area. Peary had a contrasting approach to the Polar Inuit. On one hand, he valued their methods of travel and survival above all else. He told a journalist, 'Everything they eat or wear, and everything in the way of sledges or other equipments which they possess, they have provided by long experience to be the most suitable articles of their respective kinds.' Peary spent his time in McCormick Bay learning from the hunters that supported him that winter. On the other hand, he treated them with far less respect than he might have his own countrymen. He is said to have fathered two children in the area with a married Inuit woman named Aleqasina who was rumoured to be as young as fourteen when they started their affair. A topic he avoided on his return to America. Peary would send Aleqasina's husband off on long errands so that he could make his advances. Peary was also happy to exploit the people that were so key to his successes. He returned to the area in subsequent years, taking valuable fox furs back to America as well as more illicit human cargo that included six Inuit and the skeletons of long dead Inuit that he robbed from their graves. Later, this cargo included three large meteorites that many considered sacred.

The captain indicated for us to get off and I jumped out of the boat with Bietcha and Mishookchak, my feet landing in the cold water. We waded through to the shore and headed up the shingle beach to make camp. I had brought nothing with me other than my clothes. Bietcha set up the tent that she could sleep in with her grandson – a length of canvas sheet held up in the middle by a wooden frame and lashed to rocks so that it wouldn't blow away in a wind. In an area where winds can reach over 200 kilometres per hour, this was a real danger. She threw me a small polythene bag with a lightweight modern tent inside and left me to put it up on my own.

It was clear Bietcha was in charge, and I was happy to obey as she began directing me to set out the net in preparation for the next few days of hard fishing. She couldn't speak any English and I had no Inuktitut, but we were able to understand each other through gesturing and finger pointing. When Haig-Thomas fished in the area he talked about spearing multitudes of salmon from the river at the top of the bay. Our quarry would be Arctic char and I wondered whether perhaps he was mistaken as the two species of fish share a number of similarities.

First the nets had to be laid out. We tied an old plastic milk bottle to a large rock which was paddled out and dropped about five metres off the rocky shore. The bottle acted as a float and a long rope that was attached to the net was threaded through its handle and brought back to shore before being made fast to another rock on the beach. It was simple but effective and it meant that we could pull the fish in and lay the net out without any of us having to set foot in the ice-cold water.

It didn't take much time for the fish to hit the net and they did so with a great flurry of splashing, almost as soon as we had laid it across the water. Each time we dragged in the net Mishookchak and Bietcha would shout out '*Bilbakayoo!*' I didn't know what it meant but I was quickly shouting along with them as the excitement of so many fish overtook me. We took it in turns to pull in the net. We dragged dozens of the flapping and slapping bars of silver on to the beach while they struggled to free themselves from the tangles of the net. Like salmon, Arctic char are migratory fish. They leave the rivers around McCormick Bay for only a couple of months, starting in early June and returning late August. At sea they shine with a metallic hue. As they move back to the river to spawn or escape the sub-zero temperatures their backs darken, and their bellies turn bright orange or red: a way of camouflaging themselves from predators that include polar bears, Arctic foxes and humans.

I decided to ingratiate myself with my new family by volunteering to gut all the fish we caught. It made me feel useful and would perhaps earn me a little respect. Bietcha smiled at my gesture as I waved the knife at their bellies. I crouched by the water's edge and, taking the fish, I cut from their tails along their bellies, removing the contents with a flick of the knife and watching it fall into the crystal-clear water that lapped gently against my feet. Once I was done, Bietcha told me to bury the catch under some rocks. Mishookchak led the way, and we hauled the transparent plastic bags that were bursting with fish up to a stream and buried them under a flat, heavy rock. It would offer some protection from the sun as well as the foxes and wolves. Bietcha continued fishing long into the night sun. I sat and watched her for a short while. She had lit the stove in her tent which she would visit while she waited for the nets to become full again. There was often a pot of coffee roasting on the Primus, and she would fill her mug and take the steaming cup with her back to the shoreline where she would stand and stare out across the mist-covered bay. Occasionally, she would turn and look my way, spreading out her arms like wings, her faced creased with a huge smile. 'Wonderful,' she would shout out before turning back towards the Arctic landscape. She was in her eighties and had lived in Qaanaaq all her life, yet it was like she was taking it in for the first time.

We got on well despite the language barrier. I spent the time when we were not catching fish helping with the cooking in the camp, walking up into the mountains and photographing the flora and fauna. I still felt a sense of unease in my new surroundings. My imagination conjured up paranoid illusions of large polar bears that silently stalked me. I felt as vulnerable as a migrating wildebeest navigating the crocodile-infested rivers of the Serengeti. Whenever I walked away from the camp, I carried an old .22 rifle, rusty with age, that I borrowed from Mishookchak. They laughed to each other at my paranoia. They were right to laugh. No-one had seen any sign of a polar bear and the small rifle I carried would have been useless even if they had.

In the evenings we would cut up and cook the fish we had caught in a large pan of salted water which rested above the fire. It was a common way of preparing it locally and when the temperature dropped Bietcha would invite me into their tent to get warm. Despite appearances on the outside, their tent was more spacious and cosier than mine. The Primus heater was constantly burning in the corner. Although it was summer the nights were still cold, and the Primus kicked out enough heat to cut through the chill. I was sad to retreat into the cooling evening air and head back to my plastic-lined tent each night; it felt cold and damp in comparison. I began to understand why Haig-Thomas had always tried to use the same clothing and equipment as the Inuit used.

After a few more days we had managed to fill four sacks that were now brimming with fish, almost seventy in all. I caught the high-pitched buzz of a boat engine as we cleared up our camp and soon it came into view. This time there was no fog, and we had an easy ride, zigzagging through the icebergs and racing against small groups of little black-and-white auks and eider ducks. Hans was delighted to see us on our return and was even happier when he saw the many bags of fish we brought with us.

CHAPTER 5

STAR STONES – QAANAAQ

Among the hills a meteorite
Lies huge; and moss has overgrown,
And wind and rain with touches light
Made soft, the contours of the stone

C. S. LEWIS, 'METEORITE'[9]

Peary learnt of three meteorites that had landed in the Cape York area from his Inuit companions who supported his various expeditions across the Greenland ice cap and his two-decade-long endeavours to reach the geographic North Pole. In the last few chapters of his book *Northward Over the 'Great Ice'* Peary talks about the '*Saviksue*' or Cape York meteorites. *Saviksue* means 'great irons' in Inuktitut. There were three meteorites in total, their location marked near Cape York by a large, pointed mountain that Peary named 'Signal Mountain'. The largest of the meteorites was known as 'The Tent'; the two smaller ones were called 'The Woman' and 'The Dog'. The meteorites had lain there for millennia. Local legend had it that they were originally an Inuit woman, her dog and tent that had been hurled from the sky by Torngarsuk, an evil spirit. The Inuit had been using what Peary termed 'space rocks' for iron which they chipped away to create knives, harpoon heads and other tools. It was perhaps a predictable move representative of the time that Peary would decide to remove the celestial rocks from Greenland and take them back to New York.

9 Extract used with permission from the poem 'Meteorite' by C. S. Lewis – copyright CS Lewis Pte Ltd.

Nowadays it would be akin to removing much of the accessible mineral wealth of another nation. The unassuming brown rocks had played such an important part in the culture of the Inuit. Peary was very much aware of their history but made the decision to remove not one but all three of the rocks. He was able to take two of the meteorites, 'The Woman' and 'The Dog', in 1895 in his ship the *Kite*, no mean feat with 'The Woman' alone estimated to weigh 2.7 tonnes – about the same as a pick-up truck. The third meteorite, 'The Tent', was much larger. Peary estimated that it weighed between ninety and one hundred tonnes and took two attempts to transport it in a larger ship, the *Hope*: the second attempt in 1896 and the final, successful attempt in 1897. When the larger meteorite arrived in New York it was placed on to a large truck and pulled by twenty-eight horses through the streets to the American Museum of Natural History where it went on display alongside 'The Woman' and 'The Dog'[10]. In return for their efforts in this small act of cultural genocide, Peary supplied the Inuit with barrels of biscuits, guns, knives and ammunition.

It was Henning – a middle-aged, academic-looking Dane – who introduced me to the story of Peary and his meteorites. Henning was a meteorologist from the Natural History Museum of Denmark. The museum was leading a research initiative into the Paleo-Eskimo culture, an indigenous group that disappeared around 700 years ago.

---

10 Peary also brought with him six Inuit to be studied at the museum at the request of anthropologist Franz Boas. The youngest was a boy named Minik who was around six years old at the time. They lived in the basement of the museum when they weren't on display. Sadly, four of the six died; without resistance, they fell to tuberculosis. In 1907 Minik discovered that his father's bones had never been buried but were kept in the museum. In 1993, long after Minik's death, the bones were finally repatriated to Greenland and buried in the churchyard in Qaanaaq. *Give Me My Father's Body* by Kenn Harper describes the tragic life of Minik and the fate of the other Inuit that he left Greenland with.

Peary's meteorites were an important aspect of their research and frustratingly for Henning his helicopter had been grounded by bad weather and he was stuck in Qaanaaq for the next few days. It was bad news for him but good news for me as there was very little to do while I waited for my meeting with the local hunters.

Henning invited me up the glacier above the town to look for some smaller meteorites. The route led us up a steep scree slope of a valley; below us ran a river that tumbled its way down to the Inglefield Bay. We continued walking for some time, the glacier always visible ahead of us. Along the way we looked out for extraterrestrial pieces of rock. Henning talked me through ten ways that I could spot one, but I didn't find this very helpful. It seemed to me that the ten ways applied to most of the rocks we were stepping over.

'Henning,' I shouted out across the glacier. 'This time I've definitely found one.'

Henning ran over and examined the dark-coloured rock. 'No, Edward, this is not a meteorite, it is another meteo-wrong!' he said, chastising me as a professor might a struggling student.

Despite our lack of success, looking for the elusive meteorites was a fun game and kept us occupied as we climbed the rest of the way up the steep, icy sides of the glacier. The views from the top were stunning, the vast ice cap of the glacier stretching out ahead of us as far as the eye could see. On our way back we caught sight of a Japanese party heading down to our left; they had been in Qaanaaq since spring and had been visiting the glacier every day to take samples. I imagined Haig-Thomas, Wright and Hamilton taking similar trips up the glacier back in Thule, his team laying out boards so that they could measure the extent to which the glacier had moved and in doing so shed some light as to why glaciers in Switzerland had begun to recede at such an alarming rate.

I enjoyed those days with Henning, walking the glaciers and hunting meteorites. It passed the time while I waited for Hans to arrange a gathering with the Hunters' Union. I still hadn't been able to quiz them about our route to Ellesmere Island. It was another few days before the meeting time was agreed and by that time the weather had cleared for Henning and he left town.

Sat in the confines of my room in the hotel the wait seemed long and with little to amuse me it became dull and surreal. The constant sunlight made sleep hard to come by and with such a short stay in Greenland my body clock was struggling to acclimatise. I went for a walk down to the cliffs below the town, as much for my sanity as anything else. I walked along the clear glacial river that I had spotted on my walks with Henning. Its waters bubbled and frothed as it rose and fell across the rocks below it. The river opened up at the bottom of the valley where it joined the bay. Hunters had erected a wooden structure where cuts of meat dried under the sun's warming rays. The smell of death and decay hung in the air. Hunters had cleaned and removed most of the carcass that had caused the stench. All that was left was the elongated remains of a raven-scavenged skull. The surface was still covered in tatters of yellowing meat. Large hollow sockets were all that remained of the animal's eyes and a long beak-like form protruded from below these. The skull had belonged to a narwhal that had been killed and brought up on to the shore for butchering.

The Inuit still hunted these animals from kayaks and with harpoons made of wood during the spring and summer months when the ice had retreated and the narwhals came to these bays in search of polar cod. Famed for their long, spiral teeth, these animals can grow up to five and a half metres long – not including the tusk, which can extend this length by another three metres. They are grey in colour and feed of Greenland halibut, cod, squid and shrimp. The tusk, which grows through the top lips of males and some females when they are young, are the only teeth they have. Narwhals are one of the few cetaceans in the region that don't migrate. They stay in the Arctic throughout the summer and winter months, often appearing through open-water channels that run amongst the sea ice that are known as leads. They can appear in groups of fifteen or so but sometimes in their thousands. Up to forty per cent of the animal is covered in blubber which, alongside polar bears and other species of whale, has become a delicacy for the Inuit. The blubber or 'muktuk' is carved off in chunks to be eaten raw like sashimi. It is an important source of vitamin C as fresh vegetables and fruit are expensive to source in the summer and almost impossible to find during the winter when the supply ship is prevented from reaching the area due to the thick ice. Calving glaciers can make the hunting of narwhals a perilous venture, sometimes swamping hunters into the icy seas. I was told that this had become more frequent as the climate warmed. The narwhal's most defining feature, its tusk, has created a mythology that, unlike the narwhal, has migrated across the world. It is believed by many to have inspired the stories of the unicorn. Since the time of the Vikings, merchants attributed it with everything from magic to mental health care to the neutralisation of poison.

In the 16th century a narwhal tusk[11] was gifted to Queen Elizabeth of England. Valued at £10,000 at the time it was the price of a small castle; the Queen used it as a sceptre. The reason why a narwhal has such a spectacular tusk is still unknown. Some believe it is used like a

11 More recently during the London Bridge terror attacks of 2021, a narwhal tusk was used by Darryn Frost, a British civil servant who was attending a community outreach programme organised by students from the University of Cambridge. Darryn removed the tusk from Fishmongers' Hall near London Bridge and used it to apprehend the terrorist who had already killed two people and injured three others.

sword to spar with other males, others believe it acts like a peacock's feathers, attracting would-be admirers. What is known is that there are more than 10 million nerve connections that work throughout its spiral form, making it incredibly sensitive in detecting changes in water temperature and pressure, and a useful attribute in the narwhal's ability to dive down over a thousand metres, swallowing prey whole through their toothless mouths.

I left the morbid scene and returned to the town, the image etched in my memory, a sight of death that sat so much in contrast to the beauty that surrounded it.

Hans had arranged a meeting with a man from the Hunters' Union called Rasmus to be held in the living room of the hotel. It was a pine-panelled room set apart from the guest area of the hotel. Rasmus and Hans were already sitting down, and I joined them, taking my seat on an old, comfortable sofa. Hanging on the wall above an electric heater, the length of a fishing rod, was the long, spiralled tooth of a narwhal.

Rasmus was middle-aged and tough-looking. Hans had told me that he had hunted all his life and was well respected in the community. I shook his hand and managed some brief and broken small talk before I began to walk him through our plan for the following year. Hans sat with us and translated when he sensed there was a gap. I explained that we wanted to take a dog team from Qaanaaq up the west coast to Etah before setting off across Smith Sound to Ellesmere Island in Nunavut. From there we would cross Ellesmere Island and follow the sea ice along Eureka Sound, past Axel Heiberg Island and on to Haig-Thomas Island before turning around and coming back. It was a round trip of almost 2,000 kilometres that had sounded great on paper when I had laid it out back home, but I could see from the man's reaction that it would be easier said than done.

'Smith Sound, where you cross the sea ice to the island, this is the hardest part of your journey,' he said. 'There is an area of open water on your route which doesn't freeze over any more. I have seen people try in the last few years, but they have failed and had to turn back.'

The open water he was referring to I knew as the 'Northern Water', something that scientists might call a polynya. Its open waters are an oasis for marine life in a sea of ice, but it was a problem for us. The ice charts from the previous year had pointed this out as well and Rasmus's attitude confirmed my fears. The crossing and therefore the entire expedition would be completely dependent on the state of the ice. Recently, there had been less ice coverage and the extent of the open water was increasing year on year which was not going to help with our plans. It had been the downfall of many more experienced travellers.

'It has become harder and harder to predict,' Rasmus said. 'I also think you'll find it hard to find a hunter to take you.'

The changing climate and its impact on the crossing of Smith Sound had been one factor in far fewer hunters from Qaanaaq travelling to their old hunting grounds on Ellesmere Island. The 1999 development of Nunavut, the Canadian territory that Ellesmere Island was part of, was another equally important factor. The creation of Nunavut was negotiated under Canada's policy on outstanding land claims by aboriginal peoples: a way for the Canadian Inuit to develop a more balanced and respectful relationship between themselves and the federal government. After the World Trade Centre attack in 2001, the Nunavut border, like many others around the world, was increasingly enforced. The knock-on effect was that the previously porous border across Smith Sound became more difficult for the Inuit of north-west Greenland to travel across. Okalik Eegeesiak, Chair of the Inuit Circumpolar Council, wrote in 2017: 'Our children no longer know the place names of our hunting grounds, nor have they travelled across the ice bridge that links these lands.' The result for me was that I couldn't find anyone with recent experience of the area. It was another hurdle to my plans but one that I had already had some experience of.

My initial discussions with one or two hunters had been comical, lots of head shaking and mimicking of 'hard work' as they wiped the imaginary sweat from their brows when I told them where I wanted to go. Rasmus didn't think it would be possible, and even if it was there were other things I hadn't thought about. He told me that I should have already laid provisions for food in depots along our route to support a dog team on a winter journey as we couldn't carry the amount we would need on a sledge. He also made clear that the impact of the changing climate meant the ice was melting earlier each year. 'You would be hard-pressed to make the full sledging trip in time to get back across to Greenland,' he said. 'You would be left stranded with the whole dog team on Ellesmere Island.'

I put on a brave face as my plans were slowly eroded by common sense. It wasn't that I hadn't been prepared. It was more an example of the importance of local knowledge. I was very glad that I had made the trip and even happier that I had found someone to talk our route through with. As well as the plan we spoke in detail of the changes that had happened in the community since the 1930s when Haig-Thomas had travelled to the Arctic.

The tourism that had been brought to the area was a huge help, especially tours by dog sledges and those in support of film crews and scientists. However, I was surprised to hear from Hans that since the airport came to Qaanaaq in 2001 tourism had actually decreased despite government efforts to the contrary. The cost of getting to Qaanaaq had gone up a lot, he explained. 'People always used to come by helicopter which sounds expensive but the government subsidised it so people liked it,' Hans told me. 'Most of the tourists would come from March through to May from Thule in the helicopter which used to be much cheaper than the plane is now, the hotel was always full.' It seemed a far cry from the empty rooms and halls that I had seen in the few weeks that I had been there, when it was only the odd scientist that had arrived.

The changing climate that inhibited our route also meant the ice was less predictable. It had reduced the hunters' access to traditional hunting grounds and to the animals they relied on for their income. Quotas had also made things harder, limiting the length of the season and making competition for what could be caught fiercer.

Rasmus was happy to help but was sceptical of the intentions of the many foreigners who visited. As with the forcible relocation caused by Thule Airbase, interactions with strangers driven by global forces were not always positive. Rasmus was keen to explain that while climate change had affected the way that the Inuit hunted in Qaanaaq and the surrounding towns, he was confident that they would adapt as they always did. A bigger impact, I was told, had been in the 1970s when Greenpeace led a campaign against the import of sealskins to the EU. While its intentions were positive, its implementation was naïve and ill thought through. Despite what the Inuit thought, the campaign was deemed a success by the broader international community at the time. They had targeted mass-scale commercial seal hunting, but they had failed to consult many of the smaller communities that relied on sealskin exports to support a subsistence way of life. The ban caused the price of sealskins to collapse overnight. For many Inuit in Qaanaaq who lived in modern Danish housing with the accompanying heating and water bills to pay it meant that hunting was no longer a viable profession. For those that continued to hunt, it made life much harder for them. It caused huge damage to the community's economy and its culture. The lack of an apology from Greenpeace only left resentment and a feeling of suspicion of outsiders' motivations with regards to Greenland and their own town of Qaanaaq. Although it seemed so remote up here it was clear that they hadn't been isolated from the ebbs and flows of the world around them. Many had turned to fishing to replace this income. Just as in the south of Greenland, the halibut they caught now made up a significant part of their income. It was partly because of the seal dispute and later another on fishing rights that Greenland left the EU in 1985 – only six years after gaining its autonomy from Denmark and long before the UK decided to.

I left Rasmus a much wiser person. He had added a touch of reality to what had until now been a relatively uneducated dream. Yes, I had done a lot of research and, yes, I had spoken to many in the explorer world, but those conversations carried very little weight compared to actually sitting down with someone that lived in the Arctic, hunted there and really knew the area. I realised that what we had discussed fundamentally changed both the research and the route plan. It was time to head back to London to take stock of what this meant for the expedition and to see whether it would still be possible to continue given these new challenges.

The Greenlandic weather turned in the days after that meeting, which prevented any flights coming or going. It was another week before I finally left Hans and his wife at the hotel. The delay was an introduction to the reality that out here the elements ruled. Hans and Bietcha drove me to the airport together when it was time to leave.

Waving goodbye to them from the plane felt like waving goodbye to my own grandparents. As much as I had enjoyed my brief stint in Qaanaaq, I was very much looking forward to the prospect of going to bed somewhere where night-time was a seasonal certainty and where it would be dark enough to sleep.

CHAPTER 6

BACK TO THE DRAWING BOARD – LONDON

Back in London I had some thinking to do. In terms of the research objective, I saw the changes to our plans as a positive. With only 60,000 inhabitants, Greenland is often described as one big family rather than just another country. I hoped this meant that there might be a chance of finding in Qaanaaq some of the descendants of the Inuit that had been exiled from Thule when the Airbase arrived. I had taken a short black-and-white film that had been recorded during the original expedition. The film drew blank faces from the few people I had shown it to, and my search to identify anyone in the film or find out whether there were any descendants I could speak to was a complete failure. Through the Hunters' Union, what I had established was a link to the hunting culture in Qaanaaq. Haig-Thomas's time hunting walruses, polar bears and narwhals with the Inuit took up several chapters of his book and the accounts he produced were detailed and comprehensive.

I had grown up hunting with my father in the UK and I felt that I had been provided with a legacy of understanding that might give me some affinity with the Inuit hunters, their traditions and their methods. With so many changes to hunting already in Qaanaaq I thought that it would be of much more benefit to the community to focus on this area instead and to document what we saw seventy years after the original expedition. I explained this to Zenith and the SES, my main sponsors. I was relieved and a little surprised when they signed off on the change happily.

The impact on the proposed route was a little trickier. The changing ice situation, the fact that we were clearly too late to lay depots that summer (which we would need to support a dog team on the way north) and the lack of willing locals with expertise of the Smith Sound crossing to help us were all obstacles. The unpredictable ice conditions across Smith Sound posed too great a problem to ignore and there were plenty of stories of previous expeditions falling foul of the area. I made drastic changes to the original route plan. I still felt that we needed to start in Qaanaaq as this was where we would carry out the research, but I decided that we wouldn't even attempt the sea-ice crossing which would have involved sledging past the open northern waters to get to Ellesmere Island. This meant that the original plan to use dogs and sledges had to be dropped. The desire to travel as the Inuit travelled wasn't going to work. We would have to use skis and sledges to make the route. A very modern form of travel but it had been tried and tested by many that had gone far further than we would go. Wearing the furs of the Inuit also wouldn't work. They were designed to keep you warm while the dogs did the work. They would be an added weight and we would sweat far too much in them as we pulled the heavy loads. This would become dangerous in the cold when they became damp and lost their insulating properties. While the new plan meant using modern equipment it didn't mean stepping away from the spirit of the expedition, which was to learn how the Inuit travelled in the Arctic as Haig-Thomas had done. I would have to compromise but in doing so I would assimilate the use of modern equipment and clothing with Inuit know-how about travelling in the Arctic. They could still help me to understand where to make camp, how to deal with the wildlife, the state of the ice and how to survive in its cold climate.

I did consider the use of a boat. At the awards evening in London there had even been a man from Babcock who had offered some small speedboats for the task. I almost took him up on the offer, but I worried that the fast-flowing water and the potential for getting stuck in the ice or crushed by an iceberg meant that this was too dangerous. Instead, I decided that flying across Smith Sound would be the best option. While it meant stepping away from following Haig-Thomas's journey as closely as I had planned, in particular his full route by dog sledge, it could almost guarantee that the expedition would take place the following year.

Flights from Qaanaaq to Nunavut are not a daily occurrence and so the SES were keen to understand what the likely cost would be. I did a bit of research and identified a carrier called Kenn Borek Air who flew private charters in the Arctic and in the Antarctic as well. The cost was huge, just under 65,000 Canadian dollars, the equivalent of £40,000. It would have been much cheaper to have gone from Resolute Bay in northern Canada where Kenn Borek was based, but I felt that this would undermine the story and the research. I promised the SES that I was still confident I could raise the money to cover the leap in costs even though I had no idea where to get the additional funds from at that point. I know they had their doubts. To their credit they continued to back me. The price of the charter meant that the cost of failure was much higher, but it meant that the expedition was back on track.

The plan as I now explained to Alec was to fly out to Qaanaaq at the beginning of February to establish camp. Alec would join me a couple of weeks later which also made sense in case I had forgotten anything, and he could bring it up with him from England. We would start with the research and because we would be working closely with the hunters this would also mean that, like Haig-Thomas, we could spend our time learning how to travel in the Arctic and acclimatise ourselves to the sub-freezing temperatures. This would all help prepare us for the hardest part, which was still the sledge journey to Haig-Thomas Island.

The newly chartered plane would pick us up from Qaanaaq Airport in the spring and fly us across to a Canadian weather station based at Eureka on Ellesmere Island where there was a small runway. From there we would pull our heavily laden sledges the 450 kilometres south down Eureka Sound and west along the coast of Axel Heiberg Island before heading on to Haig-Thomas Island where we hoped to find the note that Haig-Thomas had left all those years ago. If we made it that far, the plane would be our exit, taking us from the sea ice on Haig-Thomas Island before heading back to Qaanaaq where we could take the commercial flights home.

Funding was now my main concern, both for the flights and for the equipment, which meant I needed to find more sponsorship. *The Telegraph* wanted an exclusive arrangement that meant I would be providing regular articles on the expedition over the next twelve months. I was and still am an amateur when it comes to writing. Luckily, Tim Ecott, an accomplished writer and good friend, promised his help. There was one slight hitch during the discussions, however. I went along to *The Telegraph*'s offices in London's Victoria to meet Jessamy Calkin who would be commissioning the articles. Jessamy had invited her picture editor, Fred, to listen to my pitch. I arrived in an awful state, sweating alcohol and nursing a hangover brought on when some planning drinks had got out of hand the night before. Jessamy had asked me to show her some examples of my photographs, and I took out my laptop and began to run through some of the pictures that I had taken during the summer recce.

I was still experimenting with the camera, and many were out of focus or blurry, which was confirmed in no certain terms during the meeting. It was clear that I hadn't quite mastered the art of photography yet. After flicking through them, Fred came straight to the point. 'Will you be taking a photographer with you?' he asked.

'I wasn't planning to,' I said. 'Why do you ask?'

'They're not great photos,' he responded. Already in a fragile state from the night before, I was only able to muster some mumbled apologies at this latest affront to my blossoming talents. I promised them that in return for almost a year's worth of coverage I would learn how to use the camera and supply them with decent photographs. They seemed dubious but were willing to take the risk and I left the white expanses of their offices making my way down the long staircase happy in the knowledge that I now had something concrete to offer potential sponsors. The promise of it was enough to bring Haglöfs on board as our main kit sponsor. The rest came through fairly easily in a mixture of sponsored kit and through chasing up previous expeditions for their old stuff.

I couldn't imagine many people returned to the same expedition twice and so made the correct assumption that there would be a lot of kit from previous expeditions sitting in people's sheds around the country. I knocked on Sir Ranulph Fiennes's door first and he was kind enough to lend us an old tent along with some first-rate sledge harnesses and a couple of temperamental old MSR stoves (which were replaced later with some slightly newer ones by Soto, a Japanese stove maker). Vicky Nicholson from Walking With The Wounded – a charity we had supported during the Engelandvaarder expedition, then helped us out by lending us skis, poles and cooking pans that they had just finished with after their recent Antarctic expedition with Prince Harry.

The SES and Zenith had given us a huge boost with the grant but there was still a big gap in the funding needed to charter our own airplane. Some of this came from Haig-Thomas's descendants whom Alec had been discussing the expedition with. As well as Haig-Thomas's son Tony, these included his grandsons – who by coincidence were also called Ed and Al – who had both dreamt of going but hadn't managed to get there and so, along with their father Tony, were willing to contribute funds in the hopes that someone else would. The final piece of the fundraising puzzle was a contribution from the Transglobe Expedition Trust, set up by Sir Ranulph Fiennes and Anton Bowring after the Transglobe Expedition, the first north-to-south circumnavigation of the earth using only surface transport. It had been set up to support expeditions like ours and they were generous in their contributions. Haig-Thomas had got a loan in the end from a bank, but Alec and I, who had been saving like mad from our jobs, both agreed to fill the gap with personal funds. In the end we had to as we couldn't find anyone else with deep enough pockets.

It was 9th February and time to leave England again and journey to Greenland. London was bathed in the warm glow of the winter's sun. Businessmen rushed between meetings, black cabs shuffled along through the infinite city traffic and dark-glassed Middle Eastern ladies made an authoritative if not slower-paced march towards the next shopping store on the list. I was stepping away from the relative safety of London, tearing off the constraints of corporatism and stepping into a place of darkness. It was both liberating and terrifying. I packed up most of my kit and the larger items I had organised to be sent on separately. I went to Knightsbridge for a farewell lunch with Alec. In a moment of absent-mindedness, I had tricked myself into thinking I had more time than I did. Haig-Thomas had missed his boat from Copenhagen on his way to Greenland and was only saved by the kindness of a passing Dane. I couldn't imagine airlines these days being so kind and so I made my own mad rush to the airport.

I dragged a large, cumbersome Boris Bike from its magnetic lock and leapt aboard, cycling furiously through the lunchtime traffic and across an arched-back bridge to Battersea Park. All the while holding the bike handle in one hand and trying book a taxi with the other. I hit the bike terminal on Albert Bridge Road with a thud that reverberated up my wrists and into my shoulders. I leapt off and ran the rest of the way to the flat, sweat pouring off me despite the winter's chill. A black cab had already got there when I arrived. I lifted my hand to the driver and mouthed 'Two seconds' before rushing inside where I retrieved the huge waterproof bag that housed everything I needed for my journey. I leapt into the back of the waiting taxi. 'Clapham Junction station please, and fast,' I blurted out to the slightly bemused driver. To his credit he slammed his foot on to the accelerator and tore off like Senna, berating me along the way for cutting it so fine. His wheels screeched and the car jumped about manically as we raced across speed bumps to get to the station on time. We got to Clapham Junction for the 14:38 train. It was tight but if I could catch this train then I would get to Gatwick just in time to navigate the long lines of security and board the flight to Copenhagen which left at 16:20.

I made it to the airport just in time to board my plane. After the intensity of my mad dash across London I fell into my plane seat, exhausted. The steady drum of warming engines thrummed along in the background. My racing pulse settled into a steadier beat and was replaced by a feeling of trepidation for what lay ahead. I had overcome hundreds of small obstacles over the last four years to get to this point, but now here I was. The plane's wheels left the black tarmac of the runway and it dawned on me that the real journey had only just begun.

CHAPTER 7

INTO THE COLD – QAANAAQ

It was the second week of February. The sun had continued its rotations around the earth, unobserved by those living in the north of Greenland. The world here had been cloaked in perpetual darkness since November the previous year. I looked down through the frosted panes of the airplane window. In the twilight I could see all the way across Greenland's snow-covered peaks and out towards the ink-dark sea, its surface dotted with the white pinpricks of icebergs. Wisps of clouds blew over the summits of the many mountains that criss-crossed the landscape. The deep red paint of the aircraft's fuselage had developed an icy patina which stretched across its wings, like the breath marks of an unseen polar spirit. I imagined large bodies of walruses crashing through the sea ice below me, mother bears curled up with their offspring buried deep within the safety of their dens, the soft tread of lone male polar bears on their own long journeys across the frozen seas in search of prey. It was a different world to the one I had left behind in London. The pilot's voice crackled across the intercom, pulling me from my daydream. He spoke first in Greenlandic, then Danish and finally English. 'Thank you for flying with Air Greenland. We hope you enjoyed your flight. We will be starting our descent soon. We have clear skies in Qaanaaq with a temperature of minus thirty, so wrap up warm,' he said. I zipped up my down jacket and adjusted the scarf that peeked through in a gaudy orange around my neck. The lowest temperature I had experienced was in Sweden when it had been minus twenty. I had thought that was cold at the time. Minus thirty was a significant drop on that.

We touched down with a bang, the plane's air-filled tyres bouncing briefly across the gritted runway. It taxied across to the small, low terminal building where it stopped, its four large propellers spinning freely through the air. I filtered along the aisle with the other passengers, watching them carefully to see whether they turned to stone on impact with the icy air. None did and so I took my turn to step out of the plane. The cold hit me like a slap across the face, instantly removing the weariness that I had felt after three days of travelling. I took a deep breath. The air was clean and unpolluted. I recognised Hans, the hotel owner, standing in the crowded terminal, wrapped up in a grey winter coat. My boots cracked across the ice as I walked over to greet the familiar face. I placed my feet carefully, not wanting to slip on the frozen surface. I waved at him and expected to be met with a smile of recognition. He looked at me blankly. I wondered whether he had forgotten me or whether he was just pissed off that I wouldn't be paying to stay at the hotel this time. He gestured a thickly gloved finger over at another man who was deep in conversation. The man's name was Olas. He was the school's janitor who had been sent out to collect me along with a Greenlandic comedian who had come to promote his book. It could have set the scene for a memorable ride into town but a combination of my inability to speak Greenlandic or Danish and their lack of English made for an awkwardly quiet journey sat in the back seat of Olas's pick-up truck.

I stared out the window instead. The town had changed dramatically: snow covered up the sights and smells of poor drainage, bags of litter and unwashed dogs which had polluted it during the summer. The drying racks were still there along the water's edge but the boats were hidden. Either covered in snow, hauled up on to the beach or pulled into sheds to protect them from the ice that could splinter these small fibreglass boats like matchsticks. Teams of howling dogs were tethered in their places awaiting their masters for food and the next sledge journey.

Olas dropped me off at the school near the top of the town. It was one of the few buildings with more than one floor. Each one rang with the shouts and screams of the town's children battling against the teachers who were quickly losing patience. I met Troels, my host for the coming months, amongst a gaggle of these wayward souls. He was tall, well fed and, initially I thought, demonstrated many annoying qualities. He never said thank you and was sadistic in the pleasure he took from charging an extortionate rate for his lodgings and his Wi-Fi. As time went on I realised that underneath the bullish exterior, he had a heart of gold. He cared a lot for the children that he taught at the school and they seemed to adore him in return. He was a huge help in connecting us with the hunting community in Qaanaaq. Without him I think we would have struggled to make any friends at all.

Troels was part of a Danish initiative to place teachers into schools across Greenland. He had been working in Qaanaaq for over a year by the time we met. He greeted me warmly despite being in the middle of a maths class. A class that at that moment consisted of one pupil studying and the others running around in pandemonium. I sat there feeling out of place as I waited for him to finish class and show me back to the house. The general impression I got, especially after talking with some of the Greenlandic teachers in training from Nuuk, was that most of the children really weren't that interested in following the curriculum. When I looked outside the window across Inglefield Bay and Herbert Island, I could understand why. Studying maths or learning Danish seemed completely at odds with the environment they were being taught in. A nine-to-five curriculum didn't fit with the hunting pattern that many of their families still followed, which often meant weeks away from town. It also didn't fit with seasons of perpetual darkness and, in particular, perpetual light, when I had experienced children playing well into the early morning hours. The teachers were trying their best, however, and were constantly rewriting lesson plans to fit in with the culture and environment.

The bell rang to signal the end of a very long day. I was worn out by the crazed children and relieved to accompany Troels back to his house. He spoke good English and we chirped along as we walked up the ice-covered slope to an elongated red-coloured hut that rested on stilts. A large glass sliding door held together one end which led to a balcony ringed with a dark wooden handrail. Troels led the way, his heavy fur-lined boots clumping up the raised wooden stairs. He kicked the door sill on entering, handfuls of compressed snow flying off as he did so. He removed them and set them by the entrance. I followed him in, mimicking the same action. 'It will stop the snow melting on the floor inside,' he told me. I stepped inside a small boot room. It provided a type of decontamination chamber to de-kit and prevent the heat from the house being drawn out into the sub-zero temperatures outside. On one side hung a row of thick, heavy coats. The smell of sewage, partially masked by the liberal amounts of cleaning fluids, wafted from a door on the other. I guessed without looking that it must be the bathroom.

We walked into the main part of the house which felt more like a static caravan. The combination of being overheated and the lack of ventilation gave it a stuffy feel, compounded by the smells emanating from my host's bedroom, which looked like it hadn't been cleaned since he moved in. There were two bedrooms, an open-plan kitchen and living room furnished with a gigantic television and a cheap leather sofa. It was basic but it had internet and was enough for what we needed it for. That evening Troels proudly served me a plate of dry caribou meat from an animal he had shot over the summer.

I slept on the floor that night on a mat that Troels had laid out. Already developing ill feeling towards my host, I ruminated on the fact that I was paying London prices and he hadn't even bothered to provide a bed. I kept my grumblings to myself the next morning but was happy when he left for work. The temperature on the gauge read -30°C and I used the next few days to test out the equipment in the sort of temperatures we would experience in Nunavut.

Saturday finally arrived along with much-promised celebrations which I was excited to see. I headed out for the town's sports hall to witness them. When I arrived the festivities were almost over: the kids, parents and teachers had all dressed up in costume. It felt like something you might witness in a quaint village somewhere back in England. Famous figures and cartoon characters jumped out amongst the costumes; some sported Hello Kitty shirts and others full Batman outfits. I was impressed when I saw one child dressed up in full hunter's kit with a white smock and big, fluffy white polar bear pants. On his feet he wore tidy little boots called *kamiks* made from sealskin. He was the first person I had seen who was dressed in the full hunting regalia. There was also a very good impression of a fisherman – or fisherwoman, as she was a girl. She was wearing a giant fat suit and had managed to dig out some impromptu facial hair for the occasion.

With much of the culture in Qaanaaq, there was a heavy Danish influence, and these celebrations were no different. Rather than an

Inuit tradition, they were based on a historically Lutheran[12] festival called Fastelavn which had found its way over from Denmark, carried by early missionaries. The term comes from the Old Danish word *'fastelaghen'*, which translates loosely as 'fast-evening', and falls in the week before Lent. I soon learnt that dressing up in costumes was an important part of the festival. A cardboard box with the face of a cat painted on it was another common element. The box was hung like a piñata in the hall. The children had been taking it in turns to hit it as it hung spinning from a twisted string in the middle of the room. The children were blindfolded and given a stick, then spun around and sent towards the box. The first person to hit the box and make the candy spill out was called the 'Cat Queen', and the person who hit the box off the string to get the last of it was given the title the 'Cat King'. I asked one man standing next to me about the 'Cat Queen' and 'Cat King'. Many years ago, he said, the box used to house a cat, which the children beat to ward off evil, however times had changed, and it was now full of sweets. I wondered about the poor cats' luck, to have ended up in the far north with all that cold and no mice and then to find themselves in a box being knocked about by schoolchildren. Thankfully, I thought for the cat, things had changed. There was a small awards ceremony at the end with the whole town gathered in a square and prizes given to the best costumes, the prettiest and even the ugliest. I spent most of the time walking around trying to capture the moment with my camera, but it felt strange to be taking

---

12 Lutheranism is now the most practised religion in Greenland. The first missionaries arrived in 1721 and replaced many of the traditional beliefs. I have chosen to not focus on the traditional belief systems in Greenland given I had no experience of this while in Qaanaaq but it is a fascinating part of Inuit history and worth reading up on. Knud Rasmussen captured much of this during his expeditions and in his books.

photographs for an audience back home. I put my camera away and tried to be more present and less prying as the day went on.

Later that evening I followed up on an invitation to dinner at the school, which had been set up for some of the teachers in training who had travelled from Nuuk. They were leaving on the Wednesday flight the following week, and this was their farewell dinner. I took a few cans of beer up with me on the cold walk up the hill to the schoolhouse. Immediately on arriving, I was thrown in at the deep end. A long picnic table stood at one end of the room, its legs quaking under the vast quantities of grey, leathery meat that were laid across it on large, throwaway aluminium plates. Despite the banquet of boiled meats no-one was sure how to make a sauce. The headmaster, Danial, saw me as I walked in and asked me if I could do it. I was apprehensive and a little travel weary. I didn't want to ruin dinner, but I didn't want to be rude and reluctantly complied. I remembered my father making gravy back in Orford, using the juice from the meat and adding water with salt and pepper for seasoning. I took the same approach, ladling the greasy juices into a pan in the kitchen and cooking them over the burning blue hobs. The sauce began to take on a darker, thicker consistency and I was feeling pleased with the result. As I was turning the hob down on the chunky chrome cooker one of the Danish teachers came over to look. He stared at the small pan of liquid and then back at me. 'Can you make five litres of it?' he asked. I looked at him stunned until he pointed to the kitchen where there was even more meat roasting in the oven. I breathed a sigh of relief; there would be just enough to get by. It wouldn't pass for my father's gravy; it was watery and the oil from the meat fats had created a thick, bubbly film across the top. But it was better than nothing, I hoped.

With everything cooked and oily sauce at the ready we sat down at a long table in the library. Laid out in front of us were the large cuts of beef and pork with piles of rice and potatoes to match. There were even slices of chocolate brownies and ice cream for dessert. I was accompanied by a wide array of guests. Many had dressed up. Danial and his wife Rasmina wore matching Batman attire. There was a Dane dressed as a woman with a blacked-up face and wearing a fake Afro headpiece whilst his Inuit girlfriend wore a moustache and had made a fat suit out of pillows stuffed down her front and back.

After the meat and brownies had been devoured the Danish cross-dresser stood up and announced that it was time for games. Games had a role in almost every get-together I attended, whether that was out on the ice or in the warmth of someone's kitchen. Before these could begin there was a short interlude when the trainee teachers were taken out of the room, briefed and then brought back in one by one to recite a folk tale about a boy that was kidnapped. The catch was that they had to recite the story using the local lingo, much like an Englishman putting on a Scottish accent. The other teachers loved it and roared with laughter as the students blundered through their words, tripping up on unfamiliar sounds. After this was done, we got on with the other games. I would normally opt for a quiet corner out of the way but there was nowhere to hide here. The first game was to pick up where the children had left off; the box that used to house those poor cats was brought out again and hung up above the table.

Again, there was a 'Cat King' and 'Cat Queen' and even prizes for the best, ugliest and prettiest costumes. The Danish man in his short skirt managed to steal the prize for the prettiest. I forget who the awards for worst and ugliest went to but I received none. This was then followed up with a mass sing-song. Greenlandic song sheets were distributed by the headmaster, and I discovered that, unlike the choked attempts at singing I was used to back home, this was all being taken very seriously. I could see very clearly that they loved singing and they were all talented. The headmaster then donned a blonde wig as an addition to his Batman costume and he and a late arrival who had just come off a three-day bender began to expertly pluck at the strings of an electric guitar to the delight of everyone gathered there. Another late arrival to the party was the church organist who adopted a seat at a well-used piano. One of the girls then joined to lead the vocals and soon everyone was getting involved. For pure fun and enjoyment, I thought, my new friends had really hit the mark.

As the impromptu band got into the swing of it, the rest of the dinner guests began to dance. It all felt very surreal, but I was enjoying myself. It sounded very similar to the sort of thing that Haig-Thomas described during his time in Greenland. He wrote that, 'The actual dance was one learned from the Danes – for in the olden days these Eskimos never used to dance. It was something like a two-step, with a great deal of twisting and spinning round.'

From what I could see, not much had changed but there was a separate addition to the dance in that it also seemed to include a lot more clapping. Dance partners would clap right hand to right hand with each other, then left to left and finally both together. In between these movements they clapped their own hands and then got back to spinning each other around. The night ended with more games which were fun to watch, and all seemed designed to help people laugh at themselves. I joined in the first few, in which we had to clench a coin in one eye, a wooden spatula lengthways between our legs and balance a small potato on a spoon. We then had to attempt to make it around a cup at the end of the room and back again without dropping anything.

It was almost impossible, and everyone looked like mad pirates as they tried. As they started to talk about the final game they wanted to play, I decided it was probably time to go. 'The woman puts a balloon on her back whilst leaning over a chair and the man has to try and pop it with his hips,' my hosts explained. One for another time, I thought!

I woke up the next morning having weathered another night of howling from Troels's dog, made worse by the ache in my head that the beers the night before had left me with. Stepping out into the freezing temperatures was a great cure and I quickly sobered up. I was starting to acclimatise to the temperatures and the gear was holding up well. I realised that, on a calm day, just wearing some of my lightest gear was enough for anything up to -35°C. Starting at my feet and working upwards, this consisted of Baffin boots, one pair of Bridgedale socks (knee-length, otherwise the shorter ones would slip down), insulated and windproof trousers with a merino base layer on my top and bottoms, a fleece, an insulated gilet and a down jacket. On my hands I wore a set of thin under-gloves covered with thicker mittens and on my head I wore a hat and a balaclava that was pulled down around my neck but could easily be pulled up across my face if I needed it. I always felt reluctant to cover my face as none of the locals ever did. If I removed my hands from my mittens, however, they began to lose feeling almost immediately. The locals and many of the Danes wore items of modern clothing mixed with more traditional ones such as sealskin mittens, and even sealskin *kamiks* were coming back into fashion.

The light had begun to change, refracted by the clouds that had descended from the glacier above Qaanaaq, and the temperature dropped to -35°C. I managed to drag Troels down to the sea ice along with his dog, which had been howling like a manic thing ever since

I got to Qaanaaq. One night I awoke to see her slamming her chain against a wooden pillar in a bid to rid herself of her collar. In doing so she practically hung herself. It had made for some unpleasant nights trying to sleep. I thought a walk would do her good. On the sea ice next to the town there were about twelve huts that I could see from the shore; they formed a ring about three kilometres outside of town and lay all the way down the bay. Haig-Thomas didn't mention halibut in his book but since the 1980s there had been a growing industry in fish which had been quite lucrative for the local hunters. At night these huts twinkled like stars all across the bay as fishermen worked to bring their catch in.

We headed out to where Troels thought one of the hunters he knew was fishing. Last time I was here the entire place had been free of ice and now it was a few metres thick in places. A network of tracks criss-crossed the surface marking the routes that hunters had taken with their dog sledges. There was a single set of larger tyre tracks that had made deeper indentations in the snow. The town got its water from the icebergs in the bay and these tracks were made by large trucks that headed out each day to carve off chunks from the icebergs and bring them back to melt into drinking water. Walking along the tracks made by these gargantuan vehicles made me feel safe. I was still not used to walking on ice and the fact that it could take several tonnes of weight was a comfort. Stepping off towards the fishing camps was a strange feeling at first. I tried to remember some of the ways you could tell if the ice was strong enough to walk on. I knew to avoid the areas where I could see large white bubbles in the ice and to look for the areas that were white or grey, but to a person with very little experience as I was they all looked the same. We spotted some of the sledge tracks made by the hunters and followed them carefully to the fishing camps that we could see in the middle of the bay. Nookapinguaq had told Haig-Thomas that there was one 'real difference between white men and Eskimos. White men always think of ice as frozen water, but Eskimos think of water as melted ice. To us, ice is the natural state'. I tried to overcome my trepidation by thinking the same. We walked over parts where the ice had formed large ridges of broken slabs and I wondered at the incredible forces that must have caused them. In other moments I felt like I was walking through a gallery of modern art – calving icebergs had created chiselled statues of all shapes and sizes, their mirror-like features gloriously framed by the pink-coloured sky. It was a dreamlike landscape that the 18th-century philosopher Edmund Burke may have called 'sublime'. In Burke's view this is different to the idea of beauty and denotes a powerful aesthetic experience. A point where beauty is balanced with the feelings of fear, excitement and awe which can be an addictive cocktail of emotions. In a photograph, the sea ice, the icebergs and the frozen landscape that I walked through may simply be beautiful. However, if you had stood there with me, you might have felt another side to that beauty. You may have felt dwarfed by the vastness of the landscape whose horizons stretched seemingly to infinity. Or you may have tensed up when you felt an air so cold that it would bite at your uncovered skin causing you to clench your teeth in pain under its firebrand-like intensity. Your heart may have even jumped when you heard the thunderous cracks that shuddered across the mountains when an iceberg broke up. It was still very new to me and so I felt all of those things as I made my first steps across the sea ice. It was an addictive feeling and I was drawn into that landscape in a way that I hadn't experienced before.

I donned my windproof outer layer as there was a wickedly cold wind driving down the bay. As I breathed out, a thin layer of ice formed around the hair on my face and any exposed areas of skin became numb. When I pulled my balaclava up for the first time the condensation from my breath thickened it; it was like wearing a steel plate across my face. The ice-thickened garment had the benefit of better protecting my face from the wind. When we reached the hut we were aiming for we realised it was empty. Unsuccessful, we headed back to town just as the weather was turning and the fog had begun to descend across the ice. The going was a lot better on the way back with the wind behind us and it took far less time to get home then it had done to get out. My camera had suffered during the prolonged excursion. Outside, the cold drained the batteries of life within seconds. When I ungloved my hands to work the controls the freezing air chilled them to the point of agony. Stepping back into the hut the furnace-like heat caused instant condensation and covered the camera in wet drips. Operating it was something I never quite mastered during my time in the Arctic. I spent hours on the ice taking photographs of the landscape only to find that the picture had been blotted out where the camera lens had partly frosted over.

Later that evening Mikael, the hunter we had intended to meet out on the ice, came around for coffee. He introduced himself as Michael Jackson. I told him he didn't look like Michael Jackson, he said it was because of his nose. He explained that he had been out hunting for Greenlandic seal that day to provide food for the dogs and had to sledge back. His nose had gone numb and, like Michael Jackson, he thought it would fall off! He was heading back out that night but promised to drop by the next time he was going so that I could accompany him. Mikael became a great friend during my time there. The walk had calmed Troels's dog and for the first time since I had arrived in town, I got a decent night's sleep.

CHAPTER 8

THE FIRST SUNRISE – QAANAAQ

A crack opened in the curtain of dark that had covered the town of Qaanaaq for the last four months. A dim golden glow shone from behind the glaciers on the other side of the bay. The light lasted for just a few hopeful minutes during the middle of the day before the town moved back into its twilight. There was an atmosphere of excitement as the people of Qaanaaq looked forward to spring, when the sun would climb into the sky and the days would lengthen. It was a time when the temperatures rose but the ice remained. The ice was the Inuit's highway and their connection to hunting grounds and friends in nearby settlements. The growing light provided a chance to reconnect after the long winter. It was part of the reason why I travelled to Qaanaaq in early February. I wanted to witness the moment the sun rose above the horizon after months of hiding.

I had spent the last few days walking through the town and down to the bay where the constant pressure of the ice against the shore had caused it to break up into large ridges of uneven slabs. Hunters came and went, their sledges laden high with their weekly catches of halibut, each frozen stiff by the cold and covered with a thin tarpaulin sheet. They would tether the dogs at the shore's edge and push the sledges up a ramp and into the Royal Greenland shed where the hunters unloaded their catch. The sledges were stacked ten or more fish high and the entire sledge of around four metres long was completely full all the way along. A team of workers waited outside the factory unpacking the fish, sweeping the ice off them and handing them through to the factory workers who waited inside the building.

In the evenings I would walk down to the shore again and stare out across the icy expanse. The sun glowed from behind the glaciers on the far side of the bay. Not yet risen but tantalisingly close, casting shades of orange into the crisp polar air. As the light went it left behind a patina of pink and blue pastel that coloured the sky. The landscape was softened by these colours and receded into a gentle white velvet field of frozen mountains and icebergs. It gave me a feeling of easy solitude and I never tired of the view.

It was hard to imagine that in only a few months I would be dragging a heavy pulk almost 450 kilometres across the sea ice. It had always been my plan to train in Greenland rather than drag heavy tyres across sandy beaches in England as I had seen other adventurers do. I had kept up a good level of fitness carrying heavy bags across steep hills and sodden valleys in the Brecon Beacons where my reserve regiment, the Honourable Artillery Company (HAC), had a training area. My idea was to develop the specific physical attributes required for sledge hauling while I was here. Two months, I felt, would be just enough, but I needed to make sure that when Alec arrived we could start training straight away. On the way to the school I checked off a couple of tasks. I was on the search for a phone so I had some means of communication when we started training out on the ice and I also wanted to find somewhere that we could exercise when we weren't on the ice. I walked to the gym first which I had discovered existed when I was at the celebrations in the sports hall a week earlier.

On my way I saw Danial, the school's headmaster, whom I had met at the dinner. He was difficult to miss in his bright green luminous coat. He wielded a short black plastic spade in his hand which he was using to cut blocks of snow out of a large drift that led up to his house. He was joined by his young daughter who sported an equally luminous pink jacket. They were building an igloo. I headed down the track to take a closer look. He explained that each year he tried to build one or two igloos for practice and so that he could pass on his knowledge to his children. 'It's part of keeping our traditions alive,' he said. Danial was lifting the large, compacted blocks of snow and had started to place them in a circle. Each was laid at a slight inwards angle on top of each other, the idea being that they would meet at the top where he would eventually place a capping block. His delicate placement of each block was countered by the screeching sound they made as they rubbed against each other – the same sound that polystyrene makes when you drag it out of a box, and it ran through my body like fingernails on a blackboard. At the sound of this noise his daughter would run off and hide. She disliked the sound as much as I did.

Danial explained that there were still hunters in the village who could remember how to build them properly and he was still experimenting with his own version. Noticing my interest, he asked, 'Do you want to help?'

'Definitely,' I replied with childlike glee, not wanting to miss out on building an igloo with an Inuit. Danial handed me a saw and pointed me to a newly formed trench where he told me to start cutting. I cut into the snow and pulled out thick rectangular blocks almost half a metre long which I passed to Danial. Danial took the blocks and made some expert cuts, making sure they were the right shapes to fit the angles which he had already laid out from the centre of the igloo. I asked Danial questions as we worked. Was he born in Qaanaaq? Had he ever left? He told me about a meeting with the Inuit Circumpolar Council that he had been invited to attend in Europe that year.

'That sounds exciting,' I said.

'Maybe,' he replied, 'but I would have to be away from my family for two weeks and I don't think I want to do that.' I wondered how many people in England would jump at the opportunity that he had been handed. Certainly in my work I had got used to spending all week away from home with clients around the country. I found that here, in such a small community, the family unit seemed much stronger and people much closer[13]. I heard one story of a woman who gave a child to her own sister because she could not bear one herself. Something that was not unusual in Qaanaaq but would be headline-grabbing in the UK. I was continuing to rattle off questions at Danial while we worked on the igloo until he suddenly paused his work, raised his head and looked at me. 'You speak as much as a woman does,' Danial said after a short pause. I wasn't sure what to say. He wasn't being rude, it was just that people were happy to spend time in each other's company in silence in Qaanaaq. Every gap didn't need to be filled with a question.

'Sorry,' I replied, smiling sheepishly.

I was saved further embarrassment by the rest of his children who decided that this would be a great chance to join in the fun. They ran down from the house one by one. At first, they hovered around me, not quite sure of this slightly strange-looking foreigner in their midst, before building up the confidence to approach me. Soon they had me catching them like flying squirrels as they flew from the top of the

13 When Rasmussen travelled across the Arctic on the Fifth Thule Expedition in 1921 he was accompanied by three married Inuit couples. One of the most famous members of the party was Arnarulunnguaq who, despite her husband dying shortly before the trip, still accompanied Rasmussen. She was one of two Inuit to stay with Rasmussen throughout the 18,000-kilometre trip and was awarded the silver Medal of Merit by King Christian X of Denmark.

snow trench. I caught them at the bottom of one slope and then slid them down the bank on the other side. The children's enthusiasm for the game outlasted mine and I decided it was probably time to get on with the day. As Danial laid the capping stone at the top of his masterpiece I headed on to the gym.

I climbed the side stairs to the top of the hall that lay at the far end of town and entered the doorway into a small, whitewashed room. The gym was basic but it had everything that you might want. There was an ancient, rusting static bicycle, some well-worn rowing machines and a stack of old dumb-bells. A flashing stereo in the corner pumped out heavy metal music. Two men were already in there busily lifting stacks of iron. I was greeted by one of them, an athletic-looking man with the easy confidence and stance of a fighter. He casually walked up to me and advanced his hand which I took and then he introduced himself. His name was David. I had already heard a lot about him from Troels. David explained that he was a taekwondo instructor and the proud owner of the only bar in Qaanaaq, which I soon learnt to call 'Daffi's Bar'. It had a reputation amongst the Danes as being full of drunks, but David seemed like such a nice guy I couldn't believe it could be that bad. Amongst this long list of attributes, he explained that he was a teacher at the youth school at the top of the village which acted as a kind of preparatory school for young adults who were too old for school but intended to further their studies or improve their grades. He was keen to get Alec and me to come up and speak to his students about the expedition and why we were in Qaanaaq. He was genuinely enthusiastic about the benefit it would bring to his class and thought it would be a great opportunity for his students to be able to speak English with an Englishman. I was touched by David's enthusiasm for his students and his immediate kindness towards me.

I had arrived at the gym in a base layer top and insulated trousers and I wore a set of old army boots on my feet. Already, he offered to lend me gym shoes and shorts if I needed them.

My next stop after the gym was the satellite tower: a vertiginous, out-of-place structure that sat high above the one-storey houses on the lower slopes. The tower was responsible for all the town's internet and its mobile phone signal and was critical to staying connected to the outside world. There was a phone shop of sorts, and I was able to pick up a Greenlandic SIM card and number. After much discussion with the locals, I had decided that rather than using a satellite phone, a local mobile would be much cheaper. Given the small population in Greenland, the numbers were far shorter than I was used to at only six digits long, which made remembering my new number a lot easier. Having some form of communication when we started training out on the sea ice near the town was an important part of the safety plan. Very few people used VHF radios so the maritime Standard Horizon VHF radios we had been given would only really be useful for the trek to Haig-Thomas Island. Purchase in hand, I had only walked a few metres down the hill when I heard the noise of a car coming up behind me. It was the man from the satellite tower. He explained that I needed to come back with my passport before he could register my number. He had opted to drive the ten metres down the track rather than walk. It seemed that most people in Qaanaaq that had a car did the same. Because of the cold, the cars were left running all day once they had been started. I supposed it was quicker to jump into a warm car rather than pull on and take off the masses of clothing needed to walk around town in the freezing temperatures.

It was now around midday and on the way to the school to meet Troels and start our climb I realised I would get a better view from higher up the hill. I had walked its slopes when I was here in the summer and my approach was tinged with a loss in self-confidence. Much of the walk was scree and the rocks were covered with a thin layer of ice which made it difficult to get a foothold. The locals seemed content to stand at the bottom of the hill and, as there were no steep ledges, I felt that the worst that could happen was an unplanned and embarrassing descent down the side in full sight of the entire town which was just starting to emerge. However, the damage would be to my pride rather than anything more serious. There were cairns just below the crest of the hill which gave me something to aim for and I cautiously pressed on higher to reach them.

I sat down on a large boulder at the top. I could see far out into the distance from my new perch: in front of me on the other side of the bay was a wall of cliffs that lined the coast, the steep walls of rock broken only by a broad glacier that swept down to the sea ice. Out to the west stretched Herbert Island with its snow-covered slopes lit by a warm light that hinted that the sunrise was only minutes away. The rest of the town began to emerge from the houses below me. I was joined by three other intrepid adventurers, all three of whom were brothers who had also decided to walk up the slope. One of them spoke good English and had just returned to Qaanaaq from Denmark where he had been studying.

And then it appeared, that brilliant orb of orange that graced the land around it, bathing it in its warmth. It had only been a couple of weeks since I last saw the sun, but it could have been months. For the rest of the inhabitants of the town it had been months. One of the brothers described seeing the sun as something that he could feel deep down in his soul. Below us the town erupted with the sound of cheers and children laughing, as the sun finally came into view for them as well. The town's dogs went wild, their cacophony of howls spurred on by the people's excitement. The scene was visible for the briefest of moments before the sun left Qaanaaq once again in a half-light. A purgatory that was neither night nor day.

The next day I went looking for some fuel to see which type would work best in the stove I had brought. I had experimented with petrol in the balmy warmth of the winter back home but after some research I decided that I needed to find some kerosene as well. The temperatures were so low that even petrol would struggle to light with fire from a match. My plan was to compare the two to make sure what we took with us when we were dropped into the wilderness of Ellesmere Island worked. Troels told me there was a man that sold petrol in the middle of the town. I headed over, carrying the small single-litre bottles that were made of thick metal and were designed specifically for the stoves. What ensued was a Mr Bean-like attempt at the simple transaction of purchasing fuel. The petrol station consisted of a tiny hut and two small pumps. One for petrol and the other for kerosene. The man at the petrol station spoke no English and so it took me some time to understand what the problem was. The main language in the town was Greenlandic or Inuktitut, although most spoke Danish as well. Very few spoke English, and why would they? I had become a dab hand at explaining myself through hand signals which got me through the first few weeks until I learnt a few more phrases in the local language. The man was telling me that the containers I had bought were too small and he sent me off to the store to buy new ones.

I found a larger bottle at the shop but when I returned to the petrol station the man shook his head. Again, off I went to find something larger. In the shop the only other containers I could find were a couple of ten-litre tanks which I grudgingly purchased. I headed back down to the fuel pump, tanks in hand and looking well prepared to refuel a large truck rather than a small stove. The man looked at them and we both laughed at their size – after all I had only come to buy a couple of litres of fuel, clearly this was overkill. He filled one up with kerosene and the other with petrol. I thanked him and walked back up the slope, my shoulders dragged down by the weight of carrying far more fuel than I would ever use.

That evening I was invited by Troels up to the house of one of the Danish teachers in the village. She was much older than either of us and had become a veteran of the area. She had prepared coffee and cake for us which was a welcome relief from the rough cooking that I was starting to get used to at Troels's house. The views from the window of her house were immense and captured the whole of the bay. I noticed that she was still showing true Danish spirit in the décor of the house. Although I didn't see any animal skins on the floors, I saw some strong similarities with how Haig-Thomas described his experiences of the area. 'The Danish houses are a complete contrast. True, in most cases they are overheated and badly ventilated, but their walls are covered with photographs and paintings of Greenland. Sometimes harpoons, model sledges and kayaks will be hung on the walls...' Having read the extract the previous night, I smiled to myself when I noticed a cactus plant on the windowsill. 'In one way only do the Danes' homes show real character. In the windows they grow cacti and tropical plants of various kinds. The Danes are determined to show the world that, though they live in Greenland – a barren land of ice, and snow – they can grow delicate tropical species instead of the more hardy plants from home,' he had written.

I spent the final hours of the day on the porch of the house testing out the cooking stove I had brought with me from the UK. It was one of the most important pieces of equipment we would have with us when we ventured on to the ice. I knew that an expedition the previous year had failed when their stove broke and they had no backup. In the UK I had tested it with petrol which had worked perfectly. I decanted this fuel first, pouring it out of the oversized drum and into the smaller bottle. Priming the pump and shielding the stove with my glove, I put a lit match to the fuel. The petrol acted more like water and the flame went out as it touched the liquid rather than igniting the fuel. The temperature gauge read -35°C and it was only by experimenting with the stove that I discovered that by resting the match just above the fuel I could warm it enough to light it. When it did light the stove worked well but I realised I needed to try the kerosene, which had a lower burning point and should be less temperamental in these temperatures.

I left the final test for another day. I looked out from the porch, and across the bay I could see a single star shining over Herbert Island which was joined by the sliver of a crescent moon. They both hung there silently as they glistened magically over the bay. Below them the last of the sun's rays bled dark red from beneath the horizon before Qaanaaq was once again pitched into complete darkness. A feeling of contentment washed over me that night as I lay on the floor of Troels's hut. I felt very much at home here and each day I was becoming more and more comfortable with using our equipment and with living in this cold environment. I was just starting to make progress with the research element as well now that I had made enough contacts to carry out interviews with the hunters. I arranged for Troels to message Mikael, a young Inuit hunter who I had met briefly on the ice a few days earlier, and who promised to come round the next day and take me out on the sea ice with him to go fishing.

CHAPTER 9

THE COLDEST CATCH – QAANAAQ

Mikael came round the following morning while I was having breakfast. He greeted me with a wide grin and told me that he was going fishing out on the ice and wondered whether I would like to come. He was younger than the other hunters I had met. Tattoos ran down his sinewy forearms and covered his large, weathered hands. Blue etchings adorned his pale skin. Etchings, he told me later, that he had carved himself. He was clean-shaven, like many of the men I had met in Qaanaaq. What was most striking to me were his eyes. They glowed with a deeper intelligence. One was the colour of amber and the other a dark brown. A sign possibly of his dual heritage. His father was Danish and his mother an Inuit.

I had met very few people so far that could speak English. Mikael, in comparison, had a good grasp of the language, learnt from watching American blockbusters. He spoke thoughtfully and in a heavy Greenlandic accent.

While we waited in the kitchen of Troels's hut for the coffee to brew we began to discuss the expedition to the Canadian Arctic Archipelago. While Mikael's English was good, it was too early in the morning for me to explain all the details of how we were searching for a buried note that someone's great-uncle had left over seventy years ago, so I rifled through my bag and brought out a map. I had bought it back in England and it showed the whole of the archipelago including Ellesmere Island, Axel Heiberg Island and, on the far west of the page, Haig-Thomas Island. I pointed a blunt pencil at Eureka

Station and explained that we would fly from Qaanaaq to Eureka and then follow a channel called Eureka Sound south before cutting west to Haig-Thomas Island. Last summer I had been met with some very unenthusiastic responses when I had got to this point and particularly when I probed around the idea of taking a Greenlandic guide with us. Mikael was different. He looked at the map and pointing at his chest said, 'In here my heart wants to go very much, up here though I am thinking I should not.' Mikael explained that his family relied on his income as a hunter and April, one of the months that we would be away, provided some of the best halibut fishing of the year. On his best day in an eleven-hour period, he had been able to bring in 8,700 DKK worth of catch, which was something of a record. He explained that in an average month during the season it was usually more like 1,600 DKK a week. Although I liked the idea of having Mikael come with us, I knew that I wouldn't be able to match the income he received from fishing without going wildly over budget, but I was buoyed by the fact that if Mikael showed this level of interest, he must have had some hope of us making it.

Mikael asked to see some of my clothes as I would be standing about not doing much on the ice with him and he was worried I might get cold.

'I can help you with the fishing,' I said.

Mikael responded bluntly, 'I tried that before and the guy made everything look like shit.'

I took the subtle hint and went and got some warmer clothing. He didn't seem that impressed but I assured him it would do the job, having worn it for the last few weeks. I decided to take a smock as well to protect my clothes. I was used to fishing on the rivers back home and I wasn't keen on the prospect of spending a month in a tent with my poor teammate with my clothes still smelling of fish. Mikael told me to meet him down on the sea ice around midday and I spent the time in between preparing my gear as I wasn't sure how long we would be out.

Mikael was already down on the ice getting his team of dogs together when I arrived. He tied them in pairs to the handles of the ropes that were frozen into the ice. His team consisted of around six young dogs all about seven months old. The oldest member of the team had died fairly recently and Mikael said the rest were still a bit down. There was a forlorn-looking dog sitting close to the team which Mikael didn't tie to the sledge traces. 'I found it wandering down by the ice with my brother,' he said. 'When we got closer we could see that it was blind and that it would die so we saved it.'

The dogs were tied to the sledge in what the Greenlanders call a fan formation, each dog attached to a 'trace' or single piece of rope which is then attached directly to the sledge. This is different to other methods where a single piece of rope is extended out from the sledge and along to the front dogs. The rest are then tied behind the lead dogs, staggered in pairs at intervals like a ladder. As soon as our dogs were tied to the sledge traces, Mikael set off. He walked in front of the dogs carrying a whip which he cracked occasionally when the dogs threatened to push in front of him. We continued in this manner as we made our way over the shoreline, which was a jumbled-up mess of slabs where the ice had pressed against itself. It was not smooth but laced with cracks and steep shelves, making the going uneven and treacherous. We went over one particularly nasty piece which caused the sledge to rear near vertically towards the sky. It came down on the other side with a crash. At the sound of the crash the dogs took off and one of the slightly leaner dogs of the pack got caught in its own trace, falling under the sledge with a yelp as the wooden sliders ground over it. Luckily, I had already jumped off at this point, mainly out of panic at the idea of being on a runaway sledge I couldn't control. I was in a good position to quickly lift the sledge up and drag the dog away by its harness, shaken but unharmed, and it joined the others at the front.

We both jumped on the sledge as it raced across the smoother sea ice to Mikael's fishing camp and left the turbulent ice foot behind us. Mikael had set up the camp when the sea ice formed at the beginning of the season. Two years earlier, he had been unable to start until December. However, sea-ice coverage had been good this year and he had been there since October. Two other fishermen used the camp with him. The camp consisted of a traditional tent perched over a long sledge. Rope guy lines frozen into the ice were attached to each corner making the tent taut and strong enough to resist bad weather. At the entrance to the tent there was a cooking area. There was an old bench low to the ground to sit on and an ancient oil burner which sat directly on top of the ice. At the back of the tent there was a raised platform made by the sledge. Mikael either sat on this when he was cooking or else slept on it whilst he was passing the time in between checking on his fishing lines. Even in the deep minuses these tents could be warmed up to almost sauna-like temperatures with the dated Primus stoves alone.

It was another reminder of why Haig-Thomas thought so highly of the way that the Inuit approached the hardships of this environment. I had read the books of Scott and Shackleton but sitting on that sledge, almost sweating in the heat even though it was almost -40°C outside, it was easy to wonder if, had those explorers been better prepared, they would have had more success. I was keenly aware of the plight of Scott's team in particular as I had brought Apsley Cherry-Garrard's book *The Worst Journey in the World* with me. In his book he describes the unimaginable discomforts they all faced during Scott's attempt on the South Pole. Haig-Thomas was reading the same book in 1937 and commented that he felt that if they had learnt from the Polar Inuit he also believed that they would not have had to go through the hardships they had.

Close to the tent three small fishing holes had been dug out of the thick ice. One of them was Mikael's and the other two belonged to the other fishermen. Mikael's was the most used, which left me with the impression that not everyone was as hard-working as he was. I didn't see anyone else attending the other fishing holes the entire time I was there. Mikael took a metal pike out and walked over to one of the holes and began to clear away the ice that had formed over the dark water below. Once he had smashed through the larger chunks, he took a ladle which was made from a piece of wood with a plastic cup tied to the end and carefully scooped out the rest. There was already a line that had been laid the previous evening but before he began reeling it in, he started baiting another. The line was looped around a reel which was attached to a large upright metal pole. Taking the end of the line he attached it to one end of a set of hooks that he had already baited with tiny fish, and which lay fitted in cut slips that framed the rim of a large cardboard box. Mikael then attached the other end of the hooked line to a piece of metal that had been hammered flat – it was about sixty centimetres long and thirty centimetres wide and had a rock tied to one end. Mikael referred to the contraption as the 'Torpedo' and I soon saw why. First, he carefully lowered the device through the now ice-free hole and into the water below. Next, he pulled a piece of string connected to the metal plate until the metal object floated vertically beneath him. When he felt it was in position, he released the string and the Torpedo shot off under the ice, dragging the line out horizontally with it. The hooks followed first, then another weight was dropped to pull the whole thing down to the bottom and finally the large spool of line was threaded out as far as 500 metres. Occasionally, he would pause, pulling on the line with his hands so that it remained taut and the hooks could set properly. There were almost a hundred individual hooks on each of the lines that Mikael laid and in the best months he explained that he could pull up eighty flapping halibut in one go. 'Sometimes,' he chuckled, 'I spray women's deodorant on the line as it helps attract the fish.' The hooks now lay baited at the bottom of the bay. The new line would lay there for the next three hours and while we waited Mikael began to pull up the other line that had been left out the previous night.

As he pulled up the older line, he explained that it hadn't gone out well when it he had laid it before. Just as he had feared, the line had become tangled in its many hooks. 'I'm not going to work the knots out now,' said Mikael. 'I'll take it home and work on it there where it is warm and where my hands can work properly.' It was a clear Arctic-blue sky, tinged with pinks and oranges, but it was also bone-chillingly cold. Standing on the sea ice amongst the icebergs with Qaanaaq a couple of kilometres to our north I could feel the icy temperatures penetrate my clothing. First into my hands and then slowly into my legs and chest. Mikael had been working but I had been standing there watching him motionless. He saw me shivering and suggested we go inside the tent to get warm.

Once in the tent he lit both stoves, which blasted the cold air away and replaced it with hot. We sat there side by side, Mikael stepping outside occasionally to clear the hole as the ice tried to reclaim it. As we waited for the harvest of fish that the new line would bring, I asked

Mikael whether he thought things had changed at all since he started hunting. He considered the question and then pulled out an old pipe and asked me if I smoked. I shook my head. 'Don't mind me,' I said, and he proceeded to light the pipe with a match, coaxing the tobacco to flame with small puffs on the end.

Mikael turned to me and mischievously said, 'It's marijuana.' I believed him until he let out a chuckle of delight. 'Everyone always believes me when I tell them that,' he joked. 'It's only pipe tobacco!'

Mikael was older than I was. At thirty he was one of the youngest members of the Hunters' Union in Qaanaaq, of which there were thirty-one members. He had only been a hunter for five years at that point; before that he had been a bit of a wild child. His father was Danish, and Mikael had lived in Denmark until he was twelve years old. He used to box there and had won the last fourteen of his seventeen fights. Moving back to Qaanaaq was a big decision for him. 'I was angry and lost when I returned, and I spent a lot of my time drinking and getting into trouble,' he said. Mikael had been in prison twice, but he stopped drinking when he had a family. It was easy to see Mikael's Danish roots; he was above average height and although slight in build he carried a lot of strength which I found out a few weeks later when we arm-wrestled. He was energetic and driven and seemed much more willing to engage than many of his counterparts in town. I had to spend a lot of time building up trust with the others before they were happy to talk with me.

Mikael loved to fish. Although it was probably not as glamorous as walrus or narwhal hunting, it could be very lucrative to the point that it now made up a large part of his hunting calendar. 'In the last few years more and more people have got into fishing,' he said. 'Normally, at this time of year many of the older hunters would be looking for walrus but now they will fish as well.' It was also possible for hunters to make money from taking visitors to the area out on the sledges but even that didn't earn as much as fish. The price of halibut had risen that year from 12 DKK per kilogram to 16.5 DKK per kilogram. On Monday and Thursday morning each week Mikael would deliver sledges heavy with fish to the factory in town where they would weigh up his catch and pay him the proceeds.

I had read that climate change and the reduction in sea ice were having a major effect on hunting in the area. I had heard as much from the people in Qaanaaq but as Rasmus had explained when I visited in the summer, other forces beyond their control were also having an impact. When sealskin imports to the EU were banned the price of seal plummeted overnight and had a huge impact on smaller communities that relied on seal as a key part of their income. The lucrative trade in Greenland halibut to some extent had replaced this, which was why I was here with Mikael. It had changed what many of the hunters focused on. 'Some hunters will fish for halibut now until they save up enough money to go out for other more traditional species,' Mikael said. 'Mobile phones, electricity and internet have brought bills that need to be paid. Going out for the large animals means more time away from your family and there is no guarantee that you'll get one, so it is risky.'

'What about the bears?' I asked. It was something that had been weighing heavy on my mind since I had got to Qaanaaq. I had started to think that the cold was surmountable as my clothing had seemed up to scratch but the threat that I didn't feel that I had under control was the bear. I had read stories of things going very wrong.

'I often see them in the area, but it is very rare for them to attack people,' he explained.

'Do you feel safer out here with all your dogs?' I asked.

'I don't think it matters, I would hear them coming anyway and grab my rifle,' he replied. His rifle lay outside sheathed in one leg of an old pair of blue jeans.

He went on to tell me the story of an old hunter in Siorapaluk, a small settlement to the north-west of Qaanaaq. The man was hunting seals with his dogs. Finally, he managed to get one and by this time his dogs had lain down and curled up into small balls, sleeping comfortably in their traces. He walked past them and lay the seal on his sledge to keep it away from the dogs. Suddenly, from the other side of the sledge he saw a bear which stood there staring at him. It had managed to creep up on the team, stalking in from downwind to hide its smell. The dogs hadn't noticed it. The hunter looked at the bear, then down at his rifle, which lay on the sled. He looked at the bear again and as he went to grab the rifle it swiped at his arm, cutting it deeply despite the thick sealskin coat that he was wearing. He cried out with pain as the bear's claw cut into him. The bear, shocked and surprised by the noise, turned and ran away. 'It was the seal that the bear was interested in, not the hunter,' Mikael said.

Time drifted by while I sat there listening to his stories, feeling very cosy as we sheltered from the cold outside.

'Come on then,' Mikael said. 'We better get going, the line will be ready now.' Even though he had been stepping outside regularly throughout our few hours in the tent, the hole had already begun to freeze over, and the ice had to be cleared again. Once the line was free, we took it in turns to crank the handle and reel it in from the seabed. Mikael wore his thin, rubber-clad fisherman's gloves but I kept my warmer mittens on. I wondered how his hands hadn't frozen completely. I was surprised at how tiring it was to crank the handle and I was soon sweating inside my jacket. After about thirty minutes of slow reeling the first of the weights came into sight and Mikael signalled to me to stop.

We rested for about ten minutes before finally bringing in the hooks. This was important as it would give the line time to fall back down vertically through the water, making it easier to bring in the catch through the hole and avoid the hooks getting stuck on the underside of the ice. Earlier, Mikael had put a couple of handfuls of the small fish that he was using for bait into the water so that they could thaw out. The sea water was considerably warmer than the air temperature. He scooped the bait out, cut each one in half with his sharp filleting knife and placed them into a fresh bucket of water to stop them freezing again. He would slide these on to the hooks later once he had removed the halibut.

The large metal plate which acted as a weight for the line was the next thing to appear. Mikael grabbed it and cut it away from the line of hooks which still rested deep in the water. Standing over the hole he grabbed hold of the remaining line with the hooks and began pulling it out of the water. We were in luck! Dozens of fish began to appear. As they came up Mikael would remove the fish from the line, lay it behind him and then rebait the empty hook with one of the smaller fish from the bucket he had prepared earlier. The rebaited hook was then folded back neatly around the top edge of a cardboard box that he had placed beside him and the whole action was repeated for each hook. It reminded me of a magician pulling a never-ending trail of handkerchiefs from his cuff.

The fish froze instantly on the cold surface of the sea ice, their flapping bodies turning hard and motionless. Mikael rested the line every now and then to step back and gut the fish before they froze completely. Pulling their heads back by the mouth, he first made a cut down the fish's body, starting at its jawline and then slicing the knife down its body and between its fins. As he reached the bottom of the fish, he pushed the knife in further, cutting behind its guts and then flicking them neatly away. He washed the fish in the ice hole and then lay them out in a row in an area of ice that he had already brushed down away from the main working area, which was now a mess of blood and guts. I watched in quiet admiration as he carried out the same process patiently and methodically for every one of the ninety-eight hooks in temperatures well below zero.

By this time, I had been standing watching for almost two hours and the cold had begun to seep through my clothing. My toes and fingers were numb, and I tried sprinting on the spot to get warm. The result was instant satisfaction as warm blood from my core was forced to my extremities and I slowly regained feeling in my toes and hands. You can have all the layers on in the world but in these temperatures, unless you are generating heat from your body, then the cold will get through in the end.

Mikael had been feeding his dogs with some of the smaller halibut, which I thought would make a good meal for one person, so I asked to buy a couple off him for dinner. He filleted them in front of me and handed two of the freshly caught fish over to me. I offered to pay him, but he refused any offer of money. With the line brought in and a fresh line laid we tied the dogs to the sled and headed back into Qaanaaq. It was night-time now and we rode along through the cold with the sound of Mikael softly encouraging his dogs on. The stars shone out above us, and the town was lit up like an electric beacon guiding us home. I could still hear some of the other fishermen laying out their lines and pulling in their catches as we sailed along with the sound of our wooden sledge crackling along the ice beneath us.

When we got back to the shore Mikael told me there was a dog race that would take place in March. 'My team is young, but I am going to enter anyway. I've been feeding them in Qaanaaq so they know where home is. I've also begun to feed them at different points along the route to give them something to look forward to,' he said.

It had just gone nine o'clock by the time I got back to the house. The halibut fillets were frozen hard as rock. I put them into a plastic bag and laid them in some warm water to thaw them out and then I fried them in some butter. They tasted delicious and it made a change from the packaged food which was all I could source from the local store. I made a mental note to make sure I picked up more fish when I went back out over the next few months.

Looking in the mirror later that evening I noticed that one of my ears was a different colour. I had been getting frostnip on most of the days that I was out but never anything too serious. This time the lower part of my right ear had turned red and a hard, blistering swelling had developed on my ear lobe. The following day it felt like a wasp sting. I had noticed that none of the locals covered their face and so I had done the same. Clearly, my unacclimatised skin was no match for the harsher temperatures and I made sure to cover up, particularly on sledge journeys where the wind multiplied the chill factor. It was all part of learning on the job. It would be alright while I had a warm house to come back to, but it was clear that without it a minor chill could snowball into something more serious without somewhere warm to recover in. It was something to watch out for on the long trek that Alec and I had planned a couple of months from then.

CHAPTER 10

A NEW ARRIVAL – QAANAAQ

It was morning and a cold crisp blue sky had encased Qaanaaq. I woke up feeling excited about the day ahead. As I stood on the porch of the hut, icebergs dotted the frozen bay as far as I could see. I had left the UK three weeks earlier, but it felt like a lifetime. I had become used to walking out on the sea ice and found comfort in the cold. More importantly, the key ingredient for the research, a network of hunters, was very much established. The short days had lengthened, and the sun was clear above the horizon now for a good part of the day. The only thing missing was my teammate Alec who was set to fly into Qaanaaq that day. I was getting on surprisingly well with my Danish host, but I was looking forward to being reunited with my friend. I was also keen for us to start training in earnest for the trip to Haig-Thomas Island.

Getting Alec from the airport, however, wasn't going to be easy. It wasn't like I could just wave down a taxi. The school janitor who had brought me from the airport was otherwise engaged and Hans at the hotel was not at home. I had found an old sledge and made my preparations. I was intent on putting Troels's noisy dog to better use. She had been chained to one of the legs of the hut outside and had been howling almost constantly since I arrived.

The sledge itself had been made in the same way that sledges had been made in Qaanaaq for centuries. It was small, at around two and a half metres long, and made up of timber planks tied together with rope. Previously, the rope would have been string made out of seal sinew, but times had changed, and sinew had been replaced by nylon rope shipped in from outside of Greenland. The sledge sat on two long runners that ran in parallel along its base. I took it down to the ice. Each year a road formed along the ice during the winter and lasted until early spring. The ice road ran parallel to the main land road leading to the airport. Locals preferred driving the route along the ice rather than along the land road as it was faster and provided a less bumpy ride. If it was good enough for the pick-ups and 4x4s of Qaanaaq it was good enough for me. Next, I picked up the dog's harness from the hut along with some spare lines which I was going to use to tie down the mass of kit that Alec was likely to turn up with. Finally, I grabbed the dog and a bag of safety gear that I had put together (a bivvy bag, some spare warm kit and my GPS, radio and a thermos flask of hot tea) and headed down to the sledge. Mikael had been around the evening before and showed me the best knots for tying the dog safely to the trace.

I approached the dog cautiously. Having spent most of her life tethered to the hut she was looking very confused. From what I had seen she had never been walked and she had certainly never pulled a sledge before. I hoped there was still some level of natural instinct left inside her which wouldn't make me regret bringing her along. We had a few teething problems to begin with. While being tied up wasn't anything new, she wasn't used to the idea of having to pull in any particular direction. I gave up on trying to coax her forward on her own accord after my comical attempts ended in failure. Instead, I tied a second rope to her collar which I used as a lead to guide her. I had wasted a lot of time getting to that point and despite leaving plenty of time to get to the airport, we would need to get a move on if we were going to get there before the flight arrived. I didn't think Alec would thank me for having to wait around when the temperature was in the minus thirties.

Once we got going the dog pulled like a natural. We were soon managing along at a good pace as I ran beside her, guiding her with the lead. We moved out of Qaanaaq; to the left of me the icebergs dotted the bay between the near shore and the elongated shape of Herbert Island stretched out into the distance. Running along the ice road in the high Arctic surrounded by some of the most beautiful views in the world was incredible and it was hard to think of anything other than how lucky I was just to be there. To my right, laid out like a scrapheap, were old fishing boats and vehicles. It was a rich timeline of Qaanaaq history, various experiments of modernisation. There were large fishing boats sent to the village during the summer months – by those who had been lured by the possibility of halibut – and then laid to rot when the fish were nowhere to be found.

We continued at a strong pace. Occasionally, one of the local cars would pass by and the driver would wave, a quizzical look on their face as they registered the odd sight of human pulling dog. Was I pulling the dog or was the dog pulling the sledge?, I imagined them asking themselves. I rounded the final corner of the land towards the airport where I was met with an image that will remain with me forever.

Coming from across the sea ice and from the direction of Herbert Island was a hunter threading his team of dogs and a large sled through the field of static icebergs. He was cloaked in a caribou anorak, and wore polar bear trousers and a set of sealskin *kamiks*. The imagery of this lone hunter trekking across the ice invoked something powerful and heroic. A timeless figure, untouched by the modern age, stoic in the presence of an ever-changing landscape. It was easy to understand Haig-Thomas's profound respect for these people. That one man represented thousands of years of human endeavour and development within north-west Greenland. It was a contrast to the modern world that he was heading towards, a world that was furnished with the latest trappings, less suited to the same environment. I put my hand up in a high salute and I was pleased when I received one back. His professional nod to my amateur attempts.

The sound of the Air Greenland Dash 8 coming in low overhead drew me out of my stare and I picked up the pace. I got to the airport just in time to see Alec coming out of the airport terminal with his bags. He gave me a wide smile when he saw me.

'Great to see you, pal,' I shouted.

Alec looked at me and then at the sledge. 'What have you got there?'

I walked him through the basic form of transportation that was his trip back to town. 'Sorry I couldn't find a car,' I apologised.

'I couldn't have thought of a better start,' he replied.

Alec seemed excited by the prospect of stretching his legs after the long journey. We loaded the heavy bags on to the sledge. The dog strained at the new weight. By this time the knots that I had pulled together and the old, frayed harness I had put on the dog were starting to fall apart. It was becoming a pain to keep putting it back on when it fell off. I decided to let her loose and we pushed instead.

We made it back to town just as the light began to fade, turning the horizon into a burning orange flame. I climbed to the top of the steps outside Troels's hut and removed my boots outside the door before stepping inside to avoid bringing the snow in. Despite the cold, I was sweating. A combination of the run and my warm clothing. Steam poured off my thick socks as I adjusted them. A thin layer of ice had formed under my jacket where I had sweated through my fleece. I had become cold out on the ice when I had stopped, and the sweat had drawn out the heat from my body and made me shiver. It was a good lesson in the importance of striking a balance between making progress and not exerting myself. Stand still and, regardless of how many layers I was wearing, I would get cold. Move too fast and the warmth I could build up would be quickly lost through perspiration. Haig-Thomas had wondered how much more successful humans might be in the Arctic if they never sweated at all. It might have been why I never saw anyone in a hurry in Qaanaaq.

Alec was taking in his new surroundings and seemed happy, even when I broke the news to him that the floor would be his bed for the next two months. The only thing he wasn't impressed with was the toilet. The cold turned everything to ice. That meant that there was no drainage in town. Instead of a flushing toilet, we relieved ourselves into a black bin liner that was shared by the whole house. Twice a week we would draw straws for whose turn it was to take the house's excrement out of the plastic lavatory and place it by the front door for collection. It was the low point of the week for all of us. The only saving grace was the fact that it froze almost instantly. Frozen waste was much less offensive than the non-frozen kind. To welcome Alec to the house Troels had prepared a huge meal of rice, peas and reindeer meat cut from its saddle. It was the best meal he cooked for us during our stay. We talked excitedly around the table into the early hours of the morning. Alec told us what had happened in London, and I briefed him on where I had got to with the work in Greenland.

I took Alec down to the sea ice the following afternoon. The big dog race that Mikael had been training for but recently pulled out of was taking place that day. It would be a chance for Alec to see the town and to introduce him to some of the people that I had met over the last few weeks. There was a buzz of excitement in the air as some of the best hunters in the area were competing for this year's prize. The award itself was not insubstantial and included a paid trip to Ilulissat in the south where all the best teams from all around Greenland would race later that year.

Towering above the rest of the spectators was a bear of a man, dressed in the dark clothing of Greenland's national police force and sporting a huge beard. His name was Carl, and I had met him briefly at the airport during my summer recce. I couldn't think of a more suitable person to be keeping the law this far north. He told me that he had just returned from Savissivik, which lies even further north than Qaanaaq, after two days dealing with a build-up of complaints over a rise in violence in the area. It was the first time they had had to visit the area in years. Carl introduced us to his wife who was flying back in a couple of weeks as she was pregnant and the child was due soon.

We had arrived just in time to watch the dog teams being waved off by a red flag. Hundreds of people lined the ice along the shore and as the dogs raced off the whole town cheered. The race route was forty kilometres long. In the middle of the route lay a huge, rectangular iceberg, the top of which rested just beneath the summits of the mountains on the other side of the bay. It was the first of the waypoints and the teams raced towards it, quickly drawing out of sight. It would be some hours before they returned.

Games had been organised to keep the crowd entertained while we waited. The first game I saw looked like a cross between baseball and rounders. A team of fielders formed a broad circle. A long line of batsmen stood in opposition, one waiting in anticipation behind another. Like baseball, it was three strikes and then out. Every time someone managed to connect with the ball a huge cheer came from the crowd of spectators and the hitter made their way around the different bases. There was also a running race, a tug of war and a game for the children where they were each blindfolded and made to search around on their hands and knees for goodies that had been laid in front of them. Everyone fell about laughing as they scraped around and just as they almost found one of the sweets one of the adults would sneak it away from their grasps. I watched as a man wearing polar bear trousers nonchalantly walked across the ice pushing a baby pram in front of him. It was a strange scene to an outsider.

Out to my left, an old Inuit man stood atop a small iceberg with one eye shut and the other looking through a telescope. He looked like an old sea captain on the galley of his ship. Suddenly, he let out a shrill cry which signalled to the spectators that the lead dog teams had been spotted. They emerged from the icy landscape as small dots, growing larger as they neared. The final leg was a straight run back into town. The games stopped and everyone took their place in a long line of cheering, smiling faces as they called for their favourite driver to come in. It was like a very cold version of the Grand National. One man in fluffy polar bear-skin *kamiks* ran out ahead of the crowd towards the oncoming teams, waving a huge flag in the red and white colours of Greenland.

There was a real fight for first place, the hunters willing their teams on. '*Nanook!*', '*Qilalugag!*', '*Aaveq!*' they shouted as they called out the name of their favourite quarry to urge their teams on. Alec and I stood slightly to the side of the crowds. It was too close to call, the lead dog team was ahead by a nose. He maintained his lead as he passed the flag carrier and reached out to grab the flag from the hand of its bearer. The flag was raised above his head, and he began to wave it proudly to our delight. The stifled anticipation of the crowd turned into a roar. With expert precision the hunter called his team to a standstill just as it seemed they would be catapulted into the crowd of happy faces awaiting them. People ran out and grabbed the winner, hoisting him and the sledge above their shoulders and into the air. As the well-wishers gradually drew back I could see that the winner was Lars, one of the most experienced hunters in the village and seventy-one years of age. His family remained with him wearing expressions of pride on their faces.

Later, Alec and I walked up to meet Fin at his house. After a gruff first meeting, Fin was quickly becoming one of my favourites. He had lived in Greenland for over thirty years. You might wonder how someone could find themselves living in one of the most northern, out-of-the-way towns in the world. As with most things involving that level of commitment, it involved a woman and a little bit of luck. Although he never said it, I got the impression that when he was younger he was a bit of handful, which had led to him leave home to see the world. His travels had taken him across Europe to the north of Africa, where he had become involved in smuggling drugs. Having saved up enough money and with a few kilograms of cannabis stashed in the metal rim of his rucksack he left for Greenland. The relationship between Denmark and Greenland is a long and close one and perhaps coming here isn't as strange an option as it might be to a person of any other nationality.

First, he went to the capital, Nuuk, where he sold his contraband. It was also where he met his wife who was working as a nurse. He fell in love, followed her back to Qaanaaq, her home town, and had stayed ever since. It must have been hard integrating into such a closely knit society, but Fin had very much become part of the town's fabric in that time. He owned a couple of houses which he rented to visitors. These were normally scientists or teachers who were required to stay a little longer than the average tourist and didn't have a budget that stretched to living in the hotel. He had spent much of his time out on the ice with the hunters and modestly described what he had learnt during these years as only just scratching the surface.

Fin invited Alec and I to sit with him in a room that was at the back of his house, a place he called the 'Gas Chamber' where he could smoke his pipe in peace, away from the tut-tutting of his wife and the cold air outside. The room was lined from floor to ceiling with hunting tools and pieces of old animal bones, ivory and claws which he had collected on his many outings. One wall was filled entirely with rifles, an armoury that would put a national army to shame. Most were from around the turn of the 20th century and in the absence of a local gunsmith Fin had made heavy use of sealskin thread which he had used to lace many of the rifle barrels into place. He had spent a lot of time up here and had witnessed many changes. His stories were of hunting and life in Qaanaaq, narrated with the grounding of someone who had a close affinity with the Inuit.

He talked of the pleasure he got from sniffing the ears and hoofs of freshly shot caribou, growling in delight as he recounted the smell. Unbelievable stories of the sexual exploits and all-night parties of the Inuit when there was little else to get them through the long, dark winters. He had many stories of going out with the hunters, but he was hesitant at that point to tell us everything. Trust was something that took time to build in Qaanaaq and Fin had certainly been caught out before with strangers visiting the town. The stories would have to wait for another time.

After thirty years Fin was getting old. He loved Qaanaaq, but he was worried about what being an elderly person meant, especially if he got ill there. Denmark had a better care system, and it was sad to see him torn by the prospect of having to move back. My time with Fin was tinged with sadness. A great evil had begun to grow inside him. It manifested itself physically in a deep, agonising pain that permeated his lower back and legs and would occasionally surface in the briefest of grimaces across his face. Fin had begun to have dark and disturbing thoughts as he sat there in his house, hands resting on each knee, the pain from his back only partially subdued with strong painkillers. All we could do was watch as this great darkness took hold. I like to think that our presence there was a blessing for Fin. A chance to swap hunting stories and get excited about the season ahead. He rarely hunted in winter months now but waited for the ice to melt when he could take an ancient rifle from its place on the wall and search for caribou.

He had already started to look for a house to buy but his big worry was that his wife wouldn't feel comfortable in Denmark. 'The Inuit aren't always treated well by the Danes in Denmark,' he told me. Despite holding full citizenship some can face culture shock and prejudices when they arrive in Denmark. One poll taken of Danish citizens by Visit Greenland revealed that many still hold negative stereotypes. Of around the 1,000 people approached in the survey, forty per cent associated Greenlanders with binge drinking, substance abuse and social problems. Forty-three per cent believed that over half of Greenlanders were on some sort of benefit (the real figure is closer to sixteen per cent). I heard some of the Danish teachers in Qaanaaq discussing issues of binge drinking. I'm sure some of this went on but, personally, I never encountered anything worse than I had seen back home in the UK. Fin proudly took out his *kamiks* and showed us the difference between the polar bear fur-lined ones, what might be classed as top-of-the-range clothing, and the older-style seal *kamiks*. 'I won't get a new pair made,' he said. 'They don't make them like they used to.' We told Fin of our plans to go over to Herbert Island that Saturday. He suggested a route that would be safe. Fin explained that there was a small village on the island that was only used by the Inuit during the summer. The settlement had a few houses in it, and he told us that we could stay in the church overnight and make our way back to Qaanaaq the next day.

'Watch out for the thinner ice at the tip of the island,' Fin cautioned us. 'The currents are stronger there,' he said, 'so the ice won't set as thickly.' We had intended to aim for this point initially as it provided an easy marker, so I was glad he had told us as we may have found ourselves more out of our depth than we were already. The old Dane stood up and walked over to the corner of the room. He picked up a heavy, metallic, javelin-shaped pole which ended with a chisel. 'You can take this,' he said.

'What is it?' I asked.

'This is an ice chisel. If you hit the ice hard with the sharp end and it doesn't break then it will hold your weight,' he said. 'The greyer the ice, the older and stronger it will be.'

Finally, Fin also told us about the tracks left by the hunters' sledges which would guide us from Qaanaaq to Qeqertarsuaq (the local name for Herbert Island), where the hunters still stayed on their way out to the sea-ice edge. I wanted to use Qeqertarsuaq as a training run, a chance to test our gear out in a relatively safe setting. It would be the furthest we had gone from town up to that point. The dangers of the cold and the local wildlife were real, but I had chosen it as I felt it was a good place for our first adventure. It was just far enough to be remote, which would test us, but close enough for the local police and

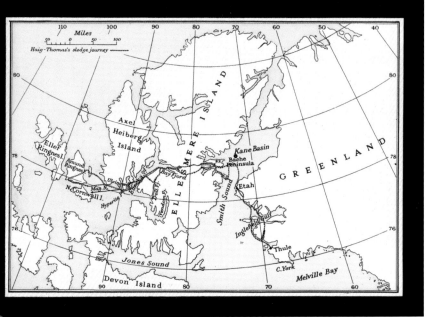

ABOVE: Original sledge route that Haig-Thomas took across Ellesmere Island in 1937–38. (RGS)

BELOW: Haig-Thomas battles Nookapinguaq, his Inuit guide, in a game of strength. (RGS)

ABOVE: Polar bear skins hanging out to dry outside our accommodation in Qaanaaq. 'The Duchess' lies below in the little red doghouse.

BELOW: Hunters relaxing after the annual dog race across Inglefield Bay.

ABOVE: Alec walks alongside the Duchess on our way to Herbert Island.

BELOW: A huge, table-shaped iceberg in Inglefield Bay.

LEFT: Mikael fishing for Greenland halibut from a hole in the sea ice.

BELOW: Qaanaaq comes out on to the ice to talk, play and watch the dog races.

ABOVE LEFT: The author standing at the cairn at the bottom of Bowdoin Glacier. (AG)

ABOVE RIGHT: A self-portrait taken in the first few weeks on Ellesmere Island. It was much colder than what we had experienced in Qaanaaq. (AG)

BELOW: Repacking the Twin Otter after we were rerouted to Resolute Bay, Canada.

ABOVE: A white wolf passes outside Eureka Weather Station in the Canadian Arctic Archipelago.

BELOW: Alec sledging down Eureka Sound towards Stor Island.

ABOVE: The author watching the bear, with the gun ready after other deterrents have failed. (AG)

LEFT: The tracks of a second polar bear that walked up to our tent. (AG)

ABOVE: The author stumbling over broken bindings and falling over the tide crack on arrival at Haig-Thomas Island. (AG)

BELOW: The view from the air as we fly back from Haig-Thomas Island and over Smith Sound on our return to Qaanaaq. The broken ice confirms the author's expectations that there can be no sledge crossing of the sound this year.

hunters to come to our rescue if we needed them. I was thankful for Fin's advice, and we finished our coffees and left him in peace. I had learnt quickly that people soon tired of the intense conversation I was used to back in England. The pace of life was slower here.

CHAPTER 11

FREEZING COLD IN QEQERTARSUAQ

We set off for Herbert Island early on Saturday morning. I had budgeted that we would cover three kilometres an hour for the day ahead. The ice was flat, but we would be towing the sledge and carrying our rucksacks. Our skis hadn't arrived yet either, they were still *en route* from the South Pole where they had been used by Prince Harry and the Walking With The Wounded team. We would be walking in our heavy Baffin boots, but I thought it would be achievable for a first run. If we could make the distance it would mean that even if the skis didn't arrive in time for the expedition to Haig-Thomas Island I would have confidence that we could walk it instead.

Mikael had mentioned that polar bears had been seen in the area recently and I was keen to make sure we had something to hand if we ever saw one ourselves. The prospect of being gnawed to pieces was helping me focus, particularly when it came to our safety equipment. I was delighted to find a large cache of emergency gear in a couple of sealed blue drums at the back of Troels's hut. They were from a British adventurer's recent efforts to reach the North Pole which had ended in failure a couple of years earlier. They were full of shotgun cartridges and pen flares, and in an attempt to preserve them for a future assault on the Pole they had all been wrapped up in plastic.

I had done my research on bear deterrents which suggested the use of pen flares: small yellow sticks which popped out a red smoking flare when the bottoms were twisted, and which had often been listed as critical. I picked up four of the small plastic devices. Alec and I

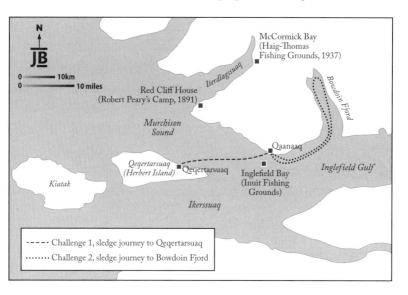

tested one before we left to make sure we both knew how to use it. I took these along with a large, chrome-barrelled .223 rifle that our host lent us. With rifle and flares in hand I felt confident that we could scare off a curious bear if we encountered one.

Mikael came round to see us off and to wish us luck as well as feed us some last-minute advice. 'Keep your head down and go slowly,' he said. 'You'll get there in the end.' With these final words of support, we pushed the sledge down the hill to the sea ice. I moved down the steep verglas roads that led from our hut to the shore, my heavy boots slipping clumsily but finding grip on the small patches of grit that poked through the icy surface.

We moved carefully through the groups of tethered dogs that lay motionless in the cold air, their bodies curled into a tight ball, noses hidden in folds of thick hair. The ice lay in pressure ridges along the shore and so we moved cautiously, pushing the wooden sledge up and down the icy slabs. The sledge's wooden frame creaked against the nylon ropes that held it together. The ice levelled out behind the ridges and stretched out to the distance.

Herbert Island sat on the horizon like the dark back of a surfacing whale. It was an impossible landmark to miss. It looked deceptively close but I had studied a map and measured twenty-five kilometres between the town and island. If we could hit our three-kilometres-per-hour target it would take us about eight hours. Along with the bears, the other thing playing on my mind was the sea ice around the eastern tip of the island, which was prone to currents and, as Fin said, could be dangerous. I made sure that we steered clear. I had brought Troels's dog with us as a further defence against the bears and in the hope that she would help us pull the sledge. I put her into the harness that I had repaired since the last trip out to the airport and tied her to the front of the sledge. 'Not a natural but better than nothing,' I said to myself. To keep her moving, Alec guided the sledge from the back and I walked alongside her at the front, coaxing her along. In this way I was able to navigate our small team over the sea ice and we were soon into a good rhythm.

A large collection of icebergs had frozen into the ice on the north-east side of Herbert Island. At a distance they appeared to us as white castles, sculpted by the harsh elements. One stood taller than others, rising high up into the clouds and protected with a tower and buttressed walls like something from a fairy tale. We stopped around mid-morning for lunch and sat, huddled on our sledge. The dog ran around us as she explored a freedom like nothing she had ever experienced before. At this point Alec had named her 'the Duchess'. Despite living a life of bondage, she carried herself with an air and grace that we had not witnessed in the other dogs in town. Perhaps it was because of her detached existence from the others that she had developed her unique character. She was graceful and aloof, and the name seemed to fit well. We left her to sniff and paw her way around the ice while we shared our rations.

Lunch consisted of tomato soup and noodles that I had hashed up that morning. As I poured from the thermos, great clouds of steam billowed from the near-boiling liquid when it met the sub-zero air. I stopped, unable to see the mug that Alec held and unwilling to coat his glove in soup. After a few spills we learnt to pour into one another's cup while the other let out a steady breath to push the vapour away. It was a windless day, but it was still too cold to sit about for long and we were soon back up on our feet.

We started off at a brisker pace to get some warmth back in our joints. Suddenly Al shouted out, 'Open water ahead,' pointing to the nearside of another giant iceberg straight ahead of us. We moved closer, our boots treading lightly on the ice as they cautiously felt their way forward. Alec's eyesight was better than mine, and it was a few metres further before I could see what he had been talking about. I was relieved to see that it wasn't an expanse but a much smaller gap in the ice that cupped the base of the giant iceberg. I walked to the edge of the icy monolith. Looking down into the clear blue water was like looking down into the window of its cold soul. The outline of its smooth edges extended deep beyond the sea ice and down into the void below.

Now, a warning to would-be ice seekers. Standing next to any iceberg, let alone an enormous one, can be perilous. Alec and I had no idea of the danger. It was only on retelling this story when I returned to Qaanaaq that I was told in short manner by the Inuit just how foolish we had been. It is believed that the explorer Gino Watkins, once touted as the successor to Scott and Shackleton, was killed when an iceberg upturned and swamped his kayak. His wet clothes and kayak apron were found on a nearby piece of ice but his body never was. It is very easy to think that an iceberg's size and the firmness of the ice around it makes it immovable, but that is only a temporary state. A state enabled by the perfect balance that exists within that iceberg at a point in time. At any moment, the ice can crack and, with the sound of a gun going off, carve off large chunks, disrupting its equilibrium. Once the balance is broken, the iceberg will tip, its colossal weight disturbed. It's a story that few live to tell. Thousands of tonnes of frozen water, tearing up the sea and ice around it as it tumbles and rolls until it finds a new balance and goes back to its misleading fortress-like state. However, at that time Alec and I were blissfully unaware, and everything was so new and exciting that we stood there in fascination.

Very soon after we moved on, the outline of the small village of Qeqertarsuaq on Herbert Island came into view. As I got closer, I began to make out individual houses. Like Qaanaaq the houses were adorned in an array of bright colours and made up of wooden boards. This settlement was much smaller and could have only housed fifty or so inhabitants. The ice on the approach to the town was very rough so we untied the Duchess from the trace and let her run off into the town to explore. Wooden towers lined the ice foot, empty of drying meat and absent of suspended kayaks. A raven hung lifeless from one of the towers, suspended by a single wind-ravaged wing and frozen in time. The place gave off a feeling of abandonment, the long, low line of hills behind it hiding the descent of the sun and creating a shadow across the town. We tugged and pushed the sledge along the shoreline, eventually hitting more even ground once we reached the land side of the ice foot. I walked into the town carrying just my rucksack and the rifle, leaving the sledge. A chill spread down my spine, a combination of my body cooling off after the effort of getting there and the shadow cast by the hill. Or maybe it was the eeriness of the place itself.

My eyes scanned the fifteen or so houses which lay at the bottom of a steep-sided, scree-covered hill. I located the small red church that was pitched to the south-west side of the settlement. It appeared to me very much like those post-apocalyptic films where the survivors come across uninhabited properties that have been left exactly as they were the day their world ended. In the same building as the church was a school room. It was still intact with a large wooden table and chairs in the middle of the room. The walls were lined with books and there were crayons and writing boards tucked tidily away in the corner. The only things missing were the teachers and the children. A bunk bed rested alongside one wall and two single beds along the others.

A worn rickety door separated the school room from the church. It creaked on rusting hinges as I pushed it open. I walked along the aisles. The pulpit, altar and pews looked as though the long-displaced congregation had only left that day. Plastic flowers adorned the petite vases that were placed around the chapel. I felt that we had stepped into another world. One inhabited by the spirits of a town that no longer existed. Mikael's teasing words echoed in my head. 'When you get there you can stay in the church but be careful, it's haunted,' he had said, without any sense of a joke. Perhaps the same ghosts that haunted this place also protected it. I shuddered at the idea and could see by Alec's ice-encrusted face that he felt the same. The sense of haunting felt very real in the post-apocalyptic surroundings. We decided to hunker down next door in the school room. Without the sun to warm it the room's temperature had plummeted into the lower minus thirties. Even in the schoolroom it felt much colder than outside. The snow and ice that we had brought with us remained tethered to our faces and clothes.

We were hungry after the walk and had only stopped once for lunch. I pulled out two bags of dried noodles. Alec got out the stove and lit it. I watched him work quickly in the cold of the room, pumping the gas bottle to get it to pressure and then opening the bottle's tap that would feed evaporated petrol along a thin metal pipe and into the stove. He unscrewed the cap that contained our windproof matches. As pressured fuel began to whistle through the stove, he struck a single match across the cylindrical top of its container and put it to the stove. The stove lit and the early orange flame turned a sapphire blue as it began to heat up. The stove burned with a reassuring intensity, and I felt the cold edge of the room fall away briefly. We placed a pot over the flame and filled it with snow which melted and began to boil. Alec poured the steaming water into cups to make tea which warmed our chilled corcs. Then I decided that we should put it out to save fuel – after all we wouldn't have the luxury of large supplies of petrol to hand on our trek across to Haig-Thomas Island. The freezing temperatures in the room resumed. I was sure that it felt colder than outside.

I threw my bag on the bed and walked outside to feed the Duchess who had miraculously appeared from her own wanderings, unperturbed by the town. Once she had finished eating, I tried to coax her into the room but while the town didn't worry her the church and schoolroom did. She ran off around the corner of the building and out of sight. With no hope of catching her I left her to her freedom. Maybe she could sense the ghosts that haunted the school and church. I walked inside, cold from standing outside. 'Sod the fuel,' I said to Alec, 'let's get this place warmed up again.' We had packed plenty of spare petrol for the journey anyway. This time there were a few problems and each time we primed the stove and turned on the fuel it would catch and then sputter out. I took the stove apart to try and clear the lines. This helped just enough for us to get our pasta cooked and water bottles filled for the following day. Then it gave up and stubbornly refused to light altogether.

Ever resourceful, Al had spotted an old-fashioned Primus in one of the other houses in the town but I decided that we wouldn't have that luxury on the expedition. We should either make this stove work or have nothing at all. Luckily, we had been provided with thick goose-down sleeping bags. I slipped inside and became warm to the point of comfort. On the table the cold made everything freeze as soon as it was put down. Even the screen of the small Kindle that I had brought would freeze with each breath and it was necessary to wipe it down every so often to clear the frost. We both slept well despite the large, open room and the lack of heat. The coldest thing that night for me were my toes. At that time, I thought it was the way that the bottom of the bed pushed against the sleeping bag and compressed the down at my feet. Sadly, that wasn't the issue. I vainly overlooked the fact that the clothing we had been provided with was only rated to -25°C. It had come from one of our few sponsors and I was adamant that we had to use it, convincing myself that with an outer bag there would be another layer of warmth and they could handle the lower temperatures in the far north. It was an act of vanity that I would regret later when we travelled to Ellesmere Island and I would suffer long nights of bone-shattering cold.

Back in the school hut I was just happy that despite the broken stove we hadn't frozen to death during the night. We decided on a casual start the following morning and awoke to find our bags covered in a thick layer of frost. I tried the stove once again, pumping the bottle while still in my sleeping bag, but it refused to light and we were left with little option other than to face the twenty-five-kilometre return journey without breakfast or lunch. The freeze-dried contents of our supplies were near useless without water. Our bodies had been burning energy all night to keep them at a survivable temperature. Without the calorific energy that the food would provide we knew that we faced a miserable journey back. I forced this to the back of my mind. Instead, I focused on the mental and physical benefits that overcoming this new challenge would provide. Like a rat abandoning a sinking ship, the Duchess – our trusted friend – decided to abandon her portage duties and ran off along the previous evening's sledge tracks and out of sight.

There was nothing left to do other than get our heads down and press on. We decided to do it quickly so our bodies, that were already feeling the lack of food, would stay warm. The system that worked best for us in the end was to tie Alec to the front of the sledge, man-hauling whilst I pushed from the back. In our deepened state of exhaustion, the icebergs that we had wondered at on the previous day's journey turned to landmarks of frustration. They created waymarks that drifted ever further away from us. At first their size made them seem so close but the longer we pressed on towards them the further they moved away. One iceberg caught my eye. It was a flat-topped mountain, larger than any I had seen previously. Its sides were funnelled into endless burrows that stretched for some 450 metres from one side to the other. Its summit pushed upwards and into the clouds. A single white bird sailed just below the apex. I felt small and insignificant. A momentary blip on a constantly changing landscape. Miraculously, after a day of sledging we made it back to the ice foot at the shore of Qaanaaq. Alec's body finally failed him, and he wanted to rest. I knew this wasn't a good idea. We still had to haul the sledge up the steep slopes that led into Qaanaaq. I knew this was the time to push ourselves. We might not have the same luxury of resting when the going got hard on the expedition. 'Come on, pal,' I said, coaxing him on. 'I can't do this on my own, just one last push.' Alec awoke to the challenge and we both pushed the sledge up the steep hill and back to the hut. It took all our remaining strength, but we arrived back at the house, hungry and exhausted but still alive. We had walked just under fifty kilometres. Importantly, we had covered the distance safely over the sea ice and without a guide. It had been an eye-opener that had given me a little more confidence about travelling without a guide in the Arctic. It had also made me understand how thin the line was between comfort and survival. A faulty stove would seal the end of any expedition across the sea ice. Importantly, we still had time to change and adapt our equipment.

Lessons Learnt

Cooking: Using the same pan to cook in as well as heat snow leads to incredibly vile drinking water for the following day.

Cleaning: Cold weather means that all water freezes and makes cleaning pots and other equipment extremely testing.

Fuel: Petrol is not a good fuel to use in low temperatures.

Beverages: A wee dram in the evening is great for morale but watch out drinking from a metal hip flask as it is far too easy for it to end up stuck on the lips.

Water bottles: Hot water in bottles before bed works great and means they won't be frozen again by morning.

Fur hoods: There is a reason why everyone in the Arctic has one. Not only do they look great, but the fur creates a fantastic microclimate around your face and is especially good for crosswinds.

Dry bags: Very necessary for gear and especially for backup warm clothes in case of immersion. The bags also freeze, however, and become incredibly rigid. Too many of these can become a bit of a hassle to work with.

CHAPTER 12
THE OLD HUNTER

Mikael came round the following morning. Alec and I recounted the story of the journey to Qeqertarsuaq like seasoned adventurers. His face was one of pure delight and a little pride as we told of the small challenges we had faced and how we had overcome them. 'And what about the ghosts?' he asked, smiling like an older brother happy in the knowledge that he had scared his younger siblings.

'The place was very creepy but we didn't see any ghosts,' I said, happy now that I knew there was no truth in the trick he had played on us. Mikael laughed and we joined him.

Planning for the upcoming trip continued alongside my daily pestering of the heroes of the local hunting community. The skis that we had missed on the march to Qeqertarsuaq were still notably absent. I didn't cherish the idea of walking 450 kilometres across the ice dragging a heavy sled. My experiences in getting the rest of our gear to us had already demonstrated the difficulties of logistics in the Arctic and the prospect of having to walk rather than ski was still a real concern. One conversation between Alec and a courier over a firearms permit summed it up well:

Alec: I need the permit to be sent to Greenland.

Courier: Is that in the US or Canada?

Alec: Greenland, it's a country.

Courier: Really? I don't think I've been asked to send anything to Greenland before. Where is Greenland?

Alec: (sigh) I'm not sure this is going to work, thank you very much for your time.

Sometimes, despite a landmass that dwarfs many of the globe's more prominent nations, Greenland seems like one of the world's forgotten countries. There are only really two options when it comes to getting gear to Qaanaaq. Either have everything planned a year in advance and send it via the ship that only comes in the summer, or pay the extortionate fees to move things by air – what we ended up doing – which comes with the additional pain that few places in the UK understand how to get things there.

I had managed to convince our friends at the Walking With The Wounded charity to lend us their skis in return for a small donation. They had been used in the trip made by Prince Harry when he led a group of armed forces veterans to the South Pole. They were in the process of being shipped from the Antarctic via South Africa to the charity's base in Norfolk. At one point they had managed to get to Greenland but had been shipped back to the UK by DHL for reasons only known to them. The logistics manager explained it was the first time in eight years he had heard of something like it happening, but our time was running out and this was no great consolation for me. I made the call to get them sent to Resolute Bay in Canada instead. I reasoned that as Kenn Borek Air, our air charter, would be coming from Canada anyway they could bring them to Qaanaaq when they came to pick us up. I was also sure that everyone knew where Canada was.

A few days later, I bumped into Rasmina, one of the English teachers at the local school. Rasmina's father was a man called Lars who was highly respected as a hunter, and I had heard people talk of him before. I had asked whether I could interview him when we first met, and she hadn't been very enthusiastic about the idea. 'He is a very busy man,' she said in the polite way that people often use to put you off an idea. She seemed in higher spirits that day and I thought the recent adventure to Qeqertarsuaq might have given us a little more credibility in the eyes of the hunting community. I tested my luck again. This time she seemed happy for us to meet him and suggested we come up later that evening as he was coming back from Qeqertarsuaq where he had been netting for seals. Al and I headed around in the evening to Lars's house, which lay at the top of the village above the museum of Knud Rasmussen. The museum still houses one of the meteorites that Peary must have missed. I was told by Fin, who was also the museum's curator, that it heaves with tourists in the summer when the large cruise ships visit.

Lars and his family welcomed us when we arrived. A caribou anorak was hanging up drying on the back of the door as we entered the hallway and a set of polar bear trousers lay on the floor with a pair of *kamiks* beside them. I thought to myself that perhaps this was the hunter I had seen on the way to the airport when I had taken the Duchess to pick up Alec. I hadn't seen anyone else wearing the full rig and it made sense if he had been going between Herbert Island and Qaanaaq a lot.

Lars was an elderly man in his seventies, but he still looked strong. His face was weathered but not wrinkly and his dark eyes glistened with life. Lars had only ever been a hunter and his late years didn't look like they would stop him any time soon. I spotted a set of barbells lying on his floor. 'Is that how you stay so strong that you can still hunt and win sledge races?' I asked.

Lars laughed. 'I have never told anyone else how I stay strong but I will tell you. I used to lift rocks and pull plants out of the ground to build up muscle,' he said.

'Surely it was all natural.' I winked at Rasmina.

'He once killed a caribou with his bare hands,' she said proudly. 'It's true, you can ask my mother, she loves telling the story.'

The inside of his house was adorned with trophies from narwhals, polar bears and even snow hares and his walls covered with diplomas and photographs of his hunting achievements. Hanging on one side of the sitting room were more pictures. Each one showed a different aspect of an expedition and in one of the older looking photographs there was an important-looking man standing amongst the team.

'Who is that?' I asked.

'That's the crown prince of Denmark,' Lars replied modestly, before explaining that he had been the prince's guide on an expedition across northern Greenland many years ago. 'He was a very good skier,' said Lars. 'Much better than the film crew that accompanied him.'

Lars pointed us towards the kitchen where Rasmina had started to take out several trays with unusual-looking meats on them. Our host offered up some of the local delicacies. Rasmina explained that one was narwhal and the other was beluga. She first demonstrated how we should eat them and, sitting cross-legged on the floor in a small circle around her, we followed suit. We each took a knife and cut a small shred of meat from the larger block. Both meats were almost opaque with a slightly pink tinge. They had been brought in from outside and were still almost frozen. We took the small chunks of meat and dipped them in the soy sauce which we sprinkled with the contents of a small pot filled with something called Aromat. Coated in blubber, the meat had a very different texture to what I was used to. It tasted buttery and made a crunch that felt like biting into a stick of celery. It was delicious and Rasmina explained that she often ate this meat in the winter as it kept her much warmer when she went out on the ice. It was interesting to see the pot of soy sauce there as well. I felt that we were sitting in a smart Japanese restaurant back in London – all we needed was some saki and a pair of chopsticks. I asked Lars where the idea for soy sauce had come from and he told me that he had seen it being used by a couple of Japanese visitors some years ago. He initially thought it was coffee but once he tried the dark mixture, he became a big fan.

As we sat and ate, Lars pointed over at a photo of a polar bear surrounded by dogs and told us the story. He had been out hunting and pulled ahead of the other hunters who had also been following the bear. Suddenly, his dogs and his sledge plummeted through thin ice and into the freezing water below. The bear was circling Lars as he floundered for his rifle, standing dripping wet on his wooden sledge which was now partially submerged beneath the surface of the water. However, the rifle had been soaked in the crash and it was now frozen and useless. He took his knife and laced it to a piece of wood, fashioning it into a spear while he waited for the bear to attack. Fortunately, the other hunters arrived and shot the bear. Lars was saved but it was a close call. As is still the custom, the hunters cut the body of the bear up and shared it out between themselves with the head and shoulder meat always going to the person who had shot or harpooned the animal first. This was the tastiest part of the animal, Rasmina explained. The other hunters would then share the rest of the body equally between them. They never killed more than they needed.

'Everyone in Greenland used to be able to hunt anything on the ice,' Lars explained. 'Then they introduced quotas and so only those with hunting licences like me can hunt now.' It didn't seem clear to Lars why the quotas had been introduced or how the government set them each year. 'They speak to the scientists,' he said. 'They don't ask us. When they introduced the quotas they also started selling dog food in the shops. Before that most hunters could feed their dogs on walrus meat alone, which was better.' I thought that Lars sounded a little distrustful of the purpose behind the quotas and how they had been implemented.

Lars was certainly living up to my expectations. He had a whole journal of stories; most of them seemed to involve close encounters with the animals that he hunted. He told us that a lot of hunters had died over the years, and I thought what a hard life it still was for many of them. Pointing to a large narwhal tooth that hung from his wall he started to tell us the story of another animal that had almost killed him. Alec and I sat there in silence like two excited schoolboys as Rasmina translated. Lars was out hunting one day in his kayak, which was still the normal way to hunt, when he saw a narwhal. Raising his harpoon above his shoulder he launched it across the water, and it stuck into the narwhal which then dived under. The narwhal took the harpoon head and the line attached to it down below the surface. On the end of the line was a sealskin bladder, which hunters used to track the animals through the water until they tired. The bladder, attached to the harpoon trace, caught on his kayak rather than running freely. As the great creature swam down to the depths it dragged Lars with it, bow first. Lars paused and mimicked taking an enormous breath before continuing his story. The animal carried on pulling against the trace, submerging the bow further and forcing water through the skin skirt which Lars wore around his waist. Normally, hunters kayak in pairs so they can look out for each other but on this occasion the hunter he was with had already gone for another narwhal and wasn't aware of the danger that Lars was in. As he got closer and closer to being completely sucked under the water, he managed to grab his knife. Cutting the line, he exploded back to the surface like a cork. Great gallons of water sloshed about inside the kayak, but it didn't sink and he managed to get to an ice floe and to safety.

I asked him the same question about walrus hunting as I had asked the other hunters, but it seemed that the stories would follow his schedule and not mine. He carried on speaking in detail about the other hunts he had been on, which sounded similar to the accounts of Haig-Thomas. On one occasion, Haig-Thomas described walking out across the new ice at night in search of walrus with a hunter from Thule called Ercko as one of the most beautiful nights of his life.

> *I saw two golden lines drawn across the ice: the phosphorescence disturbed by the runners of the sledge. I knew we were on freshly frozen sea-ice, and anywhere might come across herds of walrus feeding. We tied up our dogs, built a snow igloo in the lee of an iceberg and after cooking a meal, took our harpoons and sallied forth.*

Haig-Thomas was well aware that the tusks of the walrus they hunted could easily pierce through the thin ice they walked across. What was so inspiring to me was how he was always able to see past the danger and the hardships through to the simple beauty beneath.

> *It appeared at one of the holes and started to lever itself up with its tusks. I shall never forget the sight as this huge roaring monster climbed out on to the ice, the sea-water pouring from it in golden streams… But a walrus on the ice is like a fish out of water. Ercko ran up and drove his killing-spear into its heart. The walrus made a desperate effort to get at him with its tusks, then dropped dead on the ice and slithered back into the hole it had made. I felt sorry for it, for it was a noble animal, and had put up a wonderful fight.*

Lars explained that very little had changed since he had started hunting. He told me that in the summer months they no longer relied on their muscles alone but would take motorboats rather than the traditional *umiak*[14] to get to the walrus. They could travel further and more quickly but once the walrus were spotted the kayak would still be launched from the motorboat and then they would carry out the hunt. In the winter, though, they still did everything by sledge. Lars then told the story of his own great-uncle who had died out hunting when he was attacked by a walrus in his kayak. The walrus destroyed the little boat and although his uncle was able to reach the kayak of a friend of his he froze to death before they could get him home. It was after that uncle that Lars had been named.

He also told of a time before telephones when he would come into town from a hunt. As he drew nearer, he would run next to the sledge to show that he had caught something larger than usual. In the winter, when it was too dark to see he would flash a torch for the same reason, and it would draw great excitement from those at home.

As we left, I asked him whether he could suggest some other hunters to speak to. He gave us a couple of names and told us that there were not many left that hunted all year around. My final question was about sea ice and polar bears as I had set us a final challenge to venture out even further to a place called Bowdoin Fjord in a few days' time. He told us that we would see the bad ice and that we must be careful to avoid new ice, which was darker and often blue. Echoing the conversation we had with Fin, he told us to always test it before we walked on it. Lars stood up and said something to Rasmina who explained that he needed to go and feed his dogs.

---

14 An open boat made of sealskin that could take eight to ten rowers.

On the way to the door, he showed us some photographs on his phone of footprints that he had seen of a bear that had wandered along the cliffs to the east that led to Bowdoin Fjord. We had heard there were bears and this confirmed it. Lars warned us to be careful when firing warning shots as the bear could get aggressive – if this happened, we needed to be prepared to shoot it. We thanked him for his time, and he smiled back at us from the doorway as we left.

Despite their exile from Thule to Qaanaaq, it had become clear that many Inuit resolutely maintained many parts of their culture and traditional way of life. They had done this despite huge changes induced by their Danish masters' push towards modernism including the growth in imports of food and materials. Hunting had remained a bastion of Inuit culture, retaining a connection to the environment despite modern trappings that would pull them away as it had done in other, seemingly more developed, parts of the world.

We spent the rest of the day packing our gear for the trip and in the evening Mikael popped round to drop off a harness that he had made for the Duchess. I was still interested in understanding more about hunting some of the larger animals on the ice.

'Mikael, can you tell us a little a bit about walrus hunting?' I asked.

'Why do you want my side of the story?' he said. 'There are other hunters that are much older and more experienced than I am who can tell you more than I can,' he explained modestly. Mikael seemed more interested in fishing and so I stopped pestering and we moved on to a picture that I had seen in the book by Haig-Thomas.

'Have you ever played this game?' I said to Mikael, showing him the picture of Haig-Thomas and Nookapinguaq, fingers clasped together and with gritted, smiling faces as they tried to pull each other over.

'Yes,' Mikael said happily. 'It's a game of see who is stronger, like wrestling. I'll show you.'

This game only took one hand to play and Mikael offered me the middle finger of his right hand which I took with mine. He then planted the outside of his right foot against the outside of my right foot. The aim of the game was to pull the other person's arm into your chest, something which Mikael managed fairly easily. I heard later that the former prime minister of Greenland had lost a finger playing this game when it was pulled off at the knuckle by a competitor.

He showed me a second version of the game which seemed less likely to result in him pulling my finger off. We stood facing each with our right hands locked together and our arms wrapped in an embrace with the other. With his left hand he pressed against my left shoulder, and asked me to do the same to him with mine. Shame-faced, I felt the game go in the same direction as the last as I submitted to the quiet strength of Mikael who smiled with delight in front of me. All his years of pulling in fishing lines had clearly paid off.

CHAPTER 13

PLAYING THE WALRUS

While the ski saga continued in the background, a permit that would allow us to go on a walrus hunt with the hunters was also being elusive. There seemed to be confusion between policymakers in Nuuk and hunters in Qaanaaq over what one could and couldn't do when it came to hunting. Many worried that if they got it wrong, they could lose their hunting licences. The hunters were unwilling to take us out with them without this permit. Although we eventually got hold of a lady in Nuuk it was too late, and we resigned ourselves to hearing about hunting rather than going out on an actual hunt. It was by no means the end of the world as even if we did accompany a hunter on a walrus hunt there was no guarantee that we would find a walrus. It was hard not to be a little disappointed. Haig-Thomas's intense accounts of walrus hunting had been one of the things that had drawn me to this adventure.

One night Fin came to visit. He seemed a little down as a friend of his back in Denmark had drunk themselves to death and he had only heard the news the night before. Fin was also dealing with his own pain from something deep down in his back. He told us that he had been having his 'dark thoughts' more often. I got the feeling that he was pleased to see us. It was only later that this pain was linked to the cancer that was growing in his spine. I didn't know it then, but he was only months away from death himself.

After the initial greetings I told him how we had not had any success with the hunting permits, and I asked him whether he could tell us what he knew about walrus hunting. 'Can we make some recordings of you?' I asked innocently.

Instantly, I felt as if I had hit a nerve. 'I'm sorry, Ed,' he said apologetically, 'I've had some pretty bad experiences with people coming up here and tricking me.' Fin explained that on one occasion a reporter from the BBC had interviewed him and, in his opinion, what he said had been misused. He also described an occasion with a French journalist who asked for a fifteen-minute interview. Fin was passionate about Greenland and its people and during the interview had become emotional. 'I asked for the camera to be switched off,' Fin said, 'but when the Frenchman thought I wasn't looking I saw his hand sneak out and turn the camera back on.' It wasn't a unique perspective. I had got the feeling from a number of the people I met that they had become wary of scientists and journalists coming up to Qaanaaq for only a week or two, where they would ask questions and then go back to where they came from and write their own interpretation of a way of life that they invested little time in understanding, but that they were often happy to judge by the standards of their own cultures.

Understandably, Fin was reticent about speaking to us because of these previous experiences. 'Are you angry with me?' he asked.

'No, not at all, I can just write notes, it doesn't matter,' I said. Alec and I had grown to respect Fin and spending time with him as he told us his stories was often the highlight of our day. Having hunted and lived in Greenland for the last thirty years, as a foreigner, he was one of a kind and offered a unique perspective. With so much change in the world he may well have been the last of a kind. Fin had taken to us as well. Alec and I had both grown up hunting and I could tell Fin enjoyed swapping hunting stories with us as much as we did with him.

As I've said before, Fin lived a full life and some of his stories were far too graphic to put to paper. He had huge admiration for the hunters in Qaanaaq and especially their affinity with nature. He had to learn a lot when he moved to Qaanaaq and those lessons were not always learnt easily. He told us one story of when they were out hunting. His sledge was passing a line of pressure ice around two to three metres high where the old ice met new. Suddenly, his dogs caught the scent of something over the other side of the ice wall and immediately shot over it, taking Fin with them. The other hunters followed. Soon they spotted a polar bear not very far away at all. The experienced hunters took over the lead from Fin on the trickier new ice and started off in pursuit of the bear. As they got closer the bear crashed through the sea ice and made to swim away. The hunters jumped off their sledges and began to move in for the kill. Fin tried to follow and immediately fell right through into the freezing water below. It can be a harsh land and the other hunters took no notice despite his cries for help. His dogs, thinking it was a game, trotted over unhelpfully and began to lick his head. He shooed them away and managed to get his arms through the traces of the dog lines and pull himself up and out. He stood there, slowly beginning to freeze to death as he watched the hunters finish off the bear.

The polar bear began to attack them by charging out of the water and on to the ice. Time after time it was driven back by their shots. Fin was saddened by its plight; shot after shot rang out until eventually he saw in the bear's eyes the realisation that it was going to die. This immortal figure, master of ice and most respected hunter, slowly drooped its head and with one final breath it fell back into the water and died.

Even though Fin was soaked through and slowly freezing to death he was still not a priority. The bear was cut up first and the dogs fed. Finally, they packed the sledges up with bear meat and headed off on the sledges, which ran for some hours before they made camp. It was only once they had set up camp and lit the stove that they then helped Fin to take his now frozen clothes off and got him into a sleeping bag. Fin settled down to what he thought would be a nice long sleep, only to be woken four hours later and made to put on his partially dry clothes before they headed back. With no dry *kamiks*, he fashioned a set lent by one of the hunters into slippers which he tied to his feet. When he got home and took his boots off, his heel was black with frostbite. 'But it was a great feeling,' he said as his face lit up. 'My wife was so proud of me; I was a great Danish man who had survived the cold and brought back fresh bear meat for the table,' he chuckled.

His other story of frostbite had us both in stitches. 'I went off from the group to take a piss,' he said. 'But the other hunters kept on trying to creep up on me so they could see what a white man's penis looks like,' he laughed. 'So, I finished too quickly and got some piss on my trousers.' He looked at us with delight as he chuckled away, coughing occasionally to clear his tar-coated lungs. 'Because my trousers were wet, by the time I sledged home my penis had turned black with frostbite.' We looked at him in shock. 'But when I showed my wife, she was ecstatic – my penis had swollen to twice the size!' he cried.

Now that Fin had managed to cheer himself up with his own stories and with only a few minor prompts, the conversation moved on to walrus hunting. Fin decided that the best way to explain it was to do a mock walrus hunt in the living room of the house. Fin played the hunter and Alec and I were the walrus. First, he drew an image of a walrus harpoon and explained that the harpoon head was larger for a walrus than for a seal but the ends of both could be made from beating the metal from the tooth of a saw blade. 'The harpoon head is detachable, and it comes off when you hit the walrus with it,' he said.

'The line is attached to the harpoon head and so that is what we use to hold on to the walrus.'

Then the old Dane grabbed a broom from the corner to mimic the long wooden shaft of the harpoon and picked up a long rope. I was standing directly in Fin's eyeline and so I was the unlucky walrus that day. 'The hunter waits by the hole for the walrus to surface for air and when he sees it come up, he strikes,' Fin whispered as he hovered next to me in a crouch. Then quickly he jabbed me with the broom handle and at the same time gave me one end of the rope while he held the other.

'Surely the weight of the walrus would be too much to hold on to?' I asked.

'No,' he said, 'that's why as soon as you have the walrus you need to drop the harpoon and grab the metal pole which is chiselled at one end like a pick. You stick the pick through the loop at the end of the line, place the chiselled end on to the ice and put all of your weight on it. This stops the walrus dragging you in with it.'

'Then what happens?' I asked, slightly out of breath. I was still playing the walrus at this point and Fin was making me run around the room holding the rope.

'When the walrus is tired, he will come up for air and when he surfaces you shoot him,' Fin said, pointing to his neck to indicate where the final shot should be made.

I was surprised by his explanation as it seemed the only thing that had changed since Haig-Thomas's time was that they used a rifle rather than a spear to finish off the walrus. Running around a living room in socks wasn't quite the same as crawling across new sea ice surrounded by the electric glow of phosphorescence as Haig-Thomas had done but it was enough for me to understand. Nearly everything else in terms of technique was the same as he had witnessed over seventy years ago. The only other change that I could tell was that more recently the harpoon head would be carved from plastic rather than walrus bone.

Fin went on to explain that they would put tarpaulin sheets down between the walrus and the side of the ice hole to make dragging the large creatures, which can weigh over a tonne, on to the ice a little easier. 'For the really big ones I've even seen the hunters rig up a pulley dug into the ice so that they can use the dogs to drag them out,' he went on. The walrus is then cut up on the ice using a long knife while the carcass is still warm. The dogs are always fed first before the hunters feed themselves. The sled is loaded up with as much meat as it can hold, and any excess meat can be left under a rock or in an igloo. This doesn't always work as bears have a great sense of smell and can often find it and, if they do, they will eat it.

Fin also spoke about small but important things that are often overlooked. 'Out here you need to understand that the Inuit is the teacher, and we are just the students,' he said. He first learnt to feed dogs further south with fish; when he moved further north the others laughed. 'The hunters loved to get inside my head, they knew this wound me up and so they kept it up for hours until finally I couldn't take it any more and I got really angry,' he said, 'but when they saw me get angry, they knew they had won and they all fell about laughing.' Fin looked down, obviously feeling a little embarrassed by the memory.

He had learnt a lot from the other hunters despite some of the initial ridicule. He had noticed small things like when the Inuit fed their dogs they started with the blubber first, then the skin and finally the meat. 'Otherwise, the dogs will get full of the meat and will not want to eat the blubber,' he explained. It was also important to make sure the stronger dogs were on a shorter lead than the weaker ones which allowed the weaker dogs to get fed without hassle. The food could be thrown to the weaker ones at the back without the worry of the stronger dogs being bold enough to try and snatch it.

'In the eighties there was a horrible virus that wiped out all the local Greenlandic dogs up here,' Fin said. 'They had to import dogs from the south, so they are not as large as they used to be.' He explained that despite this the dogs had become accustomed to the region after quite a harsh selective-breeding process. One element of this selection process was based on whether the dogs swallowed their food whole or whether they chewed it. Hunters prized those dogs that swallowed as it meant that their food wouldn't be stolen from them by the other dogs. Whole pieces of meat also took longer to digest in their stomachs, which would make them feel full for longer.

'You need a lot of walruses to feed a dog team in the Arctic,' he said. 'The hunting quotas limit the number of walruses that can be killed each season which hasn't made it easy for everyone.' It was partly because of this that it was necessary for hunters to supplement their supplies with dog food purchased from the local shop. Before the quotas the more successful hunters supported the others by giving them meat for their dogs at a good rate. Since the quotas, this practice had mostly stopped. The better hunters made up the quotas first and so the poorer hunters began to lose out. This made it very expensive to keep a whole team of dogs going if someone wasn't having a very successful season. Much of this burden fell on the younger members of the community where the cost to become a hunter was already high. It also weighed heavily on some of the poorer hunters of the community who, without enough walrus meat, could struggle to sustain a team through a bad season of hunting without another source of income.

Outside interferences weren't all bad though. A few years ago, an entire guillemot population had been wiped out when they were shot at in their nests. The guillemots were killed where they lay or else fled their nests, knocking out the eggs of unborn chicks on their way. It could take five years for a bird to mature enough to give birth, which it only did once a year. An entire population could be wiped out very quickly by this short-sighted approach. A law had come in to stop this which Fin saw as a positive step.

The coffee cup in front of him lay empty, its contents drunk long ago. Fin placed two hands on the table and slowly levered himself off the wooden chair that he was sitting on with a grimace. It was clear that he was hiding a lot of pain behind his smile. He thanked us for the coffee and staggered out of the door and back into the cold. He had finally warmed to us, and we had very much warmed to him, which made it even sadder to see him struggle as he did.

CHAPTER 14

A FINAL CHALLENGE – BOWDOIN FJORD

There was just a week left until the plane was due to take us to Eureka. The last few days had been a near whiteout. In the brief moments between the roaring winds the sun burnt through the cloud, leaving a low-level mist hanging over the sea ice where the cold peaks of icebergs pushed through. I thought back to a book I had read by Gretel Ehrlich (*This Cold Heaven*). It was during these times of idle contemplation whilst stood amongst Greenland's ice that I understood what she meant in her description of Greenland as a 'cold heaven'. I had left all the complexities and noise of modern life back in the UK. When the weather made it impossible to go out and the entire town hunkered down, we would try and remain productive by practising using our electronic equipment and updating our sponsors on progress. Often though, we would simply binge-watch Troels's collection of painfully outdated action films, which included recent classics *Cop Out* and *A Good Day to Die Hard* – basically anything where a director thought the fact that Bruce Willis's name was on the credits would be enough to sell it.

The storm lasted for three days and while we made good use of the time, I was very aware of the fact that the countdown clock was ticking. Each day inside was a missed day of training. During our days in the hut, I made plans for a final training run. I heard from Hans that a French film crew had just returned from their journey to Siorapaluk, around forty kilometres north-west of Qaanaaq. They had come to make a documentary about the French explorer

Jean Malaurie. Malaurie became well known for his work in standing up for the rights of the indigenous peoples of the Arctic. He was a keen advocate of the importance of embracing cultural diversity in science. In particular, he pushed for Inuit ways of thinking to be considered at the same level as European schools of thought. His time in Greenland left a lasting impression on him. In his book, *The Last Kings of Thule*, he wrote:

> *I owe much to these exemplary men, who obliged me to discover in depth my own identity. They reminded me that a man's life should be a constant challenge that enables him to become what he truly is. They were my second – and more important – university, and I shall be indebted to them all my life.*

The French crew explained that the ice had already started to break up and they had been unable to hunt any walrus as a result because it was too dangerous. The hunters felt it could well be the end of the season. I was secretly glad that the decision to forget about the hunting permits and refocus our energies on training was the right one. It saved us a wasted trip and a lot of money.

Up to this point I was still contemplating taking a guide, a Canadian named Jerry Kobalenko, on the journey to Ellesmere Island. Unable to find a willing local during the summer, I had managed to identify Jerry as one of a handful of people who had experience of the area. With each day on the ice and through our training runs I felt more confident in our capabilities. Alec and I had listened intently to the advice of Fin and the Inuit hunters over the last few months. We had survived our trip to Herbert Island. Looking at the map I felt that the bays and fjords around Qaanaaq would be similar to the ones on

Ellesmere Island. Taking a guide would be the safer option but having someone else lead us across the sea ice on our trek would take a lot away from the challenge. To me, a rite of passage was about testing yourself without the support of the professionals in your community. Taking Jerry would mean remaining firmly in our comfort zone. We would simply be following the lead of someone already experienced in the area.

This final practice run was therefore critical. A last challenge to overcome that would confirm to me whether I was ready. I felt responsible for Alec's life as well as my own. It would be the last opportunity to test our equipment and the skills we had developed. I wasn't ready to leave Jerry out of the expedition until I was confident that I could lead the expedition across Ellesmere safely without him. It was a big decision to make.

Our plan was to leave Qaanaaq and turn east. I had chosen a place called Bowdoin Fjord, which was where Peary and his team travelled through back in 1898. We would be sleeping out in the open and completely out of sight of the town for the first time. Polar bears would also be a real threat – hunters told us that a couple had been sighted in the area only recently.

The skis were still absent, but the final pieces of equipment had arrived. Importantly, this included the bear tripwire which we wouldn't be able to go on our journey without. As the unofficial guru of expedition electronics and other fiddly things, Alec had spent the day putting together the solar-powered charging system that would allow us to communicate with the outside world. He had also been playing with the idea of using a warm box that would keep our electronics working throughout the day, but had no luck. Alec's greatest success, however, was in mastering the 'folding tent trick' which we had been trying to get to grips with since borrowing the concept from Sir Ranulph Fiennes who had explained it in one of his books. The idea was that by removing the poles from the rings that bind them to the tent on one side and maintaining that contact point on the other side of the tent, the whole thing could be neatly folded away and lain across a pulk. When it needed to go up again it could be done in a couple of minutes, compared to the ten or so minutes it took initially when we had to rethread each pole. I had already learnt how quickly frostbite could come on when I was fishing with Mikael so the time saved with the tent would be a digit saver.

We laid out our pulks on the porch and began to fill them with the essentials to set up camp that night. Bearing in mind these things were generously proportioned (Al was able to lay down in one just to prove the point), it was very tempting to overpack and fill the cavernous space. Travelling light was an idea that Haig-Thomas and, more recently, the Inuit hunters in Qaanaaq had said was key to movement in the Arctic. We restrained ourselves to only packing the key pieces of kit – tent, ice screws, sleeping system and stove – as well as some food. We then hooked ourselves up to the sledges and made our way down to the sea ice.

Our first steps with the pulks on the icy roads to the bottom of town were harder than I thought they would be. The sledges would decide they were far better off making their own way down and we were soon quickstepping as they overtook us on the slopes and dragged us along. By the time we reached the bottom we had managed to attract the attention of some of the children in town who swamped us as we stumbled inexpertly down the slope. They had a lot of fun jumping on the sledges when we weren't looking, and then picking up the back to help us along. Finally, they grabbed the sledge traces and ran off as fast as they could. We were still attached by our harnesses, and it left us no choice but to run along beside them, completely out of control.

When we got to the sea ice the children left us and remained there, halted by an invisible line across the shore where they waved us goodbye. It was a touching moment, but I felt we hardly warranted such a dedicated send-off party considering Al and I were planning on coming back in a couple of days (perhaps they knew something we didn't!).

We managed the pressure ice on the seashore with surprising ease and although our sleds were twenty to thirty kilograms shy of our expedition weight, we were very much relieved. We had never trained in pulling any weight along so we had no idea before that what it might feel like. We left the waving children behind us and headed on to a point almost exactly three kilometres out from Qaanaaq town where we would be spending the night. The spot was marked by a large iceberg to the left of which a small group of hunting camps had been set up. We had been to these camps before with Mikael. Once again Mikael had offered to provide a brotherly overview of our camp set-up when we got there. He had told us he was expecting to deliver his catch to the factory at the beginning of the next week, so he was planning on fishing around the clock to fill his sledge. I thought it was a polite excuse to give him a chance to watch over us without saying so. At least our presence there may have given him some respite from an otherwise harsh and monotonous routine.

As we got closer, I called out the Inuit welcome that I had been trying to get right ever since Fin had told me about it. '*Hag-ah-huna*,' I shouted across the ice, which was met with a mixture of amusement and confusion by Mikael. Slowly, he realised what I was trying to say and patiently corrected me when I got closer.

'*Aihiukiaq*,' he said, chuckling. '*Hain-aghunai*,' he went on in the traditional reply. He was very interested in the pulks we were dragging and was keen to try on the harness we wore to see what all the fuss was about. As soon as it was on, he shrugged his shoulders to show that he didn't think it was heavy and then set off at a run to where he thought would be a good place for us to put up camp. The place he picked was on a flat piece of ice in the middle of a field of sastrugi[15]. It was a good point, he explained, as the ice was thick and the raised lumps of the sastrugi would mean the wind would break before it hit our tent.

We went through the motions of setting up camp with him for the first time. The brittle first-year ice would shatter when I tried to hammer and turn the metal screws into it which were needed to hold down the tent. Instinctively, I moved the screws to another point, but Mikael shook his head. 'Clear the broken ice away from the hole, the ice below will not break up,' he called out. Sure enough, there was a more solid layer below, the ice didn't break, and the screws went in easily. Later he explained the best place to pitch a tent by looking at the ice around us. The wind direction was written into the ice by streaks of powdered snow that lay behind the more solid side of the sastrugi. 'Place the tent on the sheltered side of the sastrugi,' he said. 'If you face the door away from where the snow has collected you can make sure that the door of the tent stays out of the wind.' Mikael also explained how we could easily construct a snow wall which could act as a buffer against high winds. He pointed at the sastrugi and motioned that by shovelling snow from where it had collected in the lee of the frozen wave-like structure, we could clear a camp as well as

15 Sastrugi is formed when the wind cuts across areas of hard-packed snow and leaves sand-dune-like forms across the sea ice. These frozen waves are tricky to travel over on skis and I found it best to skirt around them.

build a wall by moving the snow back to the windward side of that ridge. It was all second nature to Mikael who had lived out on the ice, but it was new knowledge and very valuable to us.

Once the tent was set up, Al as 'inside man' removed his boots and shuffled inside. He would be responsible for laying out the bedding as I passed it through to him from the pulks. He was also responsible for lighting the stove, not an easy task when your hands are numb with cold. As 'outside man' it would be my job to secure the pulks, set the bear tripwire and build a snow wall to protect us from the wind. I was also the one who collected the snow which we would use to boil our water for the evening meal and to fill our canteens for the next day.

Unlike our previous attempts in Qeqertarsuaq a week earlier, with the change of fuel from 'petroleum' to 'white gas' the stove lit without a problem. Not only did we have an evening meal, but the tent also became so hot that we had to turn the stove off after a few minutes. At one point the thermometer showed 40°C, almost a seventy-degree difference to the temperature outside. It was bliss in comparison to the previous outing where everything froze, and it was only our clothing and thick sleeping bag that had kept us from succumbing to the cold. With a working stove, we could happily change into our base layers and move around comfortably without fingers going numb. Kit dried out in seconds and morale happily jumped up a few notches. I felt we had finally achieved the comfort that Haig-Thomas had managed on his winter hunting trips in the area back in 1937.

We spent the rest of the evening talking with Mikael and the other hunters who were also laying out their lines for halibut that night. As the sun slowly set behind the glimmering lights of Qaanaaq the sky came alive with stars. One of Mikael's best jokes when I had asked where the North Star was had been to point at one and then another and finally with a cheeky smile state that they were all the North Star as we were so far north! 'You must see a lot of shooting stars during the winter?' I asked Mikael.

He paused with a faraway look in his eye. 'Sometimes there are so many it is like a war is going on up there,' he replied.

Later on that evening I experimented with some long-exposure shots with my camera which took a few attempts to get right, much to the delight of the group of hunters who peered over my shoulder.

Once the stove was off and we had tucked ourselves into our sleeping systems the temperature began to drop a degree every couple of seconds and by the time we woke up the cold had dropped below the level that our thermometer would go. Haig-Thomas described some of his most comfortable nights as the ones when he was able to use animal skins such as polar bear or walrus as a mattress. Using the same principle, we both slept on the backpacking version of these: a plastic roll mat, coloured in reflective silver, on top of which lay a self-inflating mattress. The combination of the two provided a good layer of insulation between us and the ice. We would improve this set-up by borrowing a caribou skin from Fin before we set off for our trek. While the sleeping mats kept our bodies warm, the floor around the tent was freezing. As an additional weight, the skin would be a luxury, but it would act like a carpet and make the tent much warmer.

Where Haig-Thomas used a caribou-skin sleeping bag much like Scott in the Antarctic, in the interest of weight we used a down sleeping bag provided by one of our sponsors. We also carried a waterproof over-bag, and something called a vapour barrier liner to protect the bag from our own perspiration and water vapour from our breath. The idea of this was to prevent moisture building which would cancel out some of the heat-retaining properties of the goose down that the bag was filled with. Sleeping on the ice was going to take some getting used to, I thought that night. Despite being our first night on the sea ice we both managed to get enough sleep.

I awoke early the next morning feeling fresh and, unlike on the trip to Qeqertarsuaq, we were able to light the stove. Soon the tent was warm and this time we would be able to make our breakfast and avoid a long day of hauling without any food. I managed to get a decent porridge boiled up and we threw down mouthfuls of the stuff ready for the day ahead. It didn't take us long to get the tent down, pack up our pulks and get on the move. Mikael was catching a few minutes of well-earned sleep in between pulling in fish lines, and we chose not to wake him as we broke camp. The sun was just coming up over the horizon and as we walked there was a glorious sensation in my feet as warm blood began to awaken my toes that had been cold and numb since we turned in last night.

We walked along the sea ice, one behind the other. It was a clear day and we made good progress. The warm tents and safety of the fishing camp and the sleeping hunters that lay inside their tents became small dots behind us. The Duchess, whose job would be to supplement our untested bear-warning system, was being stubborn. I had attached her to my harness with a piece of rope so that she couldn't run away but she didn't really know what to do. Rather than walking forward she kept on trying to walk back towards the town, tripping me up as the rope weaved and snagged its way around my legs. We had gone roughly ten kilometres out of town and there were no signs that she was settling down, so I let her off her lead. With the town out of sight behind the headland I was confident that we had gone far enough that she would rather stick with us than go off on her own.

I was very wrong. She hesitated for only a few seconds before turning back towards Qaanaaq. We both looked at her, whistling softly and trying in vain to prevent the inevitable. She couldn't have cared less. With an attitude befitting her name she stuck her head in the air as if to say, 'I've had enough of this ridiculous idea,' and ran back towards town. She never even looked back.

'Oh dear,' I said to Alec. We both looked at each other and laughed.

'I don't think she would have made a good bear dog anyway,' he said.

'What do you think? Head on or head back?' I asked, knowing that bear tracks had been seen recently in the area.

'I'm happy to head on,' Alec said.

'We'll need to take it in turns to watch for bears,' I cautioned, but I was happy that Alec was feeling confident. I leant forward and felt the resistance of the sledge across my chest as it pulled against the harness as we continued to Bowdoin Fjord.

We carried on down Inglefield Bay, picking our way through fields of icebergs that stood like icy sculptures across the span of the bay. The long row of mountains that had been our view for over two months lay to the south and towering red cliffs rose from the sea to our north. We made good progress now that the dog was not around to distract us. We passed the time talking about the last few months and planning out the final details of the trek to Haig-Thomas Island. I was still worried about the skis not arriving in time as they made their way to Resolute Bay, but every step taken in our large Baffin boots was a positive one. It would be a lot easier to ski but we were proving to ourselves that walking would be possible as well.

The sun had to yet to reach its zenith and it cast our long shadows across the sea ice in front of us. It was like following in the footsteps of large, gangly giants. Alec spotted a hole in the ice ahead of us. Other than dead halibut or the odd snow hare it was the first sign of Arctic wildlife that we had seen. The hole, which belonged to a seal, was only half a metre or so wide and its edges of thick white ice had been rounded smooth. I could see where the seal had rested, its insulated body melting the surface of the sea ice into a glass-like sheen as it sunbathed under the Arctic sun.

We carried on walking for a few hours more, passing the peaks of the red cliffs one by one. I could see the mouth of Bowdoin Fjord in front of me. It seemed close but distances in the Arctic can be difficult to measure as there are very few reference points and this can trick the eye. We planned to make camp at the top of the fjord and head down to the glacier at the bottom the following day. Mikael had told us about a hut that had been built which we could stay in. Sure enough, as we reached the fjord after what was a longer-than-expected last few kilometres, there it was. The hut was perched on a small rocky outcrop just above the line of the sea ice. It stood in a stunning location. It was isolated and accompanied only by the beauty that surrounded it. There was a wooden board nailed to the hut. The white paint had flaked over the years, weathered by the winds, but I could just make out some writing that had dedicated it to the schoolchildren lost in an air crash several decades earlier.

I woke up the next day to see that clouds had descended across the landscape which seemed to absorb any colour and turned everything white. Visibility had reduced to the point that I could no longer see the entrance to the fjord or the glacier at the bottom where we were aiming for. The temperature had also dropped. The manageable -25°C yesterday had lowered to a cooler and, without the sun, more noticeable -30°C. It was cold but although we were now far from

Qaanaaq, I didn't feel worried. The trip was giving me the confidence I had yearned for. We left the sledges at the hut, and I packed what we needed into my rucksack which I slung over my shoulders. Alec carried the rifle that Troels had lent us in case a bear sneaked up on us. I wanted to head to Bowdoin Glacier at the head of the fjord, from where Peary had made his walk across the ice cap.

It was around five kilometres from the hut to where Bowdoin Glacier should have been: a large, sprawling mass of ice that flowed down between the valleys and looked like a giant motorway into Greenland's interior. It had looked impressive the day before but, in the mist, I could see nothing. I had hoped we might discover something of Peary's but we only found a small cairn that sat atop a rocky outcrop of land. I stood next to that cairn and looked around me. In each direction there were endless rows of snow-covered white mountains that peaked through the mist. They stood out with prominent majesty even against the ice-covered sea and cloud-covered sky. Standing there gave me a feeling of pure, unbridled freedom.

We spent a few minutes walking amongst the ice and rocks at the bottom of the fjord. I watched Alec walking, exploring the surrounding rocks through the mist. The large rifle was slung over one shoulder and I thought with some pride that we had come a long way from the early, childlike conversations that had brought us here. 'It's pretty impressive,' Alec said.

'It's a powerful place,' I responded, 'but I'm not sure if we are going to find anything in this mist.' We headed back to the hut to grab the sledges and the rest of our gear.

It was about twenty-five kilometres back to Qaanaaq, which we covered with ease. We had learnt a lot from the trip to Qeqertarsuaq and we had benefited from putting those lessons into practice. One of them was to not miss out on breakfast as we had done when our stove wouldn't light. As a result we reached Qaanaaq in much better condition than when we had crawled home in our calorie-starved state previously. Troels was glad to see us when we got back to the hut. 'I wasn't sure whether you would make it when I saw my dog come home on her own,' he said, half joking and half serious. I looked at the Duchess, who was tied back up on her chain under the balcony. She bore no sign of remorse at having left us to our fate. *Surely a few days on the sea ice with us would have been more fun than being tied up here*, I thought to myself.

I wondered what would happen to the Duchess when Troels finished his stint teaching in Qaanaaq. The hunters had their own dog teams and it didn't seem likely that she would be allowed to join them now that she was already a few years old. As my own failed attempts had taught me, training a dog to pull a sledge takes a lot of time and investment. It also didn't seem likely that she would be taken on as a pet. That was a foreign concept to most Greenlanders. The dogs were bred to work and the idea of chaining one up for the rest of their lives would have seemed alien to most. It was more likely that she would meet a sad end at the hands of the local dog catcher. I only hoped that it would be quick.

Al and I showered and were just settling in for a couple of whiskies that night when we were invited to a party in the next house. The Danish teachers were having a few drinks before going on to the sports hall where the local Qaanaaq rock band were playing. I wasn't sure what to expect of an Inuit rock band but was pleasantly surprised. When we got to the sports hall the crowd was already well on its way and a familiar Danish two-step dance accompanied the 1980s-inspired power ballads the band had created. Alec and I spent most of the concert trying to avoid being dragged into the midst of the happy crowd. We must have looked like a couple of awkward teens at our first dance.

By this time most people in Qaanaaq were aware of our expedition. That night for the first time we were approached by some of the locals who were keen to talk to us. I'm sure the reason for this was the beer as it went against the interactions I had had previously. Generally, people took a long time to warm to us. I explained that we had just come from Bowdoin Fjord and straight away one of the men said, 'My great-grandfather Peary was there.' I had read stories about a few famous Arctic explorers who hadn't been completely faithful to their wives so I was excited to meet this man. I had known that Peary had fathered two sons with his Inuit mistress, Aleqasina. One of the sons had died young; the other, Kaala, had survived and fathered five children and the family line had grown with each generation. From most accounts, Peary never publicly acknowledged the children that he had in the far north and turned his back on his Inuit family when he left Greenland. Kaala recalled wearing dog-skins when he was younger which was a sign of the poverty that he was left in. However, with the help of the community he learnt to become an effective hunter. I might have presumed that the Inuit descendants of Peary and indeed his long-term co-sledger, Matthew Henson, might have looked on their grandfathers with some bitterness, but it felt like the explorers' names still carried a sense of pride amongst those that now bore them. Soon other Inuit were stepping forward and identifying their own ancestors from the Famous Explorer handbook. Some I knew and some I didn't. 'I'm a descendant of Bartlett,' one man said. I feigned recognition but I had to look him up later – Robert Bartlett was a 20th-century American explorer who joined Peary on his North Pole attempt and led over forty expeditions in the Arctic.

Then a young man stepped forward. 'My grandfather was Nookapinguaq,' he said. We had finally found a descendant of the Inuit who had accompanied Haig-Thomas across Smith Sound to Ellesmere Island. This young man had been in Copenhagen studying and instead it was his brother who had followed in his father's footsteps, and was now a hunter in Siorapaluk, a small village further north. My lack of Inuktitut prevented the conversation from going any further and we learnt nothing of his connection to Haig-Thomas.

With the rock band finishing its final song we decided that tonight was the night to venture on to the infamous Daffi's Bar. Daffi's was a small blue hut next to the sports hall to the east of town. Inside it was dimly lit with a small dance floor to the right as we entered and a slightly larger bar on the left. I had picked up a poor impression of the place from the rumours circulating amongst the Danish expats, mainly teachers, who suggested it was violent and full of drunks.

Clearly, the Danes hadn't experienced a night out in the UK before. There was none of the rowdy drunkenness that I had expected. Everyone was incredibly friendly and seemed delighted that we were there. Alec managed to resist any attempt to get him on to the dance floor, but I wasn't as resilient. I was taken into the middle of the dance floor by an elderly Inuit lady who began twirling me around. *This is up there with some of the odder experiences of my life*, I thought hazily. I staggered around my Inuit hosts with my feet encased in their large Baffin boots, clumping unsteadily amongst the other partygoers and flashing disco lights. I gave in to Alec's sage advice to head home around midnight after the fourth and increasingly aggressive attempt to kiss me from a lady who arguably should have been in the old people's home. Alec probably felt that I might not manage to duck a fifth.

CHAPTER 15

GREEN FOR GO – RESOLUTE BAY

I woke up the next morning, in a state of catalepsy brought on by the previous night's alcohol abuse and still reeling from the thought of the brittle, dry lips of the old lady who had tried to lay them on me on the dance floor. As the local children had explained, this was what was called 'going green' in Qaanaaq. I wasn't sure whether this was because of the green label that adorned the tins of Heineken beer that were so popular or because of the colour people turned when they drank it. Yanik and Vincent, two French photographers who Alec had found to share the plane charter with us, were inbound from Ilulissat and were set to arrive in Qaanaaq at midday. Troels was in a good mood that morning and seemed pleased with himself. 'Why are you so chirpy?' I asked.

'I am making your new guests pay me rent as well,' he said with glee. Troels had agreed that they could stay in the house with us but only if they paid. The price he set was on par with the extortionate fee he was charging us. In return they would receive a pitiful amount of floor space and a blow-up mattress. Alec and I felt particularly bad about this and decided that we would vacate one of the rooms and camp together next to the radiator in the living room so they didn't feel that they were being completely fleeced.

After breakfast we went around to the house of a man called Oleg who wanted us to see a film he had made on hunting. He had a lovely house that sat next to the church on the east side of the town. Slightly raised on a mound, it was enclosed with a small picket fence, which was the only type of boundary I had seen so far in Qaanaaq. Inside, the house was decorated with pictures of friends, family and hunting. These earthly photographs were interspaced with pictures of Jesus, and I got the feeling that he was a deeply Christian man. He shook our hands briefly and then invited us to watch the television with him. There was a parliamentary meeting taking place concerning Thule and the B-52 crash which I had been hearing a bit about. Oleg's son Vittus was the foreign minister for Greenland and so we gathered around the small television in the corner of the room while he spoke. Alec and I didn't understand any of it, but I was moved to watch as tears began to fall unashamedly from the man's face, driven by the pride he felt at witnessing his son in action.

Looking around me I also noticed the awards on the wall; many were for the man's work concerning Inuit human rights. There was very little to distinguish each house from the next and so the usual traps that marked success for many in the UK – the big car, the large house, the expensive ornaments – were all absent. Despite this I knew that this was a man of status in the community. With the speech over he turned to us and spoke. 'I heard that you're looking for stories of Nookapinguaq,' he said.

'Yes,' we both replied in amazement.

The man spoke in cracked and broken English. 'When I was a child, he was in hospital with me in Qaanaaq,' he said. 'Nookapinguaq was sick but he told me stories of polar bear and seal hunting before he died in his bed. I think that his grave may be up in the cemetery at the top of the hill.'

I was amazed at the idea of Nookapinguaq being in the hospital just up the road, but it made sense as his would have been one of the families that were moved here from Thule. It seemed odd in my mind to think of him dying a death as an old man in a modern hospital bed. How much change must he have witnessed in his life? I was hoping that Oleg would mention Haig-Thomas and their great adventure to Ellesmere Island but sadly there was none.

We took our leave and walked back to the hut just in time to meet Yanik and Vincent as they were dropped off by Hans in his red Land Cruiser. It was a relief to be able to talk with them much as I liked without being admonished for it. A respite from the slower-paced and more thoughtful conversations that we had got used to. Vincent was French and a well-known photographer with a ton of awards to his name. He had been to Ellesmere Island the previous year where he had photographed the musk ox that patrolled the island. He was returning to take pictures of the white wolf which he had missed the last time he was there.

Yanik was from Switzerland, slightly smaller in stature and less reserved. He was joining Vincent as the expedition cameraman. We immediately felt a kinship with these two men, bonded by the shared sense of adventure and challenge that lay ahead on Ellesmere Island. Alec had managed to find them at the last second and, combined with the money we had saved by not taking Jerry the guide, it had been a lifesaver for our finances. More importantly, they had also made good on their promise of bringing up several bottles of whisky. Alec had refused to go on the expedition without them.

I showed them into the hut, apologising for the lack of space, and I was impressed that there were no complaints. I guess they were just happy for a place to stay as they would only be there for a night and the plane was due to arrive the next day. That was the plan, anyway. I had been in touch with the logistics company, and they had told me that the skis had not arrived in Resolute Bay yet. I had been promised they would arrive that day. I couldn't take the risk of the skis not arriving in time to be flown to Qaanaaq with our air charter. I asked Alec to take Yanik and Vincent to Fin's as the only thing they were missing was a gun which they would need for safety on the trip. I knew from experience that Fin had a serious arsenal at his disposal and could be convinced to loan them one for a small fee. While the team were away, I got in touch with the pilots at Kenn Borek Air and explained the situation.

'Do you think we could delay the flight by a day?' I asked, to give the skis time to arrive.

'We can, but it's complicated. That's going to be Sunday so someone needs to speak to the airport manager as the airport will be closed,' they replied. I asked them to provisionally shift the flight. After I hung up, I realised I had no idea who the airport manager was or where they lived.

Luckily, Troels was on hand. 'They live in the blue huts to the west of the town, but I don't know which one he lives in,' he said.

I would only have a few hours to sort things out before it was too late, so I ran out of the house and down to the blue huts. There were four, nestled in a group and newer than the other houses in Qaanaaq. I knocked on the first hut but there was no response. In the second house along, I could see lights shining through the curtains of the small window. I jogged over to it and tried again. This time there was an answer. An attractive Inuit girl opened the door and greeted me in English. I paused, both at her attractiveness and the ease with which she could converse in my language. For the last three months I had only met one or two people in the entire town other than the Danes that could really speak English. I gathered myself and asked whether this was the airport manager's house. She raised her eyebrows in the unusual way that the Inuit do when they are saying 'yes' to you and then turned and walked away. This had taken some getting used to as I always expected a verbal response and often ended up asking the same question again, misinterpreting the silent 'yes' and thinking they hadn't understood me. Conversely, people, particularly the children, would crinkle their nose when they wanted to say no. An expression that felt familiar to the face people made back home when they didn't like something.

A few seconds later a young Danish man arrived at the door. 'How can I help?' he asked. I explained the situation to him, that we were going to Ellesmere and a vital piece of equipment hadn't arrived yet. What would we need to do to delay the flight?

The man looked at me and seemed keen to help. 'I will need to stand down my team tomorrow and ask them to come in on Sunday instead as we were only opening it for your flight anyway,' he said. 'I also need to speak to Greenland air traffic control to update the flight plans,' he went on.

'Do you think it's possible then?' I asked.

'Consider it done,' he replied enthusiastically. It was the eve of our departure and after four years of planning I couldn't believe that a set of skis that could so easily be bought in a shop back home was proving such a challenge. I left the airport manager, relieved that we were back on track.

Alec and our guests were back at the house already. Fin had loaned the team a shotgun at a reasonable charge and Alec had also managed to pick up a .22 rifle as a secondary rifle to the shotgun that we already carried. At this point we considered this our polar bear defence of last resort, guided by my own research on the subject that suggested, contrary to guidance in Britain, that flares and bear bangers weren't that effective. We planned to take a variety of ammunition with us as well, which we would load into the shotgun. These ranged from the weaker shots which carried tiny ball bearings and a lower cordite charge. The intention being that if we had to use these the load would not hurt the bear too much. The strength of shot increased as each cartridge was loaded, the idea being that as the bear got closer the threat became greater. The final cartridge carried a much more powerful load including a single 'slug' of lead that would be used to kill the bear when all else had failed.

We walked outside together to test out the guns and make sure everything worked before the flight the next day. The photographers didn't seem that comfortable using their shotgun, so Alec took the gun in his hands, showed them where the safety catch was, aimed at a small tuft of grass poking through the snow and pulled the trigger. Yanik and Vincent both looked delighted when it went off and then even more excited when they got to try it out themselves.

Back at the hut I was cheered in the knowledge that everything was in place. There was a palpable feeling of nervous excitement amongst the team at the thought of the adventure on the horizon. While Alec started to make dinner for the group, I went back to the computer to confirm with the pilots that everything was in place for the following day. Just as I was about to compile the email another flew into my inbox. 'Good news,' read the note from Kenn Borek, 'your skis have arrived in Resolute!'

Bugger, I thought, and ran out of the house and back to the blue huts where the airport manager lived. I knocked frantically at the door. 'I'm so sorry, mate,' I managed to blurt out in between catching my breath, 'the skis have arrived in Resolute, are we still OK to go tomorrow?'

The man was surprisingly obliging. 'Don't worry about it, I'll need to make a few calls, but I will make sure the airport is up and running for you tomorrow,' he said. I thanked him profusely before returning to the hut. I confirmed with the pilots and the team that we were still on for the next day and then settled in for our final meal in Qaanaaq.

I woke the next morning to a flurry of activity. Yanik and Vincent were already up and gathering their gear for the flight that day. They had brought a huge amount of equipment and I wondered how much they must have paid to get it all here on the plane. There were piles of black Peli cases full of camera gear and a generous amount of camping equipment and supplies. Seeing how much stuff they had brought made me wonder whether we were taking enough equipment ourselves. 'Don't worry,' said Vincent, who must have recognised the look on my face, 'you guys will be moving a lot, but we will be stuck in the same place for a long time so need more stuff to keep us warm.'

I was reassured and, while Alec conducted some last-minute tinkering with the electronics, I cooked a hearty breakfast of porridge. I had got used to adding a few pieces of dried musk-ox meat to the concoction as a salute to some of the stories I had read of explorers like Scott eating something called 'hoosh'. The disappointed looks on our new friends' faces when I offered it to them suggested that I had crossed a culinary line.

At around ten-ish that morning Fin arrived at the house. He had offered to help us get to the airport with our gear and he seemed as excited as we were about the trip. Like an old soldier watching the younger generation heading off on their own adventure, it must have brought up many of his own memories. In the cold of the Arctic and the silence of the town, the alien noise of a plane travelled well in advance of the plane itself. Today was no different and we all pricked up our ears at the sound. 'Right,' I said, 'everyone in the truck, that's us.' I sent Yanik and Vincent off to the airport with their gear first and we headed down in the second load, arriving just in time to watch the Twin Otter touch down on the snow-covered runway of the airport.

The plane came down softly, its black bobbly tyres bouncing briefly on the slick surface as the engines picked up to a roar, slowing it until it stopped at a point just below the control tower. The pilots made their final landing checks as we watched them through the criss-cross wire of the airport fence. We would need to weigh all our gear and go through the usual customs checks before we could load it up. I was expecting to see the bearded face of Carl but a policeman whom I hadn't met before had been sent instead. He pointed us to the weighing room where we put our packed sledges on the large, flat scales. The digital read-out said eighty-five kilograms for mine. Alec's was slightly heavier at eighty-eight kilograms. It was only three kilograms more, but we still joked that he would be carrying most of the gear. Next, we weighed ourselves, mainly for posterity. We knew that we would lose a lot of weight on the trek, but it would be interesting to see just how much.

The next step was customs. The policeman pointed us to a side room which we entered one by one. The conversation followed along the same lines as someone would normally go through when boarding a plane, it was just that the answers were a bit different.

'Do you have any combustibles, weapons or drugs on you?' the man asked.

'Yes', I said, 'we have medical drugs, a shotgun, a rifle, lots of flares, some knives and fuel.' I looked at him, not knowing what was supposed to happen next. In a European airport this would have meant being marched into a small, locked room somewhere to be interrogated. It was a piece of bureaucracy that we both knew was out of place up here. It was obvious why I would have these things, and no-one would be expected to go out in the wilderness without them.

'OK,' he said, a small smile broadening across his face, 'you can go, good luck!' He shook my hand.

Next it was time to load our gear, which we did through the cargo doors that sat in the middle of the plane's fuselage. It was a strange experience having a whole plane completely at our own disposal. At the same time as the pilots helped us load up the plane, they were on the radio to Eureka weather station.

Suddenly, everything changed. 'Ed,' said one of the pilots.

'Yeah,' I replied and stopped what I was doing.

'There's a storm in Eureka, we're not going to be able to get you there today,' he said.

I wasn't sure what that meant for us. 'So what, we go tomorrow?'

'Yes, but we have a delivery tomorrow morning in Canada, so we are going to have to leave you here,' he said apologetically. I hadn't grasped the full gravity of the situation, thinking that it wasn't the end of the world, the difference of one more day didn't matter too much. Then the pilot went on: 'You should know that once we fly back to Canada and come back tomorrow it's going to cost you another twenty thousand dollars,' he said.

My jaw dropped. There was no way we could afford that. I'm not ashamed to admit that after the trials and tribulations of the last four years of planning I hit a wall. It was over. We had come so close and now we had fallen at what felt like the last hurdle. We hadn't even made it to Ellesmere Island and it was a cruel blow. I was close to tears. I walked over to Alec and explained the situation. 'Pal, I'm done, can you take this one? See if you can barter it down or something, otherwise we're finished,' I said.

Alec looked at me with sympathy and understanding in his eyes. He must have seen the pressure I was under to achieve what we had set out to achieve and not to let our sponsors or our families down. It had taken a lot to get this far. 'Alright, pal, I've got this, you finish packing the gear,' he said and then headed over to the pilots.

Fin was still at the airport watching us packing up. 'You're not taking an ice chisel?' he asked.

It broke me out of my thoughts of doom. 'What do you mean?'

'You can't walk all that way across the ice without a chisel, what happens if you come across bad ice?' he said. 'Come on, jump in the truck and I'll lend you mine.'

I raced back to Fin's house, leaving Alec to try and salvage what still felt like an impossible situation.

An hour later Fin and I returned, the long metal pole of the chisel clasped in one hand. Alec was up in the control tower with the pilots. I climbed the narrow concrete stairs until I reached the small open room at the top. He was in the middle of the two pilots and tower controller and they had gathered around a map. Alec looked at me with a glint in his eye. I could tell they had reached some sort of agreement and my spirits lifted. 'Are we back on then?' I asked.

'We're back,' he said. Alec joined me and we walked down the stairs while he explained the situation. I was mentally exhausted and could only listen in hope. 'They're going to take us back to Resolute Bay with them today,' he said, 'then when the weather clears in Eureka they will fly us out.'

'How much is that going to cost?' It seemed like this would be two trips now and not one.

'Nothing, the miles work out about the same and fuel prices have dropped since they quoted us last year so we should be square,' he said. Alec had really stepped up to the challenge and we were back in the game.

We said our goodbyes to Fin as the plane's engine roared to life. The next time I would say goodbye to him was on the way down from Qaanaaq to Kangerlussuaq for our flight home. He was sitting there at the back of the plane, hunched over in pain, wrapped in an old brown leather jacket. Those around him greeted him with affection. While he carried a smile, his eyes betrayed the fear of the unknown. He died soon afterwards from the cancer that had been growing inside him untreated for months. He was a great man and he had been a great friend.

However, Alec and I knew none of that at this point. We hopped on the plane and braced ourselves for take-off. I looked back as the plane climbed and then circled back over Qaanaaq. I could still see the small figure of Fin as he stood by his bright white truck, waving us off on our journey. The plane flew directly west, across the scattered ice of Smith Sound that Haig-Thomas had crossed back in 1938 and over the low, snowy hills of Ellesmere Island. The pilots took the plane right down to where the wheels almost touched the ground. We skimmed along from one summit to the next and then down into the valleys and back up again. The flight to Resolute only took a couple of hours but the views of Ellesmere Island gave us our first sense of what we had in store. I was relieved that the landscape looked similar to the one we had just come from, and I could see much of the sea ice was still intact.

Resolute Bay Airport was very different to the one we had just left. Large hangars and planes dotted the airport and the terminal.

Although the terminal was small it was littered with shops. In one corner by the baggage conveyor belts there stood a large, stuffed polar bear frozen in a posture of attack. It seemed like an unlikely resting place for such a magnificent animal. We were driven to a large barrack-like building that evening by one of the pilots in a big American-style truck. A small storm had hit the town and the streets were empty of life. The light from the street lamps penetrated through the ice particles that blew along the ice roads, momentarily illuminating them before they drifted out into the dark. The rooms were sparse, but they were comfortable and felt luxurious compared to our accommodation in Greenland. We were the only guests at the hotel, and we sat together and enjoyed a basic dinner of pasta. That night was the first time we had slept in a bed for a long time. We could have been restless in trepidation of what lay ahead but the false start of that day had taken a lot of that apprehension away. I've always found my own thoughts about a situation much scarier than the situation itself when it is actually happening.

We woke up to another light breakfast and had time to run to a local store just down the road. In the shop I was struck by the range of food on offer as well as its freshness. In Qaanaaq, the fresh food comes up on the ship which lands twice a year during the summer when the town is free from ice. That is when the shelves are stocked with fresh fruit and vegetables. At all other times of the year the town relies on frozen food and canned goods. Anything fresh would need to be flown up and the cost was prohibitive. For a community that had traditionally relied on what they could hunt, modern developments had forced them into a modern diet which brought along all the health ailments of the modern world like heart attacks and diabetes. In the Canadian north things were different. A total lack of fresh produce in my own diet for the last few months meant that I was drawn to the bright oranges and apples that filled the shelves. Unlike in Greenland, even though Resolute also relied on flights to bring fresh food up during the winter, they were subsidised. This meant that fresh produce still came up north during the winter so that people still had access to fruit and vegetables which, as we know, are critical to a healthy diet.

The pilots were waiting for us back at the hotel. They had been given the all-clear. Eureka was blue skies and no wind. We headed back to the airport once again. This time, though, it was for real.

CHAPTER 16

EUREKA! – ELLESMERE ISLAND

We flew through clear skies; the storms of the previous days had gone. Yanik, Vincent and Alec all looked excited as they peered through the small window of the Kenn Borek Air Twin Otter plane. Condensation had turned to ice, making the windows even smaller. Our kit was stacked up in front of us in the middle of the fuselage between the pilots and our own seats at the back. It was held in place by thick yellow straps, its volume amplified by the narrow body of the plane, and I wondered how we would be able to carry all of it once we landed. The plane flew across the frozen sea, dotted with areas of dark blue where the ice had broken apart. As we got closer to Ellesmere Island, I could make out details of the coastline and of the landscape. The island was scattered with snow-covered peaks and long glaciers which dangled like tendrils off its southern coast. It was on his journey across Ellesmere Island that once again Haig-Thomas commented that he was sure that the glaciers, just as he had witnessed in Thule, were retreating. It is an observation that has been confirmed more recently. With remote observations of Alexandra Fjord on the east coast of Ellesmere Island, researchers showed that the annual rate of melting doubled between 1959 and 2001 due to warming temperatures. A broader study of 1,700 glaciers in the north of Ellesmere Island between 1999 and 2015 showed that hundreds were shrinking and many were at risk of disappearing completely. As well as contributing to rising sea levels, the melting ice also poses a risk to the area's ecosystem. Many of the freshwater lakes, formed

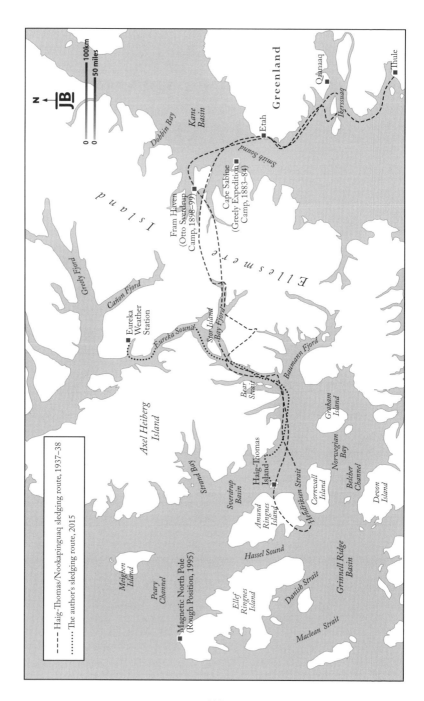

Greenland

Thule

Qaanaaq

Ikerssuaq

Etah

Smith Sound

Cape Sabine
(Greely Expedition
Camp, 1883–84)

Kane
Basin

Dobbin Bay

Fram Haven
(Otto Sverdrup
Camp, 1898–99)

Ellesmere Island

Greely Fjord

Cañon Fjord

Eureka
Weather
Station

Eureka Sound

Stor Island

Bay Fjord

Baumann Fjord

Bear
Strait

Axel Heiberg
Island

Strand Bay

Sverdrup
Basin

Haig-Thomas
Island

Graham
Island

Norwegian
Bay

Belcher
Channel

Devon
Island

Hendriksen Strait

Cornwall
Island

Amund
Ringnes
Island

Hassel Sound

Grinnell Ridge
Basin

Danish Strait

Meighen
Island

Peary
Channel

Magnetic North Pole
(Rough Position, 1995)

Ellef
Ringnes
Island

Maclean Strait

N

JB

0 ___ 100km
0 ___ 50 miles

- - - Haig-Thomas/Nookapinguaq sledging route, 1937–38
········· The author's sledging route, 2015

by the water flow from glaciers and trapped by floating ice shelves, have completely disappeared, taking with them life that has been developing for thousands of years. In the summer of 1985, a glacial lake called Dig Tsho that sat above the Khumbu valley in the Mount Everest region of Nepal burst. Water tore down the valley wrecking several villages and killing three people. In the same valley, a much larger threat containing around 73.5 billion litres of water is held in a massive glacial lake called Imja Tsho. Across Nepal and many other parts of the world these glacial lakes stand as ticking time bombs for the people below them.

In 2020, the last fully intact Canadian ice shelf on Ellesmere Island collapsed into the ocean taking forty-three per cent of its ancient frozen mass with it. Nunavut is home to twenty per cent of the world's fresh water which is held in the form of ice sheets and glaciers. This makes it the third-largest contributor to sea level rises behind Antarctica and Greenland. In human terms, there are almost a quarter of a billion people around the world who live within two metres of existing sea levels. It is predicted that with a further one-metre increase in sea levels, this number will rise close to half a billion by 2100. Melting ice sheets and glaciers have accounted for a twenty-one per cent rise in global sea levels since the turn of the millennium. These are expected to contribute to a twenty-centimetre rise in sea levels, putting millions of people at risk of annual coastal flooding by the end of the century. Europe has already seen an influx of refugees from war in the last few decades and many believe that the effects of climate change due to flooding and drought will dwarf these numbers.

Robert Peary had journeyed from Greenland up the east coast of Ellesmere Island to its most northern point in 1908 in their ship the *Roosevelt*. Ellesmere was the jumping-off point for Peary and his mixed team of Inuit and American explorers in their journey to the North Pole that he believed they had reached in April 1909. It was a claim disputed at the time and is still debated now. Amongst his detractors was an American explorer, Frederick Cook, who followed a route along the west coast of Axel Heiberg Island proposed by Sverdrup. Cook knew Peary, having served as a doctor on Peary's 1891–92 Arctic expedition where he set Peary's broken leg. Cook argued that he had reached the Pole a year before Peary with two Inuit hunters, Etukishook and Ahwelah. The ice had begun to break up on his return from the Pole and he and his team were left stranded on the east coast of Ellesmere Island for almost a year before they could make it across Smith Sound to Upernavik in Greenland and find a passage home. In Greenland, Cook met Harry Whitney, an American sportsman who he asked to take back his navigational equipment and notes. It was Peary's ship, the *Roosevelt*, that arrived first but Peary refused to take anything of Cook's back with him. Whitney buried the notes under a large rock and, although Whitney searched for these in 1910, they have never been recovered. Without his notes, Cook's claim was pulled into disrepute by Peary and his supporters. Much of it centred around a claim that Cook had made of summiting Mount McKinley in Alaska prior to his attempt at the Pole. Without the notes and with Cook's claim to have summitted Mount McKinley called into doubt, Peary was announced as the winner for the race to the North Pole. Decades later the British explorer Sir Wally Herbert, on examining Peary's logs, suggested that he had not reached it but instead came within thirty kilometres of the Pole. Herbert then claimed to be the first man to reach the Pole by dog sledge in his stead in 1969. An examination by the *National Geographic* in 1988 led to the same conclusion. Peary's claim on the Pole was something that Haig-Thomas had written of as well. Haig-Thomas met a man named Ootah who had travelled with Peary to the Pole.

'I have heard people say they didn't believe Peary reached the Pole. I tell you Davey, I was there. We must have been close to the Pole, because when Cap'n Bob went back he said we were getting close, and from there we travelled a long way. Peary twice looked at the sun. The first time he said we were near the Pole. The second time he said we had passed it. We had food for many days on the sledge. If we had wished to go on farther we could have. I can't believe that Peary, who had tried so hard to reach the Pole, would turn back without cause when he was so close.'

While there is still controversy around who made it to the Pole first, Ootah's account would suggest that Peary at least believed he reached the Pole even if later reviewers thought otherwise.

It was an American pilot, Lieutenant Colonel Joseph Fletcher, who was arguably the first to step foot at the Pole when he landed his C-47A Skytrain aircraft on the ice in May 1952. However, even this record has been disputed more recently by Russia, which claims they landed three Lisunov Li-2 transports at the North Pole four years earlier in 1948. This expedition – led by Aleksandr Kuznetsov, a Soviet explorer, along with a team of scientists – also recorded the first soundings that indicated the existence of an underwater mountain ridge beneath the ice at the North Pole.

Named the Lomonosov Ridge, this piece of continental crust in the Arctic Ocean spans 1,700 kilometres and covers the seabed between the New Siberian Islands to Ellesmere Island in the Arctic

Archipelago: an invisible, straight line of submerged mountain ranges that have been in place under the polar sea for 8 million years. The highest peak towers 3.4 kilometres above the seabed. Under the UN Convention on the Law of Sea, mountain ranges like the Lomonosov Ridge enable a country to extend their rights to activities such as fishing and extracting natural resources beyond their existing claims over the sea floor close to their own shores. It was on this basis that Russia submitted a claim in 2001 that stated that this ridge is an extension of their own shores – a claim that spans a 101,582-kilometre area around the North Pole. Denmark and Canada followed soon afterwards. As our plane banked across the settlement at Grise Fjord I wondered how much of a voice the indigenous communities that still inhabited the Archipelago had in these geopolitical negotiations.

The plane lurched as the pilots started their descent into Eureka. My hand reached forward to the chair in front, and I steadied myself against the sudden drop. The feeling of trepidation amongst the team for what lay ahead was amplified within the narrow, cylindrical container of the aircraft's fuselage. Suddenly, one of the pilots called out, 'Musk oxen to the left!' Looking down, I could make out the long, shaggy coats and thickly set bodies of these prehistoric-looking creatures. The pilot called out again. 'And there on our right,' he shouted as a group of caribou, startled by the plane's engines, started to run. Musk oxen, caribou and even Arctic hares were laid out before us. The pilots veered around again in a tight arc, and we circled down, getting lower and lower with each pass until we could see all the details of the animals below us. It was an extremely exciting start to our adventure.

The small, factory-like structure of Eureka weather station now came into view and the pilots lined the plane up for the runway before touching down on to the hard gravel surface below. We opened the metal door of the plane as the noise of the engines faded. The hit of the cold air as I climbed out shocked me after the comparative warmth of the plane.

We were on a low, snowy plateau just above the ice and surrounded by hills. The runway was barren with just a few barrels of oil grouped tightly in one corner. A small hut sat next to them and there was a sign that read: 'Welcome to Eureka'. We were in the surreal middle ground: steps away was complete wilderness with all the dangers that came with it, but right now we were in a bubble of safety.

A large American-style pick-up truck pulled up as we were unloading the kit and a man jumped out, wrapped tightly in bulky winter clothing. He walked over and greeted us with a muffle as he spoke through a thick neck warmer that was pulled up around his mouth. Yanik and Vincent had already started to unload their kit from the plane and on to the back of the truck when I joined them.

Alec had walked over to the pilots and was standing by the cargo bay of the plane deep in conversation. He was showing them the map and talking them through our route. I saw one of the pilots laugh with a slight glimmer of worry. 'Is that the map you're taking?' he said.

'It's the only one we could find,' Alec replied.

'Here, take mine, it's much more detailed and you'll find your way a lot more easily with this one,' the pilot said.

Alec thanked him and walked over to me. It was a lot better than the one we had brought along. We had looked back in London, but we hadn't been able to find one with anything near the accuracy that I could see on the paper that was now in Alec's hands. We jumped in the truck and the pilots climbed into their plane. They must have thought we were mad.

The man driving us was one of the scientists at the station. He explained that Eureka was a focal point for the scientific community, particularly academics undertaking research into climate change. During the winter there was only a small team of people keeping everything going but in the summer the team could grow to twenty or thirty people. The nearest settlement was Grise Fjord, almost 400 kilometres to the south. Like Qaanaaq there were no trees here; you would have to travel over 1,000 kilometres beyond Grise Fjord in the south to find one. The landscape was sparse, windswept and silent. We drove a short way along the track from the runway to the large blue hangar of the weather station. The truck parked up and we dragged our pulks into a concrete cargo bay where we started to assemble our kit, sheltered from the cold and daunting weather outside.

It was an odd feeling. I'm not sure what I was expecting but I hadn't thought we would see anyone when we got to Eureka, let alone be picked up by a truck and be pulling our kit together inside the relative warmth of the base. We were making final changes to the kit in our sledges when the base manager appeared. He was short and chunky with a kind but serious face. He called us over from the raised concrete steps that he stood on. 'Why don't you come in for a while before you go, and I'll show you around?' he said. Vincent and Yanik were busy working their way through a mountain of camera and film equipment while there was still good light. We looked quizzically at each other, bemused by our unexpected surroundings, and then decided to just embrace it.

The same great power politics that had been behind the creation of Thule Airbase in Greenland were also the reason why a weather station existed in Eureka. It had been established by the Americans to provide accurate weather forecasts for their long-range nuclear bombers flying across the Arctic as a deterrent against Russia during the Cold War. The station was located in the mid part of Ellesmere Island at 80°N. It experiences the lowest average annual temperature of any weather station in the Canadian Arctic, captured at a frosty -18°C. The lowest temperature ever recorded dropped to a heart-stopping -67.5°C. Eureka was established on the morning of 7th April 1947, when a six-man crew flew in from Thule Airbase, arriving with enough supplies to build a temporary post. By 19:00 the same day Eureka weather station was established. Four months later, when the ice was at its lowest ebb, an icebreaker arrived with more permanent buildings and a year's worth of supplies. Eureka has continued to provide atmospheric readings ever since. The station has survived over seventy years in the wilderness. In 1972, the Americans withdrew, leaving it under the sole responsibility of Canada. The latest upgrade happened in 2005 when the recreation rooms, state-of-the-art kitchen and additional workspaces were created. Due to its northerly situation, it is often used as the final staging point for many North Pole expeditions.

For us it was a haven from the environment around it. Hundreds of kilometres from anywhere, it had all the luxuries of the modern world and was a giant leap forward from the house we had been staying at in Qaanaaq. The halls were long and glittering in their cleanliness. There was a network of accommodation and laboratories for scientists to stay in and at the end of one of the walkways was a large room. 'I think this is probably the most northerly bar in the world,' the base manager said as we walked into the room. Its walls were lined in pine and the room full of large, comfortable brown leather chairs. As well as a bar there was a pool table, air hockey, and the white furry skin of a huge dead polar bear pinned to one wall.

'Where did that come from?' Alec asked.

'We shot it,' the base manager said. 'It had started to visit the base and had become too much of a threat to the people here.' It was bigger than the skins we had seen in Qaanaaq, and I wondered what it would be like seeing one in real life. I still thought that we would be unlikely to see any bears at all.

'It must be great being up here and getting to explore the island,' I said.

The base manager looked at me quizzically. 'Oh no,' he said, 'it's too dangerous to go outside, especially during the winter months. We rarely let anyone out.' The investment in the lazy boy chairs, widescreen TVs and Netflix subscription made more sense now.

My last night out with Alec had been at Daffi's and the temptation to not go back out into the cold and stay the night and have a drink here was overwhelming. I had to brush it off. Starting our adventure with a hangover would have been suicide.

The base manager read my mind. 'Do you two fancy a bite to eat before you head off?' he asked.

'Yes!' we said in unison, and he led us away from the siren call of the bar to the canteen. We walked down the long hallway and through the double doors at the end. The canteen was like something from another world. Vending machines stacked with chocolate and fizzy drinks rested against the far wall. A chef in a white tunic stood at a chrome mobile food counter in the corner. He had prepared a feast: there was a choice of different pizzas, chicken wings and chips and to the side there were large bowls stacked full of fresh salad and fruit. We couldn't believe our eyes. After months in Qaanaaq with only frozen food and no fresh fruit, we were now on a small rocky outcrop at the far end of the world and it felt like we had landed in the lap of luxury.

'How is this even possible?' I asked our host as we piled our plates up high.

'There isn't much to look forward to up here a lot of the time and it certainly helps with morale,' he said, 'but the reality is it costs so much to fly equipment up here that the cost of food pales in comparison. When I was in the Antarctic, we even had lobster tails and steak.'

Alec and I tore into our meal like it was our last. What a brilliant last meal it would have been, its taste heightened by months of the defrosted blandness that we had become used to. I looked up temporarily. 'Do you ever have people come here on expeditions and don't leave?' I asked.

'You wouldn't be the first,' he laughed.

I knew we had to get out of there, it would have been all too easy to stay in the temporary warmth and comfort that our new surroundings provided. Even going back to Qaanaaq at that point was starting to feel like a hardship. I nodded to Alec as I could see he was going through the same emotions as I was. 'Time to leave I reckon, pal,' I said. We finished our plates, thanked our host for his kindness and walked to the station's cargo bay to grab our sledges and get going. It was already late in the day, so we wouldn't go far, only to the sea ice that evening to set up camp.

It was important to get away from the siren call of the station that was threatening to steal away the little courage that we had managed to pluck up to get this far. Yanik and Vincent were still working through their equipment, so we grabbed the ropes that were attached to the front of ours and started to walk out in to the cold. 'Good luck, guys, we're making camp down there if you want to join us when you're finished,' I shouted. Although I had managed to pull myself away from the station, I was stepping out into an unfamiliar environment. The responsibility for our survival was on my shoulders. Moving out of the base felt like closing the door on our last means of escape. It was like someone was saying, 'Are you sure you want to do this – you can still pull out, you know?' Being near Yanik and Vincent for the first night at least would be a small but important comfort. I would know that another team would be close to us while we found our feet.

The sea ice was only a few hundred metres away from the station and it was down a slight gradient which made it easy-going. With the station so close I felt relatively carefree. We plodded down to the shore in our large Baffin boots, the harnesses of the sledge hung over one shoulder and the other arm swinging loose. More like a summer stroll than a polar expedition. I spotted a small piece of sastrugi which I pointed out to Alec, and we moved over to the spot with our gear. We pulled out the tent and set it up on a flatter part of the ice where the wind had blown it clear of snow. Just as Mikael had taught us. We clumsily threaded the aluminium tent poles through the tent's fabric, my mittens making a fiddly job more difficult. Then we secured the corners of the tent with the ice screws, shattering the brittle surface of the ice first as we had been shown before twisting the screws more securely into the harder ice below. I took out the blue aluminium shovel which I had also borrowed and began packing chunks of snow around the skirt of the tent and piled up more snow at the windward side to make a wall which would protect us if there was a storm that night. We found later that ice screws alone were enough to keep the tent securely in place even during a storm and the snow wall was soon dropped.

Alec then went to set up the bear tripwire. It had been easy in Qaanaaq but out here the cold made everything a struggle. His numb fingers stumbled over the delicate work involved in threading the small pins into the triggers that would set off the blank cartridges when the string was crossed. While Alec finished setting up the tripwire, I carried our sleeping bags and the rest of our gear that we would need that night into the tent. I was taking the final pieces of equipment out of the pulk when I noticed something out of the corner of my eye. Looking up I saw what I thought was a dog only a few metres in front of me. I looked back down at the pulk and carried on what I was doing. Then I wondered, what was a dog doing here? We weren't in Qaanaaq any more and there were no Inuit settlements nearby. I quickly looked back up, my heart beginning to race. The dog was still standing in the same position as I had seen it when I first looked up. It was large and almost as white as the Arctic landscape that surrounded it. It stood only a few metres away from us and it was clear that it wasn't a dog at all but a wolf.

'Alec, grab the gun,' I whispered, not wanting to startle the animal or take my eyes off it.

Alec stopped what he was doing and stood up cautiously. 'What is it?' he said.

'A wolf,' I replied in a slightly more urgent tone.

Canis lupus arctos – unlike their American counterparts, the grey wolves that frequent the plains of Montana or Idaho – had never borne the brunt of human expansion and the trapping, shooting and poisoning that often followed. Having experienced little interaction with humans, the wolf that had its eyes fixed on me was fearless. It was confident in its experience of taking down animals as large as musk ox, which can stand one and a half metres at the shoulder and weigh up to 350 kilograms. It seemed to understand that the small figures of Alec and myself would stand little chance against the pack.

Wolves are opportunistic predators, hunting as a group and stealing their chance to move on an animal and take it down, ideally quickly and by the throat. The lemmings and hares that scutter across the snow crust make easier prey. With a larger or less submissive animal they may start at its legs, catching them with a bite pressure nearly four times stronger than a pit bull's until the animal collapses and the wolf moves to devour the body before the animal is dead. Haig-Thomas wrote of wolves splitting open the underbelly of musk ox with their teeth as they huddled around their young in defensive circles. I knew little about the wolf at that time. They were hunted to extinction in the UK long ago. King Edward I ordered the total extermination of them during his three-decade-long reign that ran into the early 14th century. By the 15th century they were all but extinct. All that was left were rumours and hearsay. Wolves survived in Scotland a little longer, the last killed by Sir Ewan Cameron in 1680 in Perthshire.

I did not feel threatened by the wolf. It was as if an unseen thread of knowing connected us. I wasn't sure whether it saw us as prey or just something of interest. Its actions felt curious, not aggressive – but caution made me act.

I picked up the shovel and gripped it hard between my hands. Alec rushed over to the sledge and picked up the shotgun. 'Shit,' he said, 'the safety lock is still on.' The lock was a small yellow device that was threaded through the trigger guard and prevented it being pulled back far enough to fire the gun. We had attached the mechanism as a requirement for transporting the weapon before we left the airport in Qaanaaq. With the weather station still so close we had both felt safer than we were and we hadn't been paying the attention we should have. As a result, we had forgotten to remove it and, worse still, the key was buried somewhere deep in the pulks. With the lock on and no key in sight we were now completely defenceless.

The wolf looked at me and then it looked back to where it had come from. I followed its gaze and spotted another wolf, and then another. I could now see that we were surrounded by more than a dozen wolves that had managed to creep up on us while we had our heads down. It was a stand-off. The lead wolf watched us, perhaps assessing whether we were a threat before letting the rest of the pack past us. They didn't seem aggressive though, more inquisitive, and they made no move to come closer, but began to trot past one by one in a long spaced-out line, keeping their distance from the camp and following in the tracks of the wolf before them.

Once it was clear that we weren't in danger I asked Alec to try and call Vincent and Yanik who were still putting their gear together in the cargo bay back up the hill. They had come up to photograph these wolves which hadn't been seen in the area for three years and now here they were only metres away from us. I got my own camera out in the meantime and tried to do these animals justice. The sun was brushing the horizon and creating a bronze glow which ebbed from across the sea ice, framing the white winter coat of the lead wolf in a halo of light. The presence of these animals was surely a good omen for their own trip.

The wolf was there and then without a sound it was gone. The rest of the pack moved expertly and gracefully past us like a well-trained unit of professional hunters. One by one they headed away from the camp and off towards the low mountains in the distance. We had both been standing there watching them and as the last one moved out of sight I turned to Alec. 'That was insane,' I said with a chuckle of amazement.

'I know, I can't believe we saw them,' he replied. 'Vincent is going to be pissed.' We were in awe, but we had been lucky. We had let our guards down by going out on to the ice with a locked gun and no key. The wolves had been inquisitive but not aggressive, but we couldn't have known that. If it had been a polar bear, it could have been a very different story. It was a wake-up call and I understood right then that I would need to up my game and keep a better eye on what was happening around us.

We were both now shivering. The temperature in Ellesmere felt colder than Qaanaaq and the mercury in the temperature gauge read a chilling -38°C. We had been standing around not moving and so climbed into the tent. I had already laid out the sleeping bags, which rested on the caribou skin mat that would provide an extra layer of insulation against the cold below it. Alec got the stove out. It had been his favoured piece of equipment, made by a Japanese manufacturer who had given them to us for the expedition. Most people take an MSR. I had brought one as backup just in case, but I was keen to support Alec and happy for us to use it as the main stove. He tried to light it without success. It reminded me of the night we spent in Qeqertarsuaq when the stove had failed, and we had spent a freezing night in the old school hut. I grabbed the bag containing the MSR from the pulk and took it out. I had quickly gone from cold to freezing and I was keen to get warm. It was the only time the Soto stove did play up. We used it every night for the rest of the trip where it worked perfectly. It had a well-thought-out design that made it easier to regulate its flame compared to the MSR, which expelled a white-hot jet of heat that sounded like a rocket.

Inside the tent we had put on our very thick, insulated down jackets which were a horrible purple colour and we both sat around the lit stove, grateful for its heat. I asked Alec to pass me a pan which I had filled up earlier and was about to start melting down some snow to fill up our water bottles for the following day. He was looking at the map at the time and, deep in thought, he reached across the stove. The synthetic fabric of his jacket caught light instantly. Suddenly, his whole left arm went up in flames. He looked at me wide-eyed and started to pat it out with his gloves. I reached across and did the same while billows of chemical-like smoke filled the small confines of the tent. The flames went as quickly as they came, leaving only the stench of burning plastic. Examining the damage, I could see the whole left sleeve of his jacket was blackened. White feathers that formed the thickly insulated down poured out through a large hole that was all that was left of the garish outer fabric.

We had got off lightly. The only real damage was to Alec's jacket and ego. It was another reminder of how quickly things could go wrong out here. Had we panicked, the fire could have easily spread to the tent which was just as flammable. At that point we were still close enough to the station that we could have easily walked back there to safety. As soon as we broke camp, however, we would be on our own. I had brought a bivvy as a backup which would hopefully stop us freezing to death, but it would likely mean the end of the expedition. We climbed into our sleeping bags, our moods much more muted and serious after the initial excitement that we had felt from seeing the wolves. It was a mood that would set the tone for the first part of our journey as we commenced our education in the harsh realities of polar travel.

CHAPTER 17

COLD – EUREKA SOUND

I woke up cold. The freezing air had turned our sleeping breath into ice that had formed as a thin layer of frosty white across the inner sheets of the tent. I sat up and felt my head brush the damp nylon fabric of the tent. Frozen particles dislodged from its lining and rained down on me. It was like splashing cold water on my face. Alec, who was still lying down, got most of this in his eyes which he rubbed clear with the back of a silk inner glove. 'Watch out, mate,' he said.

'Morning, pal,' I replied, 'how did you sleep?'

'It was pretty cold, wasn't it?' Alec said.

'I'll get the stove on and get this place warmed up whilst we have some breakfast,' I said in agreement. I grabbed hold of the cooker which lay between us, pumped the handle of the gas bottle to pressurise it and then lit the gas with a storm match. It came to life easily, yellow flames at first which gradually relaxed into a low blue murmur once the cooker had warmed up.

The temperature inside the tent rose quickly to a toasty 25°C. I was able to move freely now that the cold that had anchored me to the thin protection of the sleeping bag had been temporarily calmed. Ice lay on the tent's fabric and on the outer layers of our sleeping bags. As the tent warmed it began to melt. Water drops landed on our bodies and on our gear, slowly soaking its way through to the down below. Lighting the cooker from within the warmth of our sleeping bags each morning soon became the routine. Each of us took it in turns to be the first one up. Being the first out of the bag was always unpleasant. It was far nicer stripping off the heavy down of the bags once the tent had warmed up. I boiled some water and filled two of the rehydrated bags up until their contents were steaming. Where explorers of old had survived on pemmican and hooch, modern advancements had given us a substantially nicer, more nutritious and broader choice of meals. I think even the Inuit would have agreed. That morning it was apple porridge, and we hugged the food bags to our chests like hot water bottles and waited for the contents to reach an edible state.

It was still very early, maybe four o'clock in the morning, but we were too close to the weather station. I was keen to get going. I worried that faced with an almost overwhelmingly long journey ahead of us it would be too tempting to run back to the warmth and safety of the station. 'I think we should get going as soon as we can,' I told Alec. 'I don't want to hang about.' Alec and I finished our meals, filled our water bottles and then started to pack up our gear. To minimise the amount of snow that could be brought into the tent I left Alec to sort everything inside and went outside to gather up the tripwire.

When Alec was done, he handed me our bags and sleeping mats through the tent's opening and I stacked these neatly into our pulks before covering them with the red waterproof shells that were attached to the rim of the sledge. Alec made a final sweep of the tent and then joined me outside where we folded the tent in half and laid it on top of one of the sledges. It was a routine that we would get very used to over the coming weeks. Although I hadn't heard them make camp, I could see Yanik and Vincent's green tent only a few metres away from ours. I could tell from the slow, muffled breathing emanating from within the paper-like structure that they were still asleep. After the friendship we had built up over the last few days I felt rude not waiting for them to get up, but standing about wasn't an option either. The icy breath of the early polar morning had already begun to seep through my clothes. I was sure they would much prefer their sleep. I put on my skis and my harness which was attached to my sled and started to pull. 'Goodbye and good luck!' I whispered as a compromise instead of a full farewell. Then I leant forward, took up the slack in the harness lines and made my first steps of the journey.

For the first few kilometres our skis slid effortlessly across the windblown sea ice that was as smooth as an ice rink. The bulk of our pulks glided easily behind us. We moved shoulder to shoulder, experiencing the initial feelings of adventure together as one unit. In front of us the empty plains of ice and snow of the fjord stretched as far as the eye could see. It was a clear day, and the now constant sun shone gently from just below the horizon. The weather station was behind us and, although it was cold, there was little wind and we warmed up quickly as we moved. There was a large hill to the left of us which marked the gateway to Eureka Sound. We stopped for lunch once we had reached it. Within a few short minutes I felt the cold starting to creep through my jacket and into my body. It was a different type of cold than the one I had become used to in Qaanaaq. A deeper and more pervasive cold. It was a warning of things to come. We finished up quickly and got moving again, soon reaching the end of the fjord where we turned south along the sea ice.

In front of us the visibility had decreased, obfuscated by a thin layer of ice crystals that had formed in the air. Then suddenly Alec whispered, 'Look up ahead.' A small grey animal emerged out of the white and trotted up to us. The tiny creature was an Arctic fox. It was beautiful and I felt slightly ashamed peering through the frosted hoods of our jackets that I had had an old lady make out of the same animal's fur. It showed no signs of fear as it approached. It had probably never seen or heard a human before and certainly didn't have the inherent flight response that other animals that cohabitate with humans have developed over the centuries.

The Arctic fox, or *Vulpes lagopus*, is native to the Arctic regions. It is similar in features to the common red foxes that grace Britain's cities and countryside. Like its cousins it is happy scavenging for food although its main prey is the hamster-like lemming. It can smell a polar bear kill from up to forty kilometres away and hear the burrowing hands of a lemming through twelve centimetres of snow. During the summer the fox will turn brown, integrating seamlessly with the rocks and heather around it. In winter it loses its brown fur and grows a glorious white coat that is one hundred and forty per cent thicker than its summer one. It maintains one of the most effective heating systems of all the animals in the Arctic. It will only start to shiver when the temperature drops to -70°C. Unlike other canids, its foot pads are covered in fur. A complex network of blood vessels are so refined that they can simultaneously provide blood flow to their foot pads while restricting it from the centre of the foot. This allows the Arctic fox to stand still on the sea ice and keep its feet above -1°C: the temperature that would cause the tissue in its feet to freeze. It can do this without pain or discomfort. Despite its miniature size, just thirty centimetres tall, it is perfectly adapted to its surroundings.

In 2019, researchers from the Norwegian Institute for Nature Research tracked a one-year-old fox that over the course of four months walked 4,415 kilometres from Svalbard in Norway all the way to Ellesmere Island. The fox had averaged 46.3 kilometres a day, a pace that any Arctic adventurer would struggle to keep up with even on their best days.

The little fox had either smelt or heard our approach. It had come to us to investigate. 'Welcome to the Arctic, chaps!' it seemed to say, before turning and dancing away. It was a lovely moment, to be surrounded by the emptiness of our environment and then witness life, completely undaunted by our presence. It was the last time I would feel like that for a long time. The next few weeks would be a nod to every terrible story I had read that recounted polar travel's less pleasant side.

We were heading for Stor Island which sat fifty kilometres south of our current position on Eureka Sound. The wind started to pick up as we moved and the smooth sledging we had temporarily experienced was replaced with the new reality of long, hard, intense days of pulling. The best surface was where there was a thin layer of snow over the harder ice below it and we could move at speed across it. Second to this was where the wind had blown away all the snow and our skis would grip the ice, preventing any glide but still putting up little resistance. Then we had the ice and snow mix. Windswept ice dotted with pockets of thick islands of snow where our skis and pulks would sink. We would either have to lean forward, digging in our skis for grip to make the sledges move, or else turn around completely to grab the harness lines in our hands and drag the pulks forward through brute force.

The whole of the southern journey down Eureka Sound seemed to be covered in the ice and snow mix. Progress was back-breaking and glacial. The worst surface was still to come and later on we would encounter fields of pressure ice that left us with no option but to drag our gear up walls of ice, sometimes taller than we were, and lower them carefully back down. At these points we would make very slow progress building up layers of sweat that soon tore the heat from our bodies.

We fell into a monotonous, purposeful trudge. We were working much harder now than we had in Qaanaaq. This was due in equal parts to the heavier sledges, which hadn't been fully loaded previously, as well as the poorer sledging conditions. As we worked, we sweated. At first this was not such an issue; as long as we kept going, we could stay warm. As the days wore on the temperatures continued to drop and our situation worsened. In his own accounts Haig-Thomas had wondered what it would be like if humans didn't sweat as he saw this as our key weakness when it came to the cold.

The effect of moisture wasn't instant but instead was a gradual process which caused our clothing and equipment to deteriorate day by day. By the time we reached camp each night our sweat had permeated every layer of our clothing, and rather than evaporating it turned to ice. Inside the tent, once we had lit the stove, the ice on our clothing that hung on strings around the tent thawed and dripped water across our sleeping bags. The vapour from our breath which expired in small clouds froze to our gear. In the morning it all warmed up again when the stove was lit, and the melted water sank even deeper into the thermal fabrics of our clothing.

The ice tied clumps of the goose down in our clothing together leaving large gaps covered in only fabric which the cold poured through. The weather didn't allow us to dry any of our kit and soon the spiralling situation gained momentum. We had very little protection now. Large blocks of ice had formed inside our sleeping bags and in our gloves and boots. At night, my toes suffered the worst. Some nights I would go to sleep, my toes having turned numb. Often, I wasn't sure whether they wouldn't have frostbite by the time I woke up. By the end of the first week, I could put a bottle of recently boiled water by my feet and by the morning it had frozen solid. My sleeping bag was so iced up that my whole body would shiver through the night in great spine-arching spasms. I would pray for the time to come when we could get up and start moving again. I don't think Alec suffered as much from the cold at night as I did. If he did, he never complained.

The mornings were equally unpleasant. Our clothing hardened during the night and getting dressed was like pulling on sheets of frosted armour. It was almost impossible to sink our feet into our large Baffin boots. We would stamp around in them on tiptoes until they warmed up and could flex just enough to be pulled on. The worst points were when we had to deal with anything fiddly. The spring-loaded firing mechanism of the bear tripwire for instance, a key item of equipment, was always a pain to pull together. Often it meant taking off a mitten which revealed the thinner lining of our silk inner gloves so that we could work our hands with greater dexterity. This exposed our hands and more importantly our fingers to the elements. The temperature had now dropped below -40°C and the pain was excruciating. If ever bare skin touched any metal, it would burn our flesh in the same way that making contact with a hot cooker would. Like my sleeping bag, my gloves also moistened and turned to ice. They were more like hard pieces of plastic and only offered protection against the wind that continued to blow in our faces. When we stopped, my hands soon turned numb until we started moving again. I had to accentuate the swing of my arms to force the blood back into my hands which caused me minutes of agonising pain as the feeling returned.

The tips of my fingers turned red at first and swelled with liquid and in the coming days turned black, waxy and numb as they succumbed to frostbite. I was so committed to completing what I had set out to do that I actively made the decision to carry on, knowing that I may lose my fingers to the painless blackness. Jerry, the guide I had spoken to before the journey, had told me that in mid-April there is a sudden jump in temperature on Ellesmere and he often wore just a shirt. I went to bed each night hoping that the following morning would be better but the weather stubbornly held to the clutches of winter. My only consolation was recalling that Haig-Thomas had suffered similarly in 1938. In *Tracks in the Snow* he described envying his Inuit friend Nookap's ability to lie motionless in his sleeping bag while

I would lie still until I couldn't bear the cold and then start turning over, trying to prevent cold air coming in through the mouth of the sleeping bag. Tucking my head into the bag I would breathe warm air over my body but it would fill the bag with moisture making the damp worse.

It was a situation that I could empathise with from experience now. While I was suffering physically from the cold, Alec was suffering mentally. I could tell he was worried and at night when we discussed it, he said he felt overwhelmed by the distance that lay ahead. Our progress at that point had been very hard won and the weather so much colder than we had thought it would be or had experienced from our training trips in Qaanaaq. He was struggling to contemplate how he could continue to take the beating that Eureka Sound was giving us for much longer. The weather seemed only to be getting worse.

I felt the same as he did but, as the expedition leader, I had to pretend that I didn't. I knew that if I voiced my own worries then we could soon talk ourselves into calling for help. We were very much living on the line of survival and the idea of doing that for a month felt insurmountable. I tried to help him come to terms with the distance by breaking it down in his mind into manageable chunks. It was a useful skill that I had learnt from my first of two failed attempts at the HAC's arduous patrol course. I explained this to Alec. 'Four hundred and fifty kilometres is a long way, but if we aim for fifteen to twenty kilometres a day by the end of this week we will be a quarter of the way there,' I said. 'And by the next we will beyond halfway.' It was how I was approaching our predicament and I was sure that if I could convince Alec to think in the same way he would feel better about it. 'In a couple of weeks it should get warmer; just focus on the next few steps,' I said. Alec told me later that this way of breaking down the journey had helped him immensely. Up to that point he had been quiet on the days, trudging behind me and battling with himself. As the days wore on and he grew more confident his mood changed and very soon we were taking it in turns to lead the way.

One of the mental challenges of modern expeditions is that by having the ability to communicate with the outside world there is always the temptation to call for help when things get hard or when you feel out of your depth, which was the case in those first few weeks. Franklin and Scott never had the option to throw in the towel. 'Don't go outside, Oates,' Scott might have said, 'I've just called Kenn Borek Air with my satellite phone, and they said they'll be here within the hour.' The heroic story of Captain Oates taking his own life for the sake of the others in the party would never have gone down in history. At any point Alec and I could have radioed Eureka or the Kenn Borek Air office in Resolute Bay and asked for help and weather permitting they could have been there within a couple of hours.

Around the fourth day I checked in with the base manager at Eureka. Alec and I were desperate for some news that the weather was improving. We thought that if anyone would know the answer to that question it was Eureka weather station. The news wasn't good.

'How are you boys doing?' came the concerned voice of the base manager over the radio.

'We're surviving,' I replied, feigning a confidence that I didn't feel.

'That's good to hear,' he said. 'We were worried about you.'

'Why, what's happened?' I asked.

'The two men you came with were evacuated last night,' he went on. 'Yanik got frostbite and Vincent broke his ankle bringing him back. They managed to make it back to base and were flown out yesterday.'

I heard later that Yanik's big toe was amputated due to the frostbite. He sent us some terrible photos of the injury when we got back to the UK, the large toe on his right foot missing, the skin around it black. Large stiches criss-crossed the closed wound. Alec and I joked that he wouldn't need the flip-flops he had left with us any more. Yanik didn't see the funny side when we told him.

The batteries that powered our gear were low at this point as Alec's jury-rigged solar panels that he had insisted on cobbling together were not working as well as he had hoped. The electrical wires that connected the panels to the rechargeable batteries had become brittle in the cold and kept snapping. Alec took enormous pleasure from tinkering with them each evening, reconnecting broken wires and coaxing his contraption back to life. I couldn't risk a long conversation, so I moved on to the weather forecast. 'Any chance it's going to warm up at all over the next few weeks?' I asked.

'Not for a while yet,' Chris responded.

I thanked him for the update and he wished us good luck and goodbye, his voice still tinged with concern. I turned to Alec and we both looked at each other in shock. Vincent had been up here before the previous year, and he was more experienced than we were in these temperatures. Yanik had grown up surrounded by the Swiss Alps and again had a lot more knowledge of cold weather environments than we did. They had also taken more gear than us as they would only be camping a few kilometres away from the weather station and so should have been comparatively comfortable. It didn't bode well.

With Yanik and Vincent gone we felt very alone. It only added to our existing sense of vulnerability. With the weather not letting up anytime soon, my main worry was being caught out in the open without shelter. Wind speeds can exceed a hundred kilometres per hour and temperatures at that time of year can be as low as -50°C. The wind chill factor was another story, but it wouldn't take much imagination to work out that in these conditions things could rapidly go south. As we skied along, I asked myself – if a storm arrived, could we battle the wind to get the tent up or would we be left to fight the elements without it? It was so cold even when we were in our tent that I knew that we would not survive for long without one.

It was partly because of this fear that we made less progress in those first few weeks than perhaps we could have. I opted to cautiously make camp whenever it looked like the weather was turning. I trekked on with this anxiety in the back of my mind until one day we did get caught out. It was late afternoon on the sixth day and Alec and I had been battling a strong breeze that had been threatening to pick up steam but which hadn't done so yet. We stopped in the lee of a large iceberg to rest and to take a light lunch. 'What do you think, Al, should we press on or call it a day?' I asked. The weather looked like it could go either way and we were both feeling unsure.

'I'm happy to press on if you are,' he replied.

Shortly after we moved off the wind started to pick up and our face masks became thick with ice. The visibility had become very poor, and it was even harder to see now that we had our goggles on, which made it difficult to make out anything at all. We carried on for a few minutes longer as the wind built to a rage. I had made the wrong decision and now we were in real danger. I pointed to a rocky outcrop up ahead which would provide some respite from the onslaught of the freezing wind. 'We can try and make camp there,' I yelled, my voice barely audible over the roar. Alec nodded and crept forward towards the spot; our bodies braced against the biting cold. The wind dropped slightly as we got closer, and we started to benefit from the protection of the rocks nearer to the shore. 'This looks OK,' I said to Alec. We shook off our harnesses and grabbed hold of the tent that was strapped down on top of one of the sleds.

The storm howled about us, and snow stung our eyes. We gripped the tent tightly between us as we unfolded it while the wind tried to tear it from our grasp. To stop it blowing away I kneeled on the middle of the shelter and one by one Alec dug the ice screws into the ground, pinning the four corners of the tent down tightly. Next, we grabbed the tent poles which were already threaded through the loops and pushed them together, creating the tent's dome. We grabbed the contents of the pulks, taking what we needed and lashing down the rest so it wouldn't blow away. I could see there was one piece of equipment missing. Fin's rifle, which he had been so reluctant to lend us at first, was missing. It must have dropped off the sledge at some point over the last couple of hours. It was only a small calibre .22 rifle that I had brought as a nod to Nookap who had fought a polar bear off with one on their expedition. Our main defence was the Mossberg shotgun that Alec carried on his sledge. Regardless, at that point every metre travelled was hard won and there was no way I was going back for it.

Once we had got most of the gear in and the tripwire was hammered in place, we dusted the snow off our clothes and crawled through the tent door. Alec lit the stove and we both took our gloves off and warmed our hands over the flames. It was a huge relief to be sat there having survived our first real test. The sound of the storm raged outside, and the wind battered the sides of the tent all around us, but inside we were now toasty and warm. 'I lost the rifle,' I admitted to Alec.

'Damn, that's not good,' he replied without judgement. It could have been easy for him to lose his temper. Although small, without it we were down to just one gun and if we were separated for any reason, it would leave one of us open to bears.

'We'll just have to make sure we keep close together,' I said.

A short while later Alec looked up from his bag. 'Ed, I've lost the charger for the satellite phone,' he said sheepishly.

'What! So, we can't charge the battery at all now?' I asked.

'No,' he stuttered, 'and there's only a little battery left in the phone.'

He knew as well as I did how important the satellite phone was, particularly if anything happened to us. What Alec hadn't grasped at that point was that without the satellite phone we wouldn't be able to message base to let them know we were OK. It was critical that we did so because it was part of the fail-safe that I had developed with Olga, the expedition's operations manager, in England. We had agreed before we left that if she hadn't heard from us in a forty-eight-hour period she would initiate the search and rescue procedure with the Canadian Coast Guard. We would be evacuated, and the expedition would be a failure, not to mention a large bill for the privilege. I told Alec none of this at the time. There didn't seem to be any point in upsetting him. 'Don't worry,' I said, biting my lip in frustration, 'we can retrace our steps tomorrow and try and find it.' I couldn't be too angry as I had lost the rifle. While Alec slept, I spent the whole night thinking about our options. I decided that the only feasible one was that if we couldn't find the charger then we would have to walk back the way we had come and get a flight back from there. Our backup, the Yellowbrick tracker, at least would show the team that we were still moving and therefore alive. However, this only had about a week's worth of charge left. The battery was supposed to last months, sending out a slow ticker of updates on our location, but unbeknownst to us at the time it was firing updates off in real time which had drained most of the battery in a matter of days.

As is often the case the situation resolved itself the next morning. The storm had cleared and, on checking his sledge, Alec found the charger underneath a bag where it had fallen the previous day. 'I found the charger,' he said almost casually. Despite not sleeping a wink, I wasn't angry; I was just relieved, but he must have seen something in my face. He looked back apologetically. 'Sorry,' he said as we carried on our journey to the bottom of Eureka Sound.

That day was a turning point for us both. We had come far too close to failure having lost and then luckily found critical items of kit. In terms of the tent, we knew that however hard it blew, we would be able to get it up. As long as we had shelter I knew that we would make it through. We were still in survival mode, but it took a lot of the fear out of the days and we started to make greater headway. We also paid a lot more attention to our communications gear as we both now understood what it would mean for the expedition if anything happened to it again.

CHAPTER 18

BEARS – AXEL HEIBERG

Almost every Arctic story has its bear. This one is no different. *Ursus maritimus*, the polar bear, is a magnificent creature, utterly at home in its environment and totally respected by anyone who encounters it. Everything I read and heard about them made me sure that we needed to take them extremely seriously. The largest polar bear ever shot weighed almost 1,000 kilograms and stood almost three and a half metres tall. A big male could weigh 700 kilograms – though 450 kilograms is the average – and stretch over two and a half metres from nose to tail. Capable of running at forty-five kilometres per hour and swimming at ten kilometres per hour (while holding their breath for two minutes), unlike all other bears they are almost exclusively carnivorous. They generally need at least one seal each week to sustain them, and their preferred method of attack is to seize prey by the head. In Qaanaaq we had talked to every Inuit hunter we met, trying to decide how we should plan for our encounter if the time came. Mikael told us that he believed that in Greenland the bears were more wary of people than in other places. From what he had heard of Canada the bears didn't seem to be so scared of people, and he thought we might be more likely to have problems once we started walking across the sea ice.

'Shouting, banging pots and pans and letting off flares, I've heard them all recommended,' I said.

Mikael answered with a wry smile. 'Maybe you'll get lucky, but the best is to shoot at them, as close as you can so that the bear sees the shot kick up some ice. Otherwise, the gun is just another noise.' Mikael, like most other Inuit, seemed to think that if the bear was already that close then there was a good chance we could die.

Haig-Thomas wrote that his friend Nookap told him that 'there are no tricks that the Eskimos can teach the bears. We have learnt everything from them. If we only had the brains of a bear we should never go hungry for a little seal meat.' Racing across the ice on their sledges at breakneck speed, Haig-Thomas described Nookap shouting a hunting chant to encourage his dog team: 'Great fat bears! We are not afraid. You shall eat their meat and blubber. I shall have new bear-skin trousers. Great bears, grr, grr, grr – bears! We are all together and not afraid!'

I hoped I would feel the same way. Unlike Haig-Thomas, we weren't interested in bear meat or hunting them at all. The thought of seeing polar bears was thrilling, but I knew enough to want them to stay at a safe distance. In the end we took a tripwire, a shotgun, flares and a .22 rifle as a final backup.

It was near the beginning of our time on the ice that we saw our first bear. Alec saw something far in the distance, just a flicker of movement among the icebergs, nothing more. Taking out our binoculars we then made out a mother and her two cubs moving towards us along the coastline, seemingly oblivious of our presence. Straight away it was actions on; Al grabbed our primary means of defence, a five-shot 12-gauge Mossberg pump-action shotgun stocked with different types of ammo, from many small pellets with a light load of cordite to the heavier SPGs which were ball-bearing sized and packed a killer punch. These different types of shot provided us with a means of escalation, so that killing or wounding the bear would be the last form of defence. I grabbed one of the pen flares and we both stepped out of our harnesses and skis so as to give us freedom of movement in case things got more serious. This would be our 'actions on' throughout the trek when we sighted a bear that might get close enough to get us worried.

Realising at this point that the mother bear was still several kilometres away, we got our skis and harnesses back on and slowly inched our way along the sea ice. It was our first bear sighting, and we were both understandably cautious. Then, as we got slightly closer, she caught our scent. Her nose was raised, and she stared in our direction, body stiffened and senses focused. With a rapid lunge she suddenly bolted up the side of a hill to safety, the cubs following as fast their short legs would allow. It had been incredible watching her and the cubs through the binoculars, and we considered ourselves lucky to have had the privilege to see one of these awe-inspiring animals out in the wild. We didn't then know it, but they were the first of more than a dozen bears we would see as we walked. Perhaps not surprisingly, many of them were in an area marked on our chart as 'Bear Strait'. The majority of the bears that we came across, on catching our scent, would run for the hills just as the mother and her cubs had done. Occasionally, one would take more interest and start to follow our scent for a while before turning away. At this point in our journey, I was still under the impression that polar bear sightings were rare. Soon enough I would get accustomed to seeing them in the distance, and lulled myself into a state of acceptance, imagining that they would always retreat from two men dragging pulks who clearly looked so out of place as to be disconcerting.

By the middle of April, the temperatures were still hovering around the minus forties. We were making good progress down Eureka Sound, and I was beginning to feel confident in our ability to survive in our new environment. During these first few weeks we had realised very quickly that there is a big difference operating in these temperatures than in the low minus thirties that we had acclimatised to in Greenland. The greatest impact was on our equipment. Anything electronic struggled to function. The only way to keep things working was to somehow store them close to our bodies, finding ways to stash the GPS and the Kindle inside our clothing so that they wouldn't die when we most wanted them. What we didn't realise was that the severe cold would also affect our polar bear defences.

It was first light when I stumbled out of the tent after enduring the howling winds and buffeting force of a blizzard. Packing up camp ready for the day's marching and pulling routine had become a semi-automatic series of well-known moves. In my oversized Baffin boots I clumsily stumbled into our tripwire system. It was supposed to set off a shotgun cartridge if anything touched the wire, but within seconds I realised that there had been no reaction at all, even though I had effectively crushed the wire against the ground with my boot. I bent down and examined the cartridge holder and mechanism. Sure enough, the cartridge percussion camp showed the telltale dent that meant it had fired – but the powder hadn't ignited. I decided it must have been a faulty cartridge and thought no more about it. Instead, I just reloaded the tripwire and gave it a test fire. Again, nothing. Silence.

The tripwire was our first line of defence, and the sure way of knowing if a bear was getting close to the tent in the night. We knew we'd never hear one coming otherwise. One manual for the Arctic warned that the only sound a bear might make was a short, sharp puff of air just before it attacked, and Al and I had both seen plenty of films of bears sneaking up on sleeping seals, even sliding along slowly on their bellies so as not to let a paw crunch the ice. Just before leaving Qaanaaq, we had heard about Jakub Moravec, a Czech tourist on Svalbard, who was dragged from his tent by a polar bear which only released him after another camper shot it three times. Even more recently I had read an interview with an American hiker, Matt Dyer, who had been snatched from his tent by a polar bear in Canada. Again, the bear had methodically disentangled him from the folds of a collapsed nylon tent and seized him around the head and neck. Listening to the snapping and crunching sounds of his own fracturing skull Dyer described the bear running, dragging him at speed towards the water where he imagined it would drown him like a seal. And all the while he was conscious of his face 'being covered in a clear, gelatinous, fishy-smelling goop – bear saliva'. More seriously he suffered paralysed vocal cords and broken vertebra as well as the skull fractures and puncture wounds to his hand and arm. That animal, which only let Dyer go when the expedition leader shot at it repeatedly with a flare gun, had ignored a tripwire system but it had at least alerted the camp that the bear was on the prowl.

It was contemporary accounts like these that made the discovery of our own equipment failure such bad news. The danger the bears posed to us was very real. And we were now over a hundred kilometres away from the nearest human being, or any chance of someone coming to our aid. Alerting Al to the problem, I decided that we had better test our last-ditch system: the shotgun.

We walked a short distance from camp to test the gun. My brooding anxiety was growing. One by one I watched Al put five cartridges into the gun and pull the trigger. And every time we heard the dull single click of the firing pin hitting the cartridge without setting it off. The cold had performed its silent work.

Logically, we decided that as the cartridges had failed in both the gun and the tripwire system, then they must be the weak link. Then I remembered a conversation with an old friend of mine who was a gunsmith. I had asked him advice about weapons in the very early planning stages of the expedition. He told me the story of Russian soldiers during World War II who had encountered similar issues with their ammunition during the bitterly cold winters in which they fought. They solved the problem by storing bullets next to their skin to keep them warm. We decided to do the same. Packing up camp we continued on down Eureka Sound, feeling rather more vulnerable than we had done before.

A few more days went by as we moved south under clear skies and down Eureka Sound. We finally turned the corner of Axel Heiberg Island to begin heading west along its southern coast. The forbidding landmass of Stor Island rose out of the sea ice to the left of us. It was a fantastic change of scenery to the narrow channel of the Sound which we had become used to over the last week, and gave us the impression of an endless Arctic wilderness that stretched out in front of us. Although it was still painfully cold, we were making good progress, and seemed to have left the strong winds and blizzards behind us for now. We were now entering territory comparable to that described in *Tracks in the Snow* and moving past familiar names on the map such as Stor Island brought home how close our experiences were to those that we had read about in the years leading up to the expedition. We could see the area where Haig-Thomas and Nookapinguaq had crossed Ellesmere Island and could almost imagine them sledging past us with their dogs on the way out to Haig-Thomas Island eighty years earlier.

It was at a similar point in his own journey that Haig-Thomas told his most dramatic account of a bear encounter. He and Nookap had been chasing a young bear for meat, as this was their primary form of food for the trip. He looked back to discover that they were also being chased by the bear's mother who, being slightly starved, was struggling to keep up with their dog team. Suddenly, as Nookap moved forward to let some of his dogs off to go after the young bear, he slipped and fell off the sledge. Just about managing to hold on with one hand he somehow kept his pipe firmly clasped between his teeth. With Nookap's weight dragging along the ice the sledge slowed, and the mother bear began to catch them up. Haig-Thomas had two choices: grab the rifle and try and shoot the mother bear; or jump off the sledge and try to get a steadier shot at her, but risk missing and being mauled to death in the process. 'We both knew that he was fighting for his life, and that if he didn't manage to pull himself back onto the sledge he would be grabbed by the bear.'

It is a mark of Haig-Thomas's humanity that he felt uneasy when the bear was finally surrounded by the dogs. Looking away as Nookap raised his rifle, he commented that 'the end of the hunt is always beastly'. He recalled, 'The bear looked so human and so pathetic as it stood to defend itself against the dogs. It seemed to give one mute appeal for help against the team.'

I've already described how the Inuit will usually try and pitch their camps in the midst of a sastrugi field on the leeward side of the ice where the snow has begun to drift. This is beneficial for two reasons: firstly, it provides ample soft snow for you to melt into drinking water; secondly, it is a fantastic natural wind barrier, allowing you to skip having to build a snow wall from scratch. Another piece of advice which was now relevant came from Mikael, who had told us to avoid camping anywhere too near an iceberg, as the sea ice is thinnest there. Thin ice attracts bears who know that it is where the seals will often create a breathing hole. It was during our second week out on the sea ice that we lazily ignored this advice, and after a particularly long slog collapsed exhausted about halfway along Stor Island. Without a sastrugi field in sight and feeling that we had gone far enough for the day, we found a very small iceberg and began to set up camp on the leeward side. The berg protected us from any sudden Arctic winds that might spring up during the night.

Al and I were tired after our trek that day, and had eaten our rations of rehydrated chilli con carne. Just as we settled into our sleeping bags I heard the sound of crunching snow. I shushed Al in mid-sentence and we both froze listening out for whatever it was I thought I had heard. With no wind there was utter silence outside. There was no mistaking the sound of slow, deliberate footsteps. We both looked at each other, before Al suggested in a whisper that it might be an Arctic fox. 'I hope so,' I muttered quietly. 'Maybe a wolf.' But I knew we couldn't just assume it was something small and relatively harmless. Something didn't feel right. 'Al, take a quick look,' I said quietly and perhaps a little selfishly.

Crawling out of a warm sleeping bag after a long day's sledging and into the freezing cold tundra in just a base layer is a struggle at the best of times. Valiantly, Al edged towards the entrance to the tent and, as quietly as possible, unzipped the door. Cautiously, he poked his head out for a moment before turning back to me and whispering the one-word warning: 'Bear!'

Bugger. I jumped out of my sleeping bag whilst Al went back to his to grab a couple of cartridges that he had been trying to keep warm. Stepping over the gun I stumbled out of the tent on all fours to see the bear about twenty metres away with its head down and looking straight at me with dark, beady eyes. I screamed at it as an almost primal fear ignited in me; Al followed behind me with the cartridges as well as our cooking pans and began to bang them loudly. The bear swayed from side to side as it walked, raising its nose every so often to sniff the air. It continued to edge closer to us, its body swaying with refined power, and then it stopped. The bear lowered its head and its black, beady eyes zoomed in on what it had seen in front of it. Me.

Our manly attempts at shouting and pot banging had not only failed to scare it off but had attracted its attention. There was another trick up our sleeves: packed away in my pulk, which was upsettingly close to the bear, lay the pen flares which I was sure would terrify this creature into changing its current opinion of us being an easy meal. I raced forwards, unzipped the bag on top of the pulk and grabbed a flare. I aimed it directly at the bear for maximum effect and fired. *Bang!* The flare erupted in red smoke and shot off like a rocket towards the animal, glancing over its left shoulder and landing in the snow. Nothing! The bear simply put its nose to where the flare was slowly sizzling itself out in the snow, sniffed it for a while and then looked back towards us and continued its steady, confident gait.

Al picked up the shotgun and loaded two shells into the breach. Putting the gun to his shoulder and pumping a cartridge into the chamber in one smooth motion he aimed at a spot close to the bear and pulled the trigger. *Click!* That gut-wrenching sound again. We looked over at each other. 'Give me the gun,' I said, and Al handed it over without a sound. I pulled the trigger. *Click!* Nothing again.

We were dressed in only our base layers – hi-tech long johns, in effect – and standing in sub-zero temperatures. We were now staring at one of nature's most prodigious hunters – without a working gun. Our final method of defence was an ice chisel just under two metres high which I had rushed back to fetch just as our plane had been about to leave Qaanaaq. The prospect of going toe to toe with a bear with a metal spear was not something I relished. Al had started to bang the pots and pans together again when an adrenaline-fuelled memory told me that I had a couple of cartridges being kept warm back in my sleeping bag.

The sleeping bag was in the tent. The bear was threateningly close by now and loping steadily towards us with an air of concentration. I rushed back into the tent, grabbed the cartridges, and loaded one into the chamber of the Mossberg. This time I aimed at the bear, knowing that could be the last act within our power to prevent us becoming the next tragic news story. I put my finger on the trigger and fired. *Bang!* The lead whizzed towards the bear, hitting it in the back. It was less than ten metres in front of me. The shock was evident, and the bear turned and ran. Holding our breath, and hearts pounding, Al and I watched as it ran into the distance, wanting to make sure that it wouldn't turn back and come for us again. The bear became smaller and smaller, a moving white hummock harder and harder to make out against the surrounding ice shapes until it was impossible to tell if I could still see it or just a ghostly image in my mind.

The threat had dissipated as suddenly as it had come and we were left standing in the snow shivering aggressively with the mixture of severe cold and adrenaline. Jumping back into the tent, Al whacked on the stove and we turbo-heated the inside whilst our shivers slowly subsided.

The whole episode had felt like a lifetime, but I imagine it could only have lasted a couple of minutes. I felt a mixture of excitement, pure elation that the threat had gone – at least for now – but also a sense of anxiety that it would be so easy to let our guard down. We were barely at the halfway point of our march. Eventually, we both calmed down to an uneasy sleep, remembering another piece of advice from our Inuit friends that when sleeping on the sea ice you always have one ear listening out for noise both from wildlife and from movements in the ice. This time the advice was easy to follow as only a couple of hours later I was startled from my sleep by a loud crack. Al was up as well and this time it was my turn to look outside the tent. The crack was unmistakeably that of the tripwire. There was nothing visible as I peered out and it wasn't obvious that anything was interfering with the tripwire. I decided that it must have been the sound of moving sea ice that had woken us. Al and I retreated into our sleeping bags once more.

Breakfast followed our usual routine: hot porridge and tea, before rolling up our sleeping bags and stepping outside to begin dismantling the tent. It was Al who rolled up the tripwire and froze in his tracks. There were bear footprints leading right up to the tent. Closer inspection revealed that a patch of snow beneath the firing mechanism showed the telltale black marks of cordite from the cartridge. Another bear had clearly come to investigate us while we slept. The tracks in the snow were confused, perhaps a sign that it had whipped around suddenly and fled at the sound of the bang.

Two incidents in one night had been unthinkable; but from that morning on, in my mind the wildlife had become as big a threat to our survival as the harsh conditions that surrounded us. I found myself constantly listening out for footsteps in the snow and I was rarely able to sleep for more than a few hours a night as a result. As leader, I was responsible for our safety, and I was determined to make sure we both got back in one piece. Alec later admitted that he had slept much better, safe in the knowledge that I was watching out for him.

Back in Qaanaaq we would describe the bears that we had seen to the Inuit hunters. They told us that, from our descriptions, the bear that had come for us was likely an adolescent male and very skinny. They thought that the red bags on our pulks could have been one of the reasons that the bears took such an interest in us. It may well have looked to them like seal blood pooling out across the snow. Skinny, adolescent and hungry was not a good combination, they explained. We had been in imminent danger, and they told us from their own experience that we had been lucky to have survived the encounter. A bear approaching in that way would take a lot to be deterred. A few metres closer, they said, and it would have been difficult to stop it before one or both of us suffered serious injury. Although I had been left with no other choice, it was comforting to know that shooting the bear had been the right thing to do. I was also glad to hear that the hunters were certain that it would suffer no lasting effects from the lighter pellets.

CHAPTER 19

ACCEPT AND ADAPT – AXEL HEIBERG

We had now travelled just over 300 kilometres and had begun to acclimatise to the environment. We were skiing between twenty and thirty kilometres per day and were well on our way to reaching Haig-Thomas Island. The weather had improved to the point that we could skim along in just a few layers of underclothing and both Alec's and my own mood had improved dramatically. I hadn't forgotten the bears that had attacked us nor the primeval anger and hunger that surged from within me when I thought of what I would do if we were attacked again. But our pulks were lighter, our bodies stronger and our minds tougher. It was as if all the guidance from Mikael in Qaanaaq and everything I had learnt from the journey before had come together. Bear Strait was behind us and we made camp at the first of two broad fjords that sat in a line at the bottom of Axel Heiberg Island. To the south the nearest piece of land was Grise Fjord which lay beyond hundreds of kilometres of frozen sea. I was used to the narrow channels of Eureka Sound where we had been flanked on either side by pointed mountains but now the view opened up. I felt both exposed and liberated. We had progressed a long way from humble, amateurish beginnings and set up camp easily that night. Without the biting cold there was no longer time wasted swinging our arms around in great windmills and dancing about trying to get warm between setting up the tripwire or unpacking our gear.

We sat in our tent with the burner on, Alec focused on boiling water for our meal. The singed sleeve of his battered jacket still bore the marks of those early mistakes, but he had learnt to move more carefully now. Alec had also managed to get the solar panels working which meant we had all the power that we needed for our satellite phone. While Alec cooked, I wrote a short update to Olga and the rest of our support team in the UK to let them know we were OK. I had been receiving concerned messages from Olga who was checking to see whether we were still alive whenever our tracker had stopped moving. It also meant that Tim Ecott as editor was getting all the content he needed to keep the newspaper interested and up to date.

The warmer climate that we had been praying for had finally arrived. The temperature had risen from lows of -40°C to around -20°C which were the temperatures that we had experienced back in Qaanaaq. I had discovered that most of our equipment worked well down to -25°C and anything below that point was when we had experienced real difficulties. We were beyond that now and so our batteries and the rest of our equipment, including our gun, had started to work – which was a relief.

The water had now boiled and, with our dinner ready, Alec and I tucked into another freeze-dried bag of chicken curry. I still looked forward to every meal and there was enough choice to keep it interesting. I scraped the bottom of the sachet with the long wooden spoon that Alec had brought along. Considering it was the fifth or sixth time we had had that same meal in only a few weeks, I was surprised at how good it still tasted. As well as the freeze-dried bags I had also brought a few blocks of butter and some digestive biscuits. The long, hard days meant that my body craved fat and so I ate the butter on top of the biscuits in thick blocks like cheese.

That night, rather than hunkering down in our sleeping bags trying to get warm, we sat up talking. We spoke about our families and how we missed them, and we talked about what we would do when we got home. I had started to think about setting up a pub near my village in Suffolk and we spoke about the food we would serve and the beers we would drink. Although there were still challenges ahead, our confidence was growing daily, and it felt like we had gone from merely surviving the Arctic to living in it.

How quickly things can change. It was in the middle of this relative bliss that once again I heard the telltale crunch of footsteps on the snow outside the tent. In an instant my dreams of the future turned back towards the danger of the present. This time I was well versed in dealing with this specific threat. I crawled out of my bag, unzipped the door of the tent and grabbed the gun which rested in its sheath on the snow outside. I pumped the grip once to pull a single cartridge into the chamber and cautiously peered around the corner of the tent. My eyes quickly rested on the culprit: a large white bear had crept up on to the land and had found its way to our camp. Two now-familiar black beady eyes stared straight at me. Its large head once again lowered to the ground. This time there was no shouting or suppressed panic. I aimed the barrel of the gun at a clump of ice two metres to the right of the bear and pulled the trigger. I had no doubt that this time it would fire. There was no dull click of a misfire, just the thunder of ignited powder as the shot rang out across the sea ice. The bullet smacked into the ground next to the bear, kicking up snow and fragments of rock. The bear turned and ran.

'Has it gone?' Alec asked from inside the tent.

'Yes, come and look,' I replied, and we both stood there silently watching as the bear ran off along the sea ice and into the distance.

The next day brought fine weather and we were able to sledge an expedition best of thirty-five kilometres in twelve hours across the mouth of the first fjord. It was one of our biggest days and I had the added pleasure of being able to stop and enjoy the sun. Previously, the contents of our water bottles had frozen solid about halfway through the day but now the weather was good enough for us to boil up fresh water when we stopped.

The sun was now always above the horizon and spiralled around us in its full 360-degree arc. We were so close to the Magnetic North Pole that compasses were useless. I hadn't quite got the hang of our handheld GPS device yet. I could work out where we were, which was useful for updating the route log each night, but I couldn't navigate very well with it. Instead, we stayed on route through a combination of handrailing the land (a method of using a consistent, static feature such as a road or river to navigate by) and checking our bearings by using the hour hand of my watch and looking at the sun which would tell me where south was. It had all seemed theoretical back in London but it was now vital to our safety and it had worked well for us. In bad weather it was a different story.

A silvery mist began to develop that evening as we made it to the second of the three fjords that we needed to cross. The visibility was already starting to reduce and a light but cold breeze was picking up. I was disappointed to see that things hadn't improved the following morning. In fact, they had got worse and the visibility at times was down to less than twenty metres or so. More disappointingly, a thick layer of snow had gathered on the ice which made it harder to pull our sledges. I could have waited for the conditions to improve but with our stores running low I knew we couldn't wait around. We had already lost a few days through storms and from the slower progress at the start. While we had managed to reclaim some of those days, I didn't want to lose the narrow margin that we had regained. I had made sure that we brought more food and fuel than we needed but if we missed the plane on the 28th and the weather turned it could be weeks before someone got to us.

I stepped out into the white of the fjord. Haig-Thomas described this part of his journey – to Surprise Ford – as his most tedious and I soon saw why. Cloaked in a thick cloud it was impossible to see any of the landscape around us. We trudged along through the whiteness, heads down, with our bodies leant against the weight of our pulks which were making hard work of the thicker snow. It felt like marching through purgatory. With no landmarks it was impossible to see how well we were doing. It was easy to doubt whether we were making any progress at all. After hours of pulling without any sights, sounds or smells to tempt our senses our minds began to wander. A strange thing happened. My mind cleared completely. I was able to recall things that I hadn't thought about for years. More than that, the memories themselves were vivid and detailed. I could replay whole films in my mind from start to finish or run through conversations with people whom I hadn't seen for years. I thought of home, of Suffolk in the summer and of walks through fields when the long grass had not yet been turned to hay. I imagined myself sailing along the river, a warm breeze blowing through the sails and on my face. My eyes squinted as beams of light twinkled across the water's surface reflecting the hot midsummer sun. Alec experienced the same thing. His thoughts turned to his family. Without the normal distractions of life our minds were completely clear and open to tours of our pasts. It didn't remove the monotony of sledging during those few days of polar blandness, but it helped.

At this point I was still concerned that we could lose our way. I was worried we might accidentally lose our bearings and ski in the wrong direction and into the open sea ice. Previously, the mountainous peaks that made up the sides of the channels down Eureka Sound had made it difficult for us to lose our bearings. There was no channel here and the sea ran for hundreds of kilometres out to our south which posed the real risk that with no land in sight we could walk off into nothingness. It would mean wasted time but more dangerously we risked hitting an area of sea ice that the ice charts had shown was perilously thin. I wasn't as confident in the use of the handheld GPS as I should have been and instead we used dead reckoning as our primary means of navigating across. While there was limited visibility and an absence of clear landmarks, we did have a mixture of small icebergs and clumps of discoloured ice to aim for. As long as you sort of knew the direction you were aiming for you could pick these out, walk towards them and then from there pick out another one that lay in a similar direction beyond.

I soon realised that Alec's eyesight was much better than mine for this task and because it was hard to see far Alec took off his sunglasses to help. We travelled for two days through the thick whiteout with Alec navigating us across the sea ice until we finally reached the other side of the final fjord. It was a huge relief.

It was 22nd April and we were now less than one hundred kilometres away from Haig-Thomas Island. We had started to think about our chances of finding Haig-Thomas's stone cairn and even wondered whether his note was still inside. At our best rate that would only take three days; however, the windless whiteout was starting to turn into a full-blown blizzard. 'We should make camp here tonight and maybe head up the coast before we cross to Haig-Thomas Island tomorrow, what do you think?' I asked Alec.

Alec had been quiet for the last few hours that day but I hadn't thought too much of it. 'I think we are going to have to, Ed, there's something wrong with my eyes,' he said. 'They're agony and I can't see much any more.'

The last few days of sledging with his eyes fully exposed to the sun had caused him to go snow-blind. With Alec not able to see, I knew it would be dangerous to carry on. He would be vulnerable to predators and regardless of the pain he was going through it would have been extremely dangerous. 'That's OK, mate,' I told him, 'we've got a couple of days of leeway so why don't we camp up for a few days while your eyes get better?'

Alec's relief was palpable.

I told him to get inside while I finished making camp. He was already in his sleeping bag by the time I had finished and his condition had worsened. He had covered his eyes with his neckcloth and he was moaning in pain. I had read about snow blindness but it was the sort of thing that happened to real explorers hundreds of years ago. I hadn't really thought it would affect one of us. Snow blindness is caused by overexposure to UV light which burns the cornea. Alec had sacrificed his eyes over the last few days navigating across the fjords and we were now paying the price. It was twenty-four-hour sunlight and there was no respite. Trying to assess how bad it was, I asked him how it felt.

'Imagine lying face down with your eyes wide open and pressed into a sandy beach,' he replied.

Not good, I thought. My only reference at that point was a book that I had with me of Scott's trip to the Antarctic and I decided to base my diagnosis and treatment of Alec's symptoms on that.

According to the book I should have been using cocaine, tucking it under Alec's eyelids to provide relief. Times had changed and cocaine was one of the few things absent from the large medical bag that Flora, our expedition doctor, had advised me to pull together before we set off. In the end I could only suggest we keep his eyes covered. I gave him a couple of tabs of codeine for the pain as he was still covering his eyes in agony. The effects of snow blindness normally last for a couple of days but can go on for weeks. Selfishly, I was keen to get going as soon as the weather improved and so I narrated to him the shorter recovery times. 'It shouldn't leave any lasting damage and you will be fine, at most it might take twenty-four hours,' I said. I was safe in the knowledge that he couldn't see and therefore couldn't check what I was telling him. His eyes were very sensitive to light now and so I covered them with a bandage and crossed my fingers.

The painkillers started to take effect and Alec drifted off to sleep. We spent the next couple of days cocooned in our bags. I made sure Alec was comfortable and I reassured him that he would get better soon even if neither of us knew when. To pass the time I read him extracts from Rudyard Kipling's book, *Kim*. It was a book that Haig-Thomas had brought out with him as well and I thought Kim's adventures in India would be a welcome escape from the pain that Alec was going through.

It had taken us almost a month to travel just under 400 kilometres to get to this point and I thought that a couple of days of rest was probably good for both of us. I cooked up double rations of food and boiled up enough water to rehydrate our worn-out bodies. We had both lost a lot of weight and our beards had grown long and scraggly. Large bags had formed under my eyes from my state of constant vigilance against the cracking ice and predacious wildlife. Alec's skin around his nose and cheeks had blistered and scabbed from the wind and cold. My fingertips were still black from the frostbite but this was only an outer layer and had already begun to peel off. With some relief I could see that underneath my fingers were starting to recover and the light pink of new skin showed through the cracks of black that protected it.

Alec's suffering continued after the blizzard had subsided and the longer it took for him to recover the more worried I got that the damage was lasting. *Have I been irresponsible not to call in a medevac as Yanik and Vincent did?*, I asked myself. It was a clear day outside and I heard rustling outside the tent. I peeked through the folds of the tent door and watched as two wolves played with each other outside. I was still surprised when I saw how unafraid of humans the wildlife was this far north. I doubted they ever really saw people, just the occasional lost scientist perhaps. While Alec continued to rest I wandered outside but still close to the tent. The sun beat down with a comforting warmth on my skin. We had camped at the bottom of a small gully and above it rose the tops of snow-capped mountains. I stood there enjoying the rugged scenery and watched a herd of musk ox climbing along the mountaintops, their large woolly coats blowing in the wind. It was an extraordinary place and a luxury to be somewhere so beautiful yet so untouched by people.

CHAPTER 20

THE FINAL PUSH –
HAIG-THOMAS ISLAND

'Are you there?' I heard Alec call from inside the tent. I had been out for only a few minutes but he must have woken up during that time and sensed that he was alone.

'I'm here, pal,' I reassured him before heading back to check on the patient.

Alec was sitting up when I got in. He had removed the makeshift bandage from his eyes and was blinking tentatively as the sunlight hit his still sensitive corneas.

'Are they feeling any better?' I asked. We had lain in the tent for two days and now only had three days to get to Haig-Thomas Island. It was enough to cover the distance but if we waited any longer we ran the risk of the weather changing on us again.

'One is worse than the other but I'll manage,' Al said valiantly. We had already had breakfast and there was no point in hanging around. I pored over the map for one last time. The next part of the journey was a sixty-kilometre slog across the sea ice. It would be the furthest that we would have to walk away from land and neither of us knew what to expect. We were both excited at the prospect of reaching Haig-Thomas Island after so long.

'Do you want any more painkillers before we kick on?' I asked.

'I'm alright,' Alec said sheepishly. I learnt later that he had accidentally double-dosed when I had been walking and was bordering on a drug-fuelled high. It was everything he could do to keep a straight face not wanting to worry me.

To get to the island we would ski along the ice foot on the west side of Axel Heiberg Island for about ten kilometres before heading directly west across the sea ice for the remaining fifty kilometres or so. It would take two days, leaving us only a day to explore the island and try and find the cairn and the note that lay beneath it. Or so we hoped. We packed up camp and were on the move in only a few minutes. It was a clear day and warm enough by now that we were able to ski wearing only a few layers of clothing. I picked a course due west for the island. Alec skied along behind me in surprisingly high spirits considering he was only partially sighted. I wasn't sure whether this was just the overdose of painkillers or because of the bond we had built up over the last few months together. It takes a huge amount of trust to follow someone blindly into the unknown.

Taking more care now to protect our eyes we put on our glacier glasses: thick black lenses held in place with a leather wrap-around. We looked like 19th-century alpinists. Alec had gone one step further now and had a thick fleece top wrapped around his head and across his most painful eye making him look more like a budget pirate than a hardened explorer. I was still wary of polar bears and so I made sure to keep close to him. My neck soon ached from the constant turning back as I checked that a polar bear hadn't sneaked up on him. The Inuit had told me that the most dangerous bear is the one that you don't see.

We made good progress across the ice as we headed away from the land. I had been worried about making the crossing as I wasn't sure how the ice would change this far away from the coast. I had checked the ice charts with Olga back in the UK but I still didn't know what to expect. I imagined open leads of water and thin pieces of dangerous ice that we might fall through along the way. My concerns eased with each kilometre that we gained and I could see the ice changed very little. It was only towards the middle of the first day that we encountered any problems. Ahead of me I could see a deep and wide field of sastrugi, the ice three metres high in places. I turned to Alec. 'Mate, looks like a wall of ice ahead of us', I said. 'I don't fancy going around so we will just have to find a way through it.'

Alec looked back at me and nodded his head in agreement.

The chunks of ice got taller as we drew nearer. It was daunting but the closer we got the easier it was to pick a way through. We skirted around the larger blocks and we clambered over the smaller pieces. Even these were almost two metres tall in places and we had to drag our pulks up near-vertical faces sometimes. Our food rations were much depleted at this stage so our pulks were lighter but it still took all that we had to carry the weight up the sheer faces and lower them safely down the other side. At one point my bindings gave way as one of the metal parts was pulled out, sticking out so that from then on it tripped me up at every other step. We repeated the process through the relentless terrain. Flatter ice appeared beyond the rubble just as it began to look like we would have to cover the remaining forty kilometres in that way.

Alec and I made camp that afternoon having covered twenty-five kilometres, just over halfway. The island was still nowhere to be seen but I knew it lay somewhere between us and Amund Ringnes Island which was just visible as a dusty haze in the distance. Although it was my first time here, I had read so much about the area that the names and landscape seemed very familiar. Haig-Thomas had spotted his island from Amund Ringnes. In his book he wrote:

> As usual, small ice-crystals were pouring down from the sky, and it was difficult to see anything very clearly. I turned my glasses to the sea-ice to the east; and there, rising out of the sea

between me and Axel Heiberg there seemed to be land. I looked at it for a long time. At first I thought it might be only a mirage, for I didn't see how an island could have been omitted from the map. Nookap, however, to whom I pointed it out, was fairly sure that it was land – indeed, more sure than I was myself.

I imagined the excitement Haig-Thomas must have felt with the prospect of discovering something completely new. Alec and I trawled through the digital copy of Haig-Thomas's book as we lay in our tent, looking for clues on where the note would be. It was hard to believe that after four years of planning, we were now just one day away from stepping on to the island's shores ourselves. The hunt for the original note left in 1938 was always a romantic ideal, but Haig-Thomas's clues gave us high hopes of locating his stone cairn: 'Unless a bear knocks down the stick, it should stand for many years. At the foot of it we left a small cairn and a note', he wrote.

The window to explore the island was narrowing quickly and so we were packed up and moving again after only a few hours of sleep. The final twenty kilometres or so made for easy sledging. We were expedition-fit now and made light work of it. I could see for kilometres across the flat, windswept ice. Alec's health had improved dramatically and so we took it in turns to lead the way. High above us in an otherwise cloudless sky floated a single, elongated cloud in the shape of an arrow which pointed straight towards the location of the island. All the pain and hardships we had been through seemed a long time ago. Although I knew we were going in the right direction, we still couldn't see land even though we should have been close. Just as I was starting to get a little worried I heard Alec shout, 'I can see it.'

'Where?' I asked as I still couldn't make it out.

'You have the worst eyes, Ed, I'm the one who's supposed to be snow-blind,' he joked.

After a little longer I could finally make out, very low on the horizon, a thick band of snow that was barely discernible from the ice that surrounded it. 'That's barely an island,' I shouted to Alec when I could see it properly, 'I mean it's hardly more than some slightly thicker snow.'

We both laughed. 'I'll race you there,' Alec challenged and shot off at pace. I followed in hot pursuit, dragging my pulk behind me. My broken binding was still being a nuisance and the faster I tried to go the more I kept tripping up. The Arctic had played a trick on us though and it was soon apparent that the island was much further away than we had thought. Alec slowed down to a more gentle pace and I came up alongside him. It was another hour before we could really start making out the details of the island that we had come so far to see. Haig-Thomas made a similar blunder, stepping off the sledge in excitement when he thought they were only a kilometre away before sheepishly rejoining Nookap and the sledge once he realised there was still five kilometres to go.

At last we reached the tide crack that separated the island from the sea ice. The land rose up ahead of us in a gradual, snow-covered slope. It was the sort of place that would be easy to miss and there were few discernible features. A small hillock marked the south side of the island and a low saddle ran the length of the island and joined it to another small hillock to the north. I marked the occasion by tripping up on my bindings and landing squarely on my back, much to Alec's delight.

'I can't believe we actually made it,' he said.

'I know, pal, we just need to find the note now!' I replied.

We camped below the highest point on the island – only ninety-six metres above sea level – and made our way up that evening in the belief that this would be where the note was. It was liberating to be able to head up on our skis without the feeling of an ungainly pulk dragging you back. As we reached the summit I was able to make out a shape that I thought was the cairn. We charged up the rest of the way to the top, only realising as we drew close that we hadn't seen a cairn but the outline of a fuel drum. Unbelievable! There was no note here, just this drum and a few old whisky crates from some unknown occupant who had been there before us. Haig-Thomas and Nookap had stood where we were. Neither of us could believe that there was no trace of the cairn.

Deflated, we trudged back down the hill and decided to go back to the book, burn the wooden crates and have a glass of whisky of our own. Whisky was one thing we had packed in quantity. There were almost three litres of the stuff which had been untouched up until then. We had been so far beyond our comfort zone during the trip that I was afraid that the debilitating effects of alcohol would have been tantamount to suicide. I had also been warned that alcohol made it much harder to tell when you might be getting frostbite. One of the more elderly Inuit in Qaanaaq had learnt this the hard way when he passed out in the snow one night and ended up losing his whole hand to the cold. I was delighted when Alec cracked open the first bottle. We stood around the burning crates and made several toasts to the fact that we had reached our destination. It was soon evident why it had been a good idea to abstain until now. I stumbled into the tent, tripping over the flap and landed heavily on my sleeping bag. I had got away lightly. Alec came next.

First, he broke the tent zip by pulling on it too hard. The zip snapped in his hand and we had to sew the door closed. He then fell into the stove while the pot was on and sent boiling hot water across all our gear. He looked at me sheepishly. I looked back at him saying nothing. We knew it was time for both of us to sober up. We still hadn't found the note and the window of opportunity was closing. Reading Haig-Thomas's words again, I thought that he might have found it difficult to distinguish between the northern and southern parts of the island when he had ventured on to the island. Our modern map gave us a much greater picture and so we planned to search the northern side the following day. It was only when I got back to the UK that I reread the story and realised my mistake. I had been looking for a cairn at the top of the island. The book made it clear that it was buried on the flat surface at the southern end. It made sense. Travelling by sledge they would have moved across the flattest part of the island and it would have been easier to make a cairn there. Exhausted from the journey and the nights spent sleeping with one ear always listening for bears this critical fact was lost on me.

Waking at four o'clock, we threw down our porridge and broke camp. We headed north along the coast of the island first. At one point Alec thought he had spotted what looked like a new piece of land. The prospect of discovering his own island was overwhelming and he began skiing off at pace. I chased after him but couldn't keep up and he skied along for a full hour in a straight line towards what turned out to be the eastern side of Amund Ringnes, twenty-five kilometres away. The lack of a reference point had played a trick on him. Alec was carrying the GPS tracker and we were told later by people watching our progress updates at home that they had thought that he had been taken hostage by a polar bear. Realising I wouldn't catch up and with Alec completely deaf to my shouts I decided to start scouring the island. We had meant to split up anyway to try and cover as much of the island as we could in the short time we had left so I didn't begrudge him. I checked every stone that looked like a cairn without luck. There was no ski pole and no sign of any note. By this time Alec had rejoined me and told me that he had had no luck either.

Suddenly, the crisp silence that we had become so used to was broken by the alien sound of an aircraft engine cutting across our senses. It was the Twin Otter of Kenn Borek Air and, without the note, I made the difficult decision to turn back to camp. There was still one more hill to be checked on the way back. 'You're the better skier, why don't you go up and I'll head back?' I shouted to Alec. While he skied up to the southern summit, I hurried back to meet the pilots. The plane flew low overhead as I raced back to camp. I felt like I was running late for a bus. I was worried that they would need someone to walk out a landing strip for them but I needn't have been. I watched as the glistening Twin Otter came in for a sharp landing at the edge of the tide crack, throwing up snow as it kicked back its engines, and stopped just metres from the wall of pressure ice in front of it.

I was just starting to pack up camp when Al finally arrived from a far-off hill, albeit with no news on the note. We were both disappointed not to have found it. Looking back now I think Haig-Thomas would have laughed at us rushing about, getting very sweaty trying to find it. I hope he would have enjoyed hearing about the adventure we had been on to get there. 'I left our own note,' Alec said when he returned. 'I liked the idea that one day one of our children might come back here and find it on their own adventure.'

The pilots helped us pack up camp and load the plane. We hadn't washed for almost a month but the pilots were too polite to say anything. Our challenge was just ending but Haig-Thomas and Nookap's ordeal had just started at this point. They were already facing hunger after their food supplies had run out. Although it was still socially acceptable in those days to eat their dog teams, it wasn't something that Haig-Thomas was willing to do. Instead, they faced starvation. Bears had broken into the food depots that they laid for the route back home, leaving just bones and broken igloos. They were lucky to stumble across a bear that walked up to their tent and provided just enough food for them to feed the team and get back to Thule.

We had got off lightly in comparison and we were soon ready to leave. The pilots had taxied the plane around and we sat in the empty hold, proud of what we had achieved and very relieved to have survived. We were a very different pair to the people who had set off only a month earlier. Physically, Alec's eyes were still bloodshot from his snow blindness and the skin around his nose and cheeks was blistered and peeling. My own state was no better, I had large bags under my eyes from the lack of sleep and my fingers still bore the marks of frostbite. We had lost a lot of weight and bore scraggly, ill-kempt beards and greasy hair. As our clothes and equipment warmed up the extent of the smell of our unwashed bodies became clearer. You know it's bad when you can smell yourself.

The plane gathered momentum and we soared steeply into the air, the body of the plane shaking vigorously around us. Haig-Thomas Island and the sea ice that had become our home receded into the distance. I wondered again where the note might have been. The plane set a course for Greenland, retracing our journey below it with ease. Distances that had taken us days were covered in minutes. Once the engine had settled down into a steady rhythm one of the pilots turned to us. 'You're lucky you got out when you did,' he said with some concern. 'Two guys have just gone missing south of here. You're the last pick-up, we're on search and rescue now.'

The two men they were talking about were seasoned professionals from Holland who were exploring the impact of climate change on the sea-ice coverage that year. It took three days for their last location to be found. All that was left was a sledge and their dog. Their bodies were never recovered. I knew we had been fortunate. I only knew of three expeditions to the area that year. Ours, the two Dutchmen and Vincent's. We had achieved what we had set out to do but the other two teams were either dead or had suffered life-changing injuries. We had faced our own challenges with the wildlife and the cold and were lucky to be alive.

There was now another note on Haig-Thomas Island that paid tribute to the man. Perhaps in another seventy or eighty years one of our descendants might make a similar journey and, like us, perhaps they will be able to measure the health of the high Arctic, learn from its inhabitants and overcome their own challenges.

CHAPTER 21

THE JOURNEY BACK – LONDON

There was a week to go until our flight would leave for London. Fin had collected us from Qaanaaq airstrip on our return like a proud father. I had dreaded telling him that I had lost his rifle but even this passed over him with only the briefest moment of annoyance. Alec couldn't wait to get back to the UK but I was hesitant. I had grown fond of the community that had taught me so much about the Arctic environment. They had given me, a polar novice, a privileged insight into the culture of a highly respected and knowledgeable people. This knowledge had helped us to survive a steep learning curve: -40°C temperatures, strong blizzards and intimidating wildlife, all of which tested our equipment and our bodies to their limits. Each challenge had come with its own overwhelming sense of accomplishment that I cherished. It had provided me with a deeper sense of confidence and understanding of myself and it felt at the time as though I had found the single test of manhood that I had longed for.

We spent our days trawling through Troels's collection of cheap American adventure films and eating vast quantities of food rich in carbohydrates from the supermarket. Qaanaaq's version of fast food. The town felt different now. The feeling of being an outsider had been replaced by a sense of acceptance. It became clear from my conversations that many in the town had thought that we wouldn't survive the expedition. I had commissioned some artwork from Ecko, one of the local artists. A few small pieces, hewn from caribou bone to keep as memories of my time in the north. Ecko had been happy to make them for me and I had spent hours in the hut drawing out ideas with him while Troels translated the finer details from English to Danish. I had promised to pay him when we got back and agreed it with a handshake. I messaged Ecko when we returned, hoping they would be ready, but he didn't respond. I was surprised until I bumped into him in the supermarket.

'Ecko!' I called out at the entrance of the shop. He carried two bags laden with imported cans of food and air-sealed meats. I explained that we had just returned from Nunavut and he seemed pleased for us. 'Did you manage to make those pieces we talked about before I left?' I asked.

'No,' Ecko replied without any embarrassment. 'We thought you would die out there and it didn't make sense to create something for a dead person.'

I shouldn't have been surprised. I had barely scratched the surface in understanding the culture in Qaanaaq but thinking back to Fin's story of the polar bear hunt it made sense. In England people were always happy to air their opinions on whether they thought we would make it or not. Most didn't think we would even start. Here, the Polar Inuit kept those types of thoughts to themselves. It was better to step back and allow someone to make their own mistakes. Maybe they thought that they would be more likely to learn from them. It struck me then that no-one had told me before I left that they didn't think we would accomplish what we set out to do. If they had, I wondered whether I would have had the courage to go. I didn't mind ignoring the naysayers back home – most who had commented had never been to the Arctic. If an Inuit had told me that we were unlikely to succeed with the years of experience that they had then it would have been foolhardy to have continued unsupported as we did.

The week flew by and soon it was time to leave once again. This time for home. Troels organised a farewell *kaffemik* and many of our friends came to say their goodbyes and hear tales of the adventure to Nunavut – a place that few had been to since the change in ice conditions at Smith Sound and because of the invisible border that ran through it. A man walked in as many were leaving. His name was Olenguak and he wore a face stained deep brown from working out in the summer's sun. The rest of his skin was pale where it had been protected from the elements by the thick furs that he wore. He looked like he had been dunked head first into a mug of tea. Olenguak had won fame as a great hunter and although I had heard his name many times, I had never met him. I was honoured that he had come to meet us in the hut. We showed him pictures of the bear that Alec had taken after it had attacked us. 'You were very lucky to survive,' he said as he examined the pictures from my camera. 'It is a very hungry young male.' I was relieved. Olenguak had seen many bears. The fact that he had come to the same conclusion went some way to putting my mind at rest.

Fin did not come to the *kaffemik*; I had heard that his pain had become too great. He was the last one to board as Alec and I sat on the plane bound for home. He limped down the aisle wearing an old leather jacket, his mouth pulled into a weak smile that barely hid the grimace of pain beneath. As he walked, he was greeted by men and women who grabbed his hand or waved. Fin took his seat at the back of the plane, his hands pushed hard into his knees and his knuckles white where they clutched the fabric of his jeans.

'Where are you going?' I asked.

'I'm going to a hospital in Nuuk,' he said. 'They are going to see where my pain is coming from.'

When I left the plane in Kangerlussuaq I had the feeling that this would be the last time I would see Fin. Two months later he was dead. The cancer had flowed through his body unchecked. I like to think that he passed in peace but I have seen cancer patients die and it is rarely a painless death.

In Qaanaaq I had begun to be accepted. In London I felt like an outsider. The world moved around me as if on fast forward. Busy workers ran from place to place, talking hurriedly as if to thin air, their voices carrying to invisible participants on the other side of the white plastic earphones that protruded from each ear. It was a sharp contrast to the slow and methodical way of life that I had become used to. Where every action had a purpose and every word had a meaning. In London so much effort seemed to be driven towards simply being busy. On the way to meet Olga at a café near Piccadilly I stumbled across an old friend. I walked up to her still carrying my rucksack and sporting a scraggly, ill-kempt beard. She stepped back in shock until she recognised me. I looked like a wandering tramp, unwashed and out of place. The reception from Olga was the same. 'You look ridiculous,' she said, examining the frostbitten scabs that were starting to heal across my face. 'There's nothing to you and you stink,' she went on.

'I think you mean "lean",' I replied jokingly. I had lost almost thirteen kilograms of weight during the journey and my fast-food diet since returning had barely made an impact.

'So, what are you going to do now?' she asked.

'The first thing I am going to do is have a bath,' I said, 'then I am going back to work.'

I had gone to Greenland in search of answers to my questions. I had wanted to understand how the lives of the people had changed since Haig-Thomas had made his journey to the region. My time there had been short and I had barely scratched the surface but as a hunter I felt that I had seen Qaanaaq through a more empathetic lens than some of the foreign scientists or intrepid explorers who had ventured to the icy north. Through my conversations with the Inuit and by accompanying them on the ice I had witnessed a transient society, weathering the outside influences of modernism and still practising forms of hunting that had been passed down through the centuries. Hunting was one of the ways in which they had maintained a fragile thread to their cultural traditions. Their spears, kayaks and sledges were a way to survive – literally, in providing sustenance, but also by preserving a way of life that was being eroded by the tat of modernism. Electric appliances, overheated houses and carb-rich ready meals. I had heard how climate change was affecting the cycle of the seasons. The waning sea ice altered their frozen highways and made travel to other settlements more precarious and the Inuit's access to their quarry increasingly unpredictable. The seasons when they could hunt across the ice had also become shorter. But I understood that life in Qaanaaq was always at the mercy of the climate. The weather that came was not something that could be fought against but needed to be adapted to.

I felt that the actions of outside forces had an equal impact on their way of life. It was the US ambition to counter a Russian threat in Thule that had forced the exile of the population from Thule to Qaanaaq, not climate change. It was Greenpeace's activism in the 1970s that had caused the ban on sealskin imports and destroyed a key source of income for the Inuit hunters of Qaanaaq. It was the border along Smith Sound that had come into force after 9/11 which separated them from large swathes of their traditional hunting grounds on Ellesmere Island. It wasn't just because the summers had become warmer or the winters shorter.

I didn't believe climate change would be the death knell for the last vestiges of hunting culture in the region. Climate change is a much slower phenomenon. Like the overnight creation of Thule Airbase, I do worry about the more immediate impact of commercial activities in the Arctic, expansionist policies of foreign governments and the meddling of activists. These all pose a more immediate threat to the Polar Inuit than climate change does. Modern ways of living are already pulling many in Qaanaaq away from the land and have reduced the numbers of people willing to hunt. My hope is that the increased understanding in the West of our own relationship with our environment will help policymakers better understand the Inuit's relationship with theirs. There are lessons to be learnt from how they have managed to live sustainably since their arrival in Greenland and have such minimal impact on their environment. We might be less quick in the future to dictate how other cultures should live and perhaps more willing to learn how indigenous cultures can teach us how to live more sustainably and in tune with our own environments.

Alec and I went our separate ways in London. He had been the best companion on the journey that I could have wished for. Our time together, learning from the Inuit and battling the harsh conditions of the Canadian Arctic Archipelago, had formed an unbreakable bond between us. We had both found something in that challenge. Alec had proved that he had what it took to follow in his great-uncle's footsteps. The challenge had almost broken me but I had found contentment in the hardship. A sense of peace.

Weeks later the sounds of cushioned footfall on the surface crust of frozen sea ice still haunted me as I slept. In the safety of London it struck me how close to death we had come, but Alec and I had prevailed. The journey had been a personal rite of passage to manhood and, perhaps more than that, it had given me the gift of clarity and fulfilment. The powerful wanderlust that had dogged me for so long had left me. I wanted to try and live my life with harmony and meaning. Not to fight the bad weather but to understand my place in the environment and to adapt to it. To be content with what I had and to prioritise the things that really mattered. My family, my friends and my community. I had learnt that from the Polar Inuit.